"You deny what is Jewish in you,

and that is too, **too Jewish!**"

("Missachten, was man

'jüdisch' nennt,/Ist leider, leider jüdisch!")

FRITZ LÖHNER,
Israeliten und andere Antisemiten, 32–33

"But when your name

is Wendy Wasserstein

and you're from New York,

you are the walking

embodiment of

'too Jewish.' "

WENDY WASSERSTEIN,
Reform Judaism
(Summer 1993), 45

"People said I was **too Jewish**—and I

even suffered from anti-Jewish prejudice

from Jews themselves."

JACKIE MASON,
quoted in Sander L. Gilman, *The Jew's Body,* 26

"And *never* have we American Jews

thought, let alone asserted, 'Yes I am

beautiful. I come from a beautiful race.'

And we would say, with the irony which

has been our most prized and useful

possession for quite a few millennia: 'I'm

not going to say that—too arrogant . . . ,'

i.e., 'too Jewish.' "

DAVID MAMET,
The Decoration of Jewish Houses, 11

EDITED BY
NORMAN L. KLEEBLATT

TOO JEWISH?

CHALLENGING
TRADITIONAL
IDENTITIES

THE JEWISH MUSEUM, NEW YORK
UNDER THE AUSPICES OF THE JEWISH THEOLOGICAL SEMINARY OF AMERICA

AND

RUTGERS UNIVERSITY PRESS, NEW BRUNSWICK, NEW JERSEY

This book has been published in conjunction with the exhibition Too Jewish? Challenging Traditional Identities *held at The Jewish Museum, New York, 10 March 1996–14 July 1996.*

Too Jewish?: Challenging Traditional Identities *has been supported, in part, by grants from The Nathan Cummings Foundation, the National Endowment for the Arts, a federal agency, Barbara S. Horowitz, Israel Discount Bank, New York State Council on the Arts, Joan and Hyman Sall, Maureen and Marshall Cogan and the "21" International Holding, Inc., Foundation, Linda and Ronald F. Daitz, Ellen Schloss Flamm, the Andy Warhol Foundation for the Visual Arts, William S. Ehrlich and Ruth Lloyds, and Ulrich and Harriet Meyer.*

Exhibition Curator: Norman L. Kleeblatt
Consulting Curator: Maurice Berger
Assistant Curator: Mira R. Goldfarb
Project Assistant: Jonathan P. Canning
Manuscript Editor: Sheila Schwartz
Curator, Art Video Program: Robin F. White

Designed and typeset by Jenny Dossin
Printed by Worzalla Printing
Manufactured in the United States of America

Library of Congress Cataloging-in-Publication Data
Too Jewish? : challenging traditional identities / edited by Norman L. Kleeblatt.
p.   cm.
Issued in association with a traveling exhibition opening at the Jewish Museum of New York in March, 1996.
Includes bibliographical references.
ISBN 0-8135-2326-5 (cloth: alk. paper)
ISBN 0-8135-2327-3 (pbk : alk. paper)
1. Jews—United States—Identity.   2. Jews—United States—Intellectual life.   3. Jewish artists—United States—Exhibitions.   I. Kleeblatt, Norman L.   II. Jewish Museum (New York, N.Y.)
DS143.T65   1996
305.892'4073—dc20   95-50861
                                                                                       CIP

British Cataloging-in-Publication information available

CONTENTS

Jewish identity in the 1990s takes many forms, from a renewed comfort with a familiar past, to a search for meaningful new forms of ritual. The artists in *Too Jewish?* examine and represent a wide spectrum of concerns from the secular and the spiritual, yet all relating to an identification with Jewishness. Their art reflects the ways Jews have been seen and identified by the world, and how Jews see themselves. Some works use humor to deflate or deconstruct Jewish stereotypes. Others demand and even invent a readjustment of tradition in order to claim a recognized place within the practice of Judaism. Thus, more than a simple acknowledgment or celebration of Jewishness, these works are active, often brassy forms of communication, an insistent engagement with the viewer in a conversation about identity that is confrontational, funny, and poignant at the same time.

In looking at the whole Jewish experience in the world over time, The Jewish Museum's exhibitions reflect a perpetual combination of continuity and change within the realm of Jewish culture. In the historic objects of the Museum's permanent exhibition, one can see the results of this dynamic interchange. In this exhibition, one sees less the results and more the process of search and reinvention. An active Jewish identity in the contemporary world requires one to be thoughtful and creative. In this context, these artists have provided models for consideration.

Many thanks to Norman Kleeblatt, Susan and Elihu Rose Curator of Fine Arts, who has shown foresight and imagination in bringing together the multiple voices and complex issues within this important exhibition, and this richly absorbing book. I thank him and the staff of the Fine Arts Department of The Jewish Museum for their commitment and excellent work in directing and managing this project.

was just my attempt to dilute the impact of the paintings. Ultimately, I realized that my twinge of discomfort reflected the undeniable mindset of an assimilated Jew, even one who is a curator at The Jewish Museum. Indeed, my past exhibitions reflected that ideology, one on which I and so many American Jews had been raised.

During the two years after my first viewing of *The Chapter Paintings*, I visited a number of other artists who were treating the subject of Jewish identity in new ways. Jewish iconography and content was, in itself, not a new phenomenon, yet there was something different about the way these artists presented their identity. No longer an apologia for conspicuous Jewishness, these works were for the most part confrontational and often embarrassing. In seeking to celebrate subjectivity, these artists were compelled to challenge the authority and hierarchy of both the art world and the Jewish communities, two of the many coordinates that circumscribe their complicated personal identities.

While multicultural exhibitions have abounded in the years since 1989, there has been little focus on Jewish artists or Jewish subject matter. The interrogation of this absence—and of what makes Jewish artists less marginal than other groups—was integral to the formulation of this exhibition. Jewishness is ultimately only one of the many marginalities that most of these artists experience. In the exploration of personal identity, the issue of religion emerges only after a number of other aspects are addressed.

The dilemma of exhibiting Rand's project at The Jewish Museum finally forced me to confront my own cultural *difference* as a Jew and to attempt to figure out how different my "otherness" was from the "otherness" of any number of diverse minorities. Therefore, the exhibition *Too Jewish?* evolved both from my scrutiny of self and from the scrutiny of self as reflected in the work of the eighteen artists in the show. This book and the exhibition it documents by no means attempt to codify issues of identity in general and Jewish identity in particular. Such an approach would be counterproductive to the acknowledgment of the complexity of issues of personal identity and antithetical to the inevitable flux of current scholarship. This project serves more as a means of asking questions and beginning a dialogue, of shedding prejudices, not only about others, but also about ourselves.

The essays in this book frame Jewish identity from both contemporary and historical perspectives; each reflects the themes and strategies of the artists shown in the exhibition. In her Foreword, art historian Linda Nochlin introduces the discussion of the intricacies of postmodern Jewish identity with an analysis of the reception of fashion designer Jean Paul Gaultier's Fall 1993 Hasidic-inspired collection. Examination of contemporary Jewish identity requires a close investigation of the modern attitudes about the Jewish body, a topic central to the work of a number of artists in the show. No one is more qualified to articulate the scientific and historic theories that ensured the Jew's difference than Sander Gilman, who has presented here one aspect of his extensive research on the Jew's body. Art theorist

Rhonda Lieberman has contributed "Jewish Barbie," a clever lament over the Jewish princess whose frustrated ambitions are attributed to her ethnic body type. And sociologist Riv-Ellen Prell examines the internal and external constructions of this stereotype as it has evolved in American popular culture. Cultural critic Maurice Berger scrutinizes the stereotypes inherent in characterizations of Jewish masculinity in American television. It is precisely in the midst of all these cultural notions and attitudes that the Jewish artists in the exhibition came of age.

Equally important for the artists' choice of subject matter are the aesthetic theories of modern art historians. The artists challenge the strategies of those critics and artists who singularly tried to separate identity from art—ironically, a large number of them were Jews. The renowned critic Clement Greenberg held such sway in distilling aesthetics from subjectivity that his theoretical approach might now be seen as an assimilationist tactic. Margaret Olin, who has worked extensively on the nationalism and prejudice that permeate the work of a number of major twentieth-century art historians, here examines Greenberg's assimilatory practice.

"Notes on Akiba" was originally written for *The Third Seder*, performed at The Jewish Museum on the night before the first Seder, 1995. Initially it had been scheduled as part of the programming for the *Too Jewish?* exhibition. With signature humor and painful honesty, playwright Tony Kushner carries on the Passover tradition of reinterpreting the story of Exodus through contemporary Jewish experience.

While the exhibition tries to be as inclusive as possible, there are some self-admitted deficiencies. Undoubtedly, it would have benefited from the presence of a Sephardi artist and of an Orthodox Jew who shared the same strategies and attitudes as the other *Too Jewish?* artists. Although I reviewed the work of a small number of artists of Sephardi origin, none seemed to fit with the prevailing critical and interrogatory attitude of the other artists in the show. The absence of the latter is understandable given the fact that, by definition, Orthodox Jews must accept certain authority and hierarchies that are in large measure incommensurate with the kind of critical self-examination exemplified by the exhibition.

A number of non-Jewish artists have also been drawn to difficult Jewish subject matter. One of the toughest moments in the organization of the show was when I concluded, for the sake of clarity, that I would limit the roster of participants to Jewish artists. The exhibition is nevertheless intended to be part of a greater and ongoing cultural project: the understanding that the different racial, ethnic, religious, sexual, and gender groups that make up our diverse society are all struggling with the complexity of their difference and using their perceptions to gain greater sensitivity.

NORMAN L. KLEEBLATT
Susan and Elihu Rose Curator of Fine Arts
The Jewish Museum

For a contemporary art exhibition, *Too Jewish? Challenging Traditional Identities* has had an unusually long planning period. As frustrating as such a delay was for my zeal to introduce recent art in a new context, there were nevertheless rewarding consequences. The most indisputable has been my associations with the many individuals who have generously participated in the organization of the show.

I am most grateful to Joan Rosenbaum, Helen Goldsmith Menschel Director of The Jewish Museum, who recognized the timeliness of the *Too Jewish?* question and its expression in the work of the artists I selected. Her confidence in this project has been vital, and her intelligent support deeply appreciated. The exhibition has benefited greatly from her thoughtful observations and suggestions and her concerns that the show be comprehensible to as broad a public as possible. My initial idea for the show must be credited to the numerous conversations about the role of contemporary art at The Jewish Museum with former Assistant Director of Programs Ward Mintz. His spontaneous enthusiasm for the idea and his wisdom and insight during its germination were crucial to the show's conceptualization and its positive reception here.

The exhibition could not have evolved without the prescient insights of Consulting Curator Maurice Berger, Senior Fellow, The Vera List Center for Art and Politics, New School for Social Research. He is a treasured colleague and friend with whom I deliberated the many aspects of this project during the last two years. Maurice contributed significantly to the discussions surrounding the complex philosophical and aesthetic issues that the exhibition addresses. I thank him also for his useful editorial comments on my essay and the catalogue bibliography. His wise counsel, genuine enthusiasm, and loyalty have been invaluable both to me and to the project. Thomas Sokolowski, Director of The Grey Art Gallery at New York University, offered valuable perspective and advice at the time of the project's inception. I am very grateful to him for his advice, encouragement, and friendship.

I am proud to have organized this exhibition for The Jewish Museum, and ever grateful to its staff and volunteers for their talents, commitment, and for their confidence in me. Eric Zafran, Deputy Director for Curatorial Affairs, provided guidance and useful comments about my essay. As I sit writing this, I know he will continue to support the project and guide it through its final phases of installation. Sharon Blume, consultant to the Museum's curatorial department during 1993 and 1994, was a wonderful supporter, advisor, and friend. I greatly appreciated her understanding of the ideological aspects of diversity for both Jewish artists and the various Jewish communities, and her regard for humor as central to both the exhibition and the "Jewish psyche."

The exhibition and its attendant publication would not have been possible without the devotion, intelligence, and plain hard work of Mira Goldfarb, Curatorial Assistant in this department. In essence, she became the de facto Assistant Curator for *Too Jewish?* Mira joined this department during the middle of the planning period for the project and actually kept it alive as I was asked to quickly turn my attention to the details of a major international exhibition of Camille Pissarro. During this time, she picked up the myriad details of the exhibition, soothed the disappointed spirits of the artists who had planned to show their work at The Jewish Museum a full year earlier, and provided me with the peace of mind that, even though I had to temporarily turn my attentions away from *Too Jewish?*, it was in good hands. Much of the success of both the exhibition and catalogue must be credited to her. Mira's intelligent analyses of both ideological and aesthetic issues, as well as her friendship and good humor, aided me and the exhibition greatly. I am enormously grateful to Project Assistant Jonathan Canning, who is a doctoral candidate in medieval art at Columbia University. For three long days each week, Jonathan made the intellectual leap into contemporary art, Jewish identity politics, and American popular culture. With much cleverness and humor, Jonathan embraced the unique challenges that the coordination of this exhibition and catalogue presented.

Special thanks go to the cherished colleagues of the Fine Arts Department: Susan Chevlowe, Assistant Curator; Lisa Leavitt, Exhibitions Assistant; and Irene Z. Schenck, Research Associate; and former Curatorial Assistant Emily Whittemore. Their enthusiasm for, support for, and even initial skepticism about this exhibition were vital to its realization. They have shown exceptional dedication over the years. I am very grateful for the efforts of Anthony Cate, Alex Cigale, Deena B. Fiedler, Julia Goldman, Gail Mandel, volunteer Elizabeth Kardos and interns Rachel D. Bonk, Karen Davis, Stephanie Dick, Madelyn Jordon, Suzanne Karsch, Jennifer Lager, Rachel Natelson, and Stephania Rosenstein, who have all enthusiastically and intelligently offered their time and energy.

Deepest thanks go to Dennis Szackas, former Manager for Program Funding, whose superb knowledge of contemporary art, distinctive creativity, and tireless efforts led to the exhibition's funding by the National Endowment for the Arts. I am also grateful to Lynn Thommen, Deputy Director for Development; Evan Kingsley, consultant to the Museum's Development Department; Breena Solomon, Director of Program Funding; and Clare Garfield, Grants Coordinator, who eagerly continued those efforts. Exciting programs and lectures were conceived and organized by Jack Salzman, Deputy Director of Media and Programs; Judy Siegel, Director of Education; and Aviva Weintraub, Manager of Public Programs. Dr. Salzman also shared his wisdom, expertise, and valuable time in providing suggestions for my essay and the book in general. Special thanks go to Kim Bistrong, Media Coordinator, for significant assistance on the media components of the show. I am grateful for the resources of the National Jewish Archive of Broadcasting. Publicity was ingeniously handled—as usual—by Anne Scher, Director of Public Relations. Robin Cramer, Cooper Shop Director of Product Development and Merchandising, enthusiastically created products to complement the exhibition. Jane Dunne, Deputy Director for Administration, and Ann Applebaum, Counsel, The Jewish Theological Seminary of America, devoted expertise to contracts and legal matters. Thanks also to former Assistant Director for Administration Claudette Donlon. Samantha Gilbert, Administrator, provided important guidance. Geri Thomas, former Administrator of Exhibitions and Collections, played an integral part in the initial phases of organizing the show. I greatly appreciated her intelligent and collegial support. Susan Palamara, Registrar, and Kathryn A. Potts, Coordinator of Exhibitions and Collections, accommodated the complicated details of arranging for the Museum installation and the travel of this show with practical wisdom and creativity.

I am ever grateful to the *Too Jewish?* exhibition designer, whose enthusiasm for the project resulted in a dynamic design. The regulations of another institution prevent me from naming the designer of the installation of the exhibition. He cleverly and coolly embraced the numerous challenges posed by this multimedia exhibition. Thanks also to Al Lazarte, Director of Operations, for realizing the design and installation at the Museum.

With dynamism and creativity, Jacqueline Klugman lent her advice and assistance for *Too Jewish?* from across the Atlantic. As always, I am grateful for her intelligence, encouragement, and warm friendship.

Special thanks to Robin White of Owen Electric Pictures who is in the process of curating the video art program. She eagerly researched a very new field, assembling the work of important voices.

This book sets the art of *Too Jewish?* in the broader context of cultural studies. Its contributors are leading writers in their respective fields, and their essays remind us of the ever profound cross-pollination between disciplines. My thanks to Maurice Berger, again, Sander L. Gilman, Tony Kushner, Rhonda Lieberman, Linda Nochlin, Margaret Olin, and Riv-Ellen Prell for their enthusiasm and commitment. I am ever grateful to Peter Prescott for his intelligent comments on the exhibition, on my essay, as well as his constant encouragement. David Joselit and Catherine Sousslof also provided valuable insights and support. It has been a privilege to work with Leslie Mitchner, Editor in Chief, Marilyn Campbell, Managing Editor, and the staff at Rutgers University Press, whose enthusiasm, sensitivity, and professionalism were constant. Publication designer Jenny Dossin creatively and skillfully translated the sensibilities of the exhibition onto the look of these pages. Special mention goes to Matthew Baigell, who, with his signature prescience, forged our connection with Rutgers.

NORMAN L. KLEEBLATT
Susan and Elihu Rose Curator of Fine Arts
The Jewish Museum

FOREWORD
THE COUTURIER AND THE HASID

Growing up in Brooklyn, Crown Heights to be specific, in the 1930s and '40s, meant living in a world where almost everyone was Jewish. Not for me the depressing experience of "otherness" or marginalization or alienation described by so many who have written on growing up Jewish. In my basically secular, culturally ambitious, secure middle-class neighborhood, being a Jew was considered a good thing, when it was considered at all, although there were, of course, better and worse examples: Einstein was better, Louis Lepke was worse. But "too Jewish"? What could this mean in a world in which being Jewish exhausted the possibilities of existence?

Yet, paradoxically, living in a homogeneous society produces fine discriminations within the hegemonic discourse: in my secular but Jewish-identified community, it was clear, if almost always left unstated, that some people, some looks, some modes of behavior were less than desirable—shrugging, loudness, dirty fingernails, sidecurls—well, these were just "too Jewish." There weren't many Hasidim around in those days, before World War II brought them in droves to my old neighborhood. But I remember quite early peering down into a kind of basement assembly room below street level and seeing Them crowded together, like black beetles, bowing and mumbling, little men wearing odd, identifiable garments, so different from my emancipated doctor-grandfather's white linen summer suit and jaunty straw boater. It was clear that Grandpa's opinion of Them

LINDA NOCHLIN *is Lila Acheson Wallace Professor of Modern Art at the New York University Institute of Fine Arts. Her latest publication is* The Jew in the Text, *edited with Tamar Garb (Thames and Hudson, 1995). She has published extensively in the fields of nineteenth-century art, contemporary art, and feminism and art.*

wasn't high. This was precisely what he had come to the United States to escape—this darkness and superstition. Not that he ever wanted to assimilate, to forget that he and his artistic cronies at the Café Royale were Jews. It was simply that the Hasidim and their ilk were "too Jewish," Jewish in the wrong way: retrograde, uncultivated, narrow, rule-ridden, and authoritarian, rather than open, rational, literary, politically and culturally left, up on the latest in art and theater.

None of this may seem particularly relevant to the issue of Jewishness and *haute couture*, but these childhood memories made my reactions all the stronger when I first saw pictures of couturier-provocateur Jean Paul Gaultier's explosive "Hasidic" collection, a collection that made waves in the fashion world both here and abroad in Fall 1993. If ever there was an incident within the realm of popular culture that figured the Jew as excessive, as "too Jewish" with a vengeance, this was it. Broad felt hats with synthetic *pais* attached; man-tailored caftans for women. The "show was a campy sendup," declared *New York Times* fashion critic Amy Spindler. "Manischewitz wine was served, the invitations were lettered in Hebraic-looking script, and models' heads were adorned with exaggerated curls and yarmulkes. . . . Mr. Gaultier himself came out wearing a blue-and-white striped one, to match his signature Breton fisherman's shirt." Given the Jewish origins of many key figures in the fashion

Jean Paul Gaultier, Fall Collection, 1993.

LINDA NOCHLIN

world, the generally positive reception of the collection was striking. "He did it with taste and charm and dignity. In fact there was a great effort to give respect," said Kalman Ruttenstein, fashion director of Bloomingdale's Paris collection. And Ellin Salzman, fashion director of Bergdorf Goodman, was equally approving. "As a Jewish-American Princess, I wasn't offended at all. I just cut through all that Judaic stuff and looked at the clothes." Barbara Weiser, the Jewish owner of Charivari, said: "Gaultier shows always have a sense of humor. Perhaps this was a reaction to the neo-Nazism in Germany, or to political rightism in France. The clothes were so elegant and beautiful. It was just a vehicle to present the clothes. . . . I'm a person who cares about my religion, and if it were offensive I would have gotten up and walked out."[1]

Others were less tolerant, especially when French *Vogue* had the bright idea of photographing the collection in Borough Park, a center of Hasidic and Orthodox Judaism. "The whole thing is very offensive," said Rabbi Morris Shmidman, the executive director of the Council of Jewish Organizations of Borough Park. "To take men's mode of clothing and make that into a modish thing for women is extremely inappropriate in this community."[2] It was obviously the cross-dressing aspect of the collection that hit religious Jews most heavily, and, not coincidentally, it was exactly this transgressive gesture of Gaultier's collection that gave me the biggest thrill.

My first reaction to Gaultier's chutzpah was, I must admit, mixed. Not that I hadn't been prepared: Barbra Streisand had already breached the seemingly unbridgeable gap between couturier gorgeous and Orthodox ugly in her *Yentl* costume (represented in this show by Deborah Kass's *Triple Silver Yentl* of 1992). On the one hand, there is no way I can deny my first, almost instinctive, negative reaction to the collection as anti-Semitic. But then again, almost immediately, I delighted in the fact that these exquisitely crafted caftans and elegant beaver hats dripping synthetic *pais* were camping up just exactly that aspect of (excessive) Judaism that I had always disliked: its deliberate uglification and desexualization of the human body; the segregation of the sexes, signaled by the archaic clothing, which seemed, unlike the similar quaint practices of the Amish and Mennonites, for instance, to implicate me in its strategies. Above all, the collection sent up the authoritarian postures of Orthodox Jewish men and their insistence on positioning masculinity and femininity as absolute difference, with femininity equated with secondary citizenship. This, to me, was and is the root of what is literally "too Jewish," and this was what Gaultier, and his tribe of adorable *shiksa* models, flaunting their sidecurls with a difference, was blatantly calling into question. The rigid gender separation essential to Orthodox Judaism was blown sky-high by gorgeous models in male drag that was, at the same time, patently feminized, to be read as a gendered signifier and one that calls into question the whole authoritarian structure of Jewish fundamentalism. It seems to me as though Jewish women have always suffered a double oppression: one as Jews, from the society at large, the other as Jewish women, within Judaism itself, which typecast women for certain roles but denied them access to the heart of Jewish theory and practice. Gaultier's transvestite imagination brought that out into the open.

Critical theorist Homi Bhabha's notion of the ambiguous function of mimicry seems essential here—its role in both sustaining and undermining the power of dominant discourse to maintain a social order.[3] Yet the undermining functions of mimicry cannot be understood in the case of the Gaultier collection without the intervention of the notion of gender transgression. To borrow Homi Bhabha's locution, but to place it in another context: "The success of [Hasidic] appropriation depends on a proliferation of inappropriate objects that ensure its strategic failure, so that mimicry is at once resemblance and menace."[4] What better way of describing Gaultier's achievement in his "too Jewish" collection, which fails as resemblance (who would ever mistake these high-class female models in their elegant caftans for actual Hasidim?) just as it succeeds in menace, its undermining of the Jewish laws of sexual identity and difference? To be "too Jewish" in the case of Gaultier's costumes, is emphatically not to be Jewish, above all, not to be a Jewish *man*.

But before we rate the Gaultier Hasidic collection as an unqualified success, we must ask: Is imitation the sincerest flattery or the least sincere? Isn't there just the shadow of bad faith hovering about the adulatory reviews, the gush over the charm and the fine sewing? Where does inspiration end and parody begin in the mimic-world of high fashion? Gaultier and his fans are surely aware of the transgressiveness involved in borrowing from below—in borrowing specifically from a group that can only resent such blatant trampling on their most cherished values (values that I, as a secular Jewish woman, find distasteful and oppressive, it is true). This is the only way, of course, a major dress designer can be "too Jewish." False hooked noses, a plethora of silver fox, bowlegged models with huge bosoms and bulging bellies—the standard repertory of anti-Semitic caricature—would be well—just *too* "too Jewish."

The admirable achievement of the *Too Jewish?* show, both as an exhibition and as a concept, is that it destroys or sends up Jewish stereotypes (for better or for worse) at the same time that it powerfully and wittily evokes the range and variety of modern Jewish identities. This is no small achievement. From high theory to mass media representation, from kitsch menorahs to *haute couture, Too Jewish?* raises the questions without providing easy answers, and gives us a good measure of provocation and visual pleasure in the process.

NOTES

1. Amy Spindler, "Patterns," *The New York Times*, March 16, 1993, B8.
2. Pener Degen, "Egos and Ids," *The New York Times*, August 1, 1993, 4.
3. Homi K. Bhabha, "Of Mimicry and Man," in *The Location of Culture* (London and New York: Routledge, 1994), 85.
4. I have substituted the word "Hasidic" for "colonial" in this sentence. Ibid., 86.

LINDA NOCHLIN

NORMAN L. KLEEBLATT

"PASSING" INTO MULTICULTURALISM

> We are not, in fact, "other." We are choices.
>
> TONI MORRISON[1]

> In today's debate over multiculturalism, Jewish self-identification
> is all too often left to those who define Jewish culture in terms
> of an exclusivist, religious tradition and reject the possibility of a broader,
> secular Jewish culture as a legitimate form of human culture.
>
> DAVID BIALE[2]

THIS ESSAY PLACES THE WORKS IN THE EXHIBITION WITHIN THE CONTEXT OF A GROWING AWARENESS OF JEWISH ETHNICITY AS A MISSING LINK IN THE DISCOURSE ON DIVERSITY AND DIFFERENCE. IT EXAMINES HOW THE COMPLEX HISTORY OF ASSIMILATION AFFECTED THE EXPERIENCE OF "JEWISHNESS" IN POST–WORLD WAR II AMERICA.

BACKGROUND:

ART, IDENTITY, AND THE ABSENCE OF THE JEWISH QUESTION

Observers of art produced in the United States during the last fifteen years could hardly miss the centrality of issues relating to identity. Artists from marginalized positions—social, racial, gender, sexual, ethnic, and geographical—and, most recently, religious—have created work about personal and often hybrid subjectivity. In doing so, they have replaced modernism's universalist notion of "style" with often politicized versions of the postmodern alternative, "subject matter."

Since the early 1980s, a host of articles, books, and group exhibitions has dealt with identity issues in general and those of certain marginalized groups in particular. Exhibitions have ranged from modest shows in alternative spaces, which pioneered exposure of much of this type of art, to more recent, often large and elaborate exhibitions in major museums.[3] Art about identity is now virtually canonized—it is even beginning to appear in art history survey books.[4]

Fueled by theoretical discussions and practical applications of multiculturalism, the new attention to diversity began in the 1980s to secure places for artists who previously had been denied access to the gallery and museum systems. Women, a variety of Latinos, African Americans, Native Americans, Asian Americans, lesbians, and gay men found representation in the American art world in numbers unthinkable even ten years earlier. Not only did these artists, now partially empowered, exhibit within the confines of the formerly white, male-dominated system, but the art they showed was predominantly self-representational. Apart from its subjectivity, their work often censured the values of earlier exclusionary systems, challenging both the canons of Western art history and the cultural status quo. As with the academic pursuit of marginalized histories, their art tried, as Cornel West has so concisely observed, "to recast, redefine, and revise the very notions of 'modernity,' 'mainstream,' 'margins,' 'difference,' 'otherness.'"[5]

Acknowledgment in the art world of identity and issue-based subjects is a direct, albeit delayed, result of the struggles of both civil rights and feminist movements that began in the 1960s. In addition, the consideration of subjectivity and self-representation sprang from a number of preoccupations in academia. These include the study of poststructuralist philosophy, with its focus on self-reflexiveness, a critique of dominant power structures, and attention to psycho-analytic movements—especially as based on the writing of Jacques Lacan, which focused on visuality and issues of the self and the Other.[6] This issue-based and identity-specific art also reflects the new examination of media technologies, with their confusion of image and information.

Postmodern thought and aesthetics have played a major role in the turn from objective authority to subjective interrogation. Postmodernism's admiration for history and tradition, its advocacy of allegory and parody, its rejection of master narratives, its dismissal of modernity and progress, and its critique of representation were initially positioned as an apolitical and highly aestheticized movement.[7]

By the mid-1980s, however, especially as evidenced in the work of a number of women artists, the postmodern movement was becoming politicized, as its scrutiny of representation began to encompass the feminist critique of patriarchy (authority).[8] The conjunction of politics with postmodernity offered new currency for the art of marginalized groups. Andreas Huyssen cogently summarized: "It was especially the art, writing, film-making, and criticism of women and minority artists with their recuperation of buried and mutilated traditions, their emphasis on exploring forms of gender- and race-based subjectivity in aesthetic productions and experiences, and their refusal to be limited to standard canonizations, which added a whole new dimension to the critique of high modernism and to the emergence of alternative forms of culture."[9]

As with other white, ethnic minorities, Jewish identity has until now played a minor role in both the writing about and the exhibition of identity-based art.[10] While Jews certainly have been included in some of the exhibitions of this art, it has not been for their Jewishness, but for their primary public identities as, for example, women, Holocaust survivors, lesbians, or gay men. Some Jewish artists have been included in identity exhibitions because their art examined other marginalized cultures or provided a critique of the established order.[11]

Within the framework of diversity and identity-based art, the self-representation of Jews as a religious, ethnic, and cultural minority thus proves both problematic and paradoxical. During the early decades of this century, Jews had to fight for a place in the emerging world of American art. They had to overcome prejudice, battle the powerful voices of anti-Semitic critics, and fight the nativism that rejected the art of

NORMAN L. KLEEBLATT

immigrants and first-generation Americans.[12] In postwar America, however, Jews—especially Jewish men—came to hold prominent places as artists, collectors, dealers, and critics.

Indeed, the enterprise of such Jewish critics and painters as Clement Greenberg, Harold Rosenberg, Mark Rothko, and Barnett Newman did much to create the postwar dominance of American art in the international domain.[13] The New York School of painting and criticism, which emerged in the early 1940s, eventually came to represent "Jewish" in the popular consciousness, though its participants kept their frequently deracinated voices entirely within a secular domain.[14] Yet, at the same time, critic Cornel West sees the Jewish entrance into "anti-Semitic and exclusivistic institutions" as a highly significant development that "initiated the slow but sure undoing of the male WASP cultural hegemony and homogeneity."[15] Furthermore, in other social aspects of postwar America, Jews as a group were also conspicuously successful, professionally and economically.[16] Hence, this formerly reviled and often physically threatened minority, posited as a racial other in nineteenth- and twentieth-century Europe, now emerged in America as a highly visible and empowered group.

Radical assimilation and clear separation of public persona from private self became standard strategy for Jews who sought entry to humanist and commercial professions. A publisher recently reflected that when he began his career in 1958, the industry "still thought of itself as a respectable profession. The business was being run, for the most part, by men in suits or donnish tweeds, with pipes, who were either Ivy League WASPs or Jews whose highest ambition was to be mistaken for WASPs."[17] The Jewish community thus achieved visible success while its individual members were becoming invisible.[18]

Enfranchised as full participants in the American art world, Jewish artists have not so far been considered a marginalized group worthy of representation within the new identity-based order. Through the process of assimilation and under the formalist hegemony of postwar modernism, many Jewish artists, writers, performers, and theater, film, and television producers—like many other successful Jews—lost their culturally distinctive voices. Admission into the mainstream had required the shedding of that very ethnic and cultural specificity upon which the new identity-centered art is based.

The new order in the art world, engaged with issues of marginality, has left assimilated Jewish artists confused in their search for an ethnic and cultural subjectivity. And there is one further complication: the critical difference between Jewish self-representation and the self-representation of other diverse racial, ethnic, and marginalized cultural groups. These latter artists have, in their work, promoted the positive aspects of their communities while critiquing the authority structures that often threatened their individual and communal rights and well-being. Jewish artists seeking self-representation, by contrast, came to view their identities through a paradoxical mirror. Naturally, they were eager to claim affirmative facets of their American Jewish experience. Yet, in the interrogative strategies gleaned from the work of other minority artists, Jews found themselves scrutinizing the very formation of the assimilatory values of their own communities, Jewish participation within the contested power systems, and the general taboo against Jewish self-presentation in American avant-garde art during the postwar period.[19] So, for example, while women were critiquing external systems, Jewish identity-centered artists were looking at both external and internal issues of self-representation. This attitude of critical self-examination has certain analogues in the Jewish contribution to postwar American literature. To be a Jewish writer in postwar America usually meant to be a critic. It was rare, until recently, for major Jewish writers to celebrate their Jewishness.[20]

The great shift of multiculturalism has forced Jewish writers and artists to radically rethink their place in society, a place marked by the complicated definitions of American and Jewish identity. Jews entered the multicultural art world at a time when the positions of identity construction were themselves being seriously reexamined. Earlier versions of subjectivity posited more monolithic identities, as if each member of one of the various hyphenated-American groups was identical to the other.[21]

More recent writings about identity acknowledge that it is constructed in complicated and critical ways. Scholars now try to explore highly faceted positions at the interstices of various identities.[22] For example, Henry Louis Gates, Jr., cautions against "policing the borders of identity and acknowledg[es] [their] fluid and interactive nature." He claims that "selves are seen as fragmented and multiplicitous. Identities are not stable attributes but labile sites of contestation and negotiation. The construction and articulation for such identities is seen as itself a political act."[23] Along with his colleague Kwame Anthony Appiah, Gates has observed that these newer and complex interactions of race, class, and gender—to which one might add ethnic and religious—have been pioneered within the areas of feminist and gay and lesbian studies.[24] These unstable—if sometimes confusing—models of identity formation are actually extremely useful in examining the complicated trajectory of identities that exist for American Jews.

JEWISH IDENTITY COMES OF AGE

The 1980s witnessed the emergence of Jewish themes among a group of mainstream, predominantly secular artists. These themes were primarily celebratory, sometimes nostalgic—familial ancestry and religious heritage, Jewish liturgy, biblical narrative, and the Holocaust as a shared Jewish past.[25] However, with the exception of R. B. Kitaj, whose paintings critically examined the Diaspora experience and the impact of Jewish subjectivity on art and Western history, few artists during the early 1980s scrutinized the complicated notions of identity that recent criticism proposed. But by the beginning of the 1990s, a number of Jewish artists—most spanning an age range from twenty-five to fifty—were using strident, provocative, Jewish subject mat-

NORMAN L. KLEEBLATT

ter to assert a personal ethnicity and culture. Artists in this group operated from vantage points entirely associated with individual identities and located within an American, and often popular, culture.

The artists discussed here are mostly women and men who have rediscovered their Jewish identities by circuitous routes. Their stylistically heterogeneous art, encompassing a wide range of media and aesthetic strategies, includes painting, drawing, sculpture, installation art, set design, and performance. As individuals, some have lapsed in their religious observance. Many observe piecemeal, and some create new modes of "ritual" through their art. Others, who came from non-observant homes, use their art to interrogate the reasons for their parents' high degree of assimilation.

Most have come to examine aspects of their subjectivity through personal struggles in certain arenas—political, gender, or sexual—only to realize that their identities were more intricate, and that religious and cultural issues still remained unresolved for them. In general, the artists confront the promotion of an American Jewish identity with all the ethnic and cultural erasure that was part of the assimilatory package. What binds artists in the group is not a stylistic homogeneity, but rather their predilection for repeated, and often appropriated, images or framing devices. The artists also share a confrontational zeal for Jewish identification, deploying irony, paradox, and, not least, humor. These qualities may be seen as visual kin to the writing of novelist Philip Roth, who pioneered the examination of conflicted identity for an earlier generation of American Jews.[26] Initially, the American Jewish community reacted negatively to Roth's writing, though it has since ensconced him as a cultural maverick. This pattern may forecast a trend with respect to today's visual artists, who have experienced individual and communal resistance to their subject matter.[27] Yet they are engaged in a struggle for a complex personal identity that has ramifications within the Jewish world, the art world, as well as for the ongoing human rights debates around the globe.

The *Too Jewish?* artists recast their Jewish past in the matrix of postwar America, including both positive and negative aspects of growing up as a white Other in what was formerly seen as the munificent melting pot. Few pay attention to earlier Jewish pasts—the shtetls and ghettos of Europe or New York's Lower East Side, places about which previous generations still wax nostalgic. And the Holocaust, which occupies a central position within the construction of contemporary Jewish identity, is addressed ambivalently or critically, if it is addressed at all. The experiences of the artists in this exhibition have involved the conflicted messages of middle-class, suburban values. They belong to the first generation to have grown up watching their American and Jewish reflections on the television screen.[28] Mostly third- and fourth-generation Americans, they have reaped the contentious rewards of assimilation and Americanization, while nevertheless experiencing marginalization, alienation, and the subtle anti-Semitism that still permeates American culture.

Subject matter explored by this diverse group of artists can be divided into three distinct categories: a confrontation of ethnic stereotypes of the Jewish body; a challenge to the absence of Jewish representation in American popular culture and art; and new models for ritual. Each of the artists in the exhibition deals with at least one of these categories, and there is a great deal of overlap.

RECONSIDERING THE ETHNIC BODY

Body issues have played a dominant role within the realms of recent cultural criticism and art. Minority, feminist, and gay and lesbian studies have made the body a location of oppression and resistance, a means to undermine stereotypes and the authoritarian voice.[29] A significant corpus of identity-based art questions the historical and prevailing stereotypes of ethnic-, racial-, gender-, and sexual-specific bodies. Such work often confronts viewers with well-known, embarrassing, tired, and often painful images, forcing them to recognize the long-extant insidiousness inscribed within these representations.

The cultural construction of the Jewish body as seen in the work of a number of artists reflects the considerable recent scholarly attention to this subject. These include studies of the nineteenth-century medical and scientific theories that helped guarantee the racial and physical otherness of the Jew. The physical construction of Jewish masculinity and femininity within American popular culture, with all its attendant complexities and contradictions, has also been the focus of critical and penetrating study. Most recently, there have begun to appear analyses of the religious-specific body as read in biblical commentary and Talmudic exegesis. These latter analyses shift the old, internal stereotype of "the people of the book" to a consideration of observant Jews as physical and sexual entities.[30] Stereotypes, and particularly the societal pressure to negate or eradicate them, are in fact constantly recurring themes in the works of many of the artists under discussion.

Hannah Wilke, who died in 1993, produced one of the earliest works in the show. Her 1985 *Venus Pareve* (plate 36) is a group of twenty-five hand-modeled sculptural self-portraits, with some cast in edible chocolate. The sculpture shows a predilection for wordplay, use of food as art material, and a central concern with the body, sexuality, and narcissism. Puns and double entendres have always been essential elements in Wilke's art.[31] In *Venus Pareve* she has titled her self-portrait busts with two foreign words, one Latin, one Hebrew. The Latin name for the goddess of love has become part of English vocabulary; its mythological history has, for that matter, become central to Western art and culture. The Hebrew word *pareve*, however, is entirely foreign to nonreligious Jews and immediately identifies Wilke, who is both artist and sitter, as Other. (*Pareve* is a term used in Jewish dietary laws. It indicates the neutrality of ingredients, i.e., that the food in question can be eaten with either dairy or meat.) Indeed, Wilke's chocolate is made with neutral (*pareve*) ingredients, the irony of which is apparent in her Venus's sexy pose.

NORMAN L. KLEEBLATT

Wilke's painted plaster figures are modeled, then cast and painted, while her chocolate figures are simply cast. The interchange between the physical work—with its dualistic play between the permanent and transitory, the visual and edible—and the multiple readings afforded it through its oracular title situate Wilke as an heir to Marcel Duchamp.[32] Purposely locating herself within the interstices of numerous contemporary art movements, Wilke here addresses the manipulation and specularity of the female body as it is visually consumed by the male gaze. This tyrannical, if passive, masculine eye has been a major concern within feminist art and criticism for the last two decades.[33] In *Venus Pareve*, Wilke teases the viewer into becoming proactive by indulging the assumed baser, and performative, function of eating, which must now coexist with the more privileged and detached sense of vision. Visual and verbal, physical and abstract aspects that sustain the formal function of this sculpture position Wilke herself as a Jewish Venus, with all the irony and contradiction such a designation might call forth. The work exploits the stereotype of Jewish women as sexually permissive, navigating the sexual connotations of the beautiful, exotic Jewess in the classic observation of Jean-Paul Sartre.[34] Through its image of the self-proclaimed Jewish artist and sitter, mirrored in its identity-specific title, the work challenges the representation and the exclusionary aspects of Venus's supposed classical Western origins. *Venus Pareve* has catapulted Wilke's Jewish body, with all its "oriental" implications, into the canon of Western art, making Wilke, both the sculpture's subject and its creator, the first Jewish Venus.

Deborah Kass celebrates the formerly marginalized, ethnically identified, Jewish female superstar. Kass, whose early feminist work questioned the heroic masculine style of such twentieth-century "masters" as Pablo Picasso, Jackson Pollock, Jasper Johns, and David Salle, calls her silkscreen series of Barbra Streisand "Jewish Jackies" (plates 8 and 9) (referring, of course, to Andy Warhol's famous "Jackie" Kennedy series). She has purposely borrowed the format of Warhol's celebrity portraits to call attention to the one major female Jewish superstar whom Warhol omitted from his cosmopolitan Hollywood register. Such omission may have transpired because Streisand's ethnically specific features and voice were too un-American for the cool, nationalist intimations of the Pop master. Through Barbra Streisand, Kass proudly presents the physical stereotype of Jewish female ethnicity. Cultural critic Maurice Berger sees these works as "question[ing] the codes of beauty and normalcy that underwrite the subliminal anti-Semitism in American culture."[35] Kass's series of large-scale *Yentl* paintings (fig. 1), showing Barbra Streisand cross-dressed in the cinematic role of Yentl, articulates issues of sexual and gender ambiguity. For Kass, Yentl is essentially a Talmudic student in drag: a woman who had to pass as a man in order to obtain a Jewish education.[36]

The 1962 story by Isaac Bashevis Singer on which the Yentl tale is based can, for Kass, be read from a homosexual vantage point. This sexually deceptive image of Yentl adds a third, now lesbian element to Kass's earlier exploration of her feminist and Jewish identities. The image of Barbra Streisand, Kass's hero from her

Fig. 1. Deborah Kass, Triple Silver Yentl

(My Elvis), *1992.*

teenage years, acts as the surrogate for the artist's Jewish identity. And it confronts the problem of representing Jewish bodies in American popular culture, given "Streisand's unWASPy looks, a big nose, and a reputation for business shrewdness (read in the ethnic stereotype of 'pushy')."[37]

Of all the stereotypes in the above quotation, the notion of the "Jewish nose" has become most important for a number of Jewish artists in the show, as in Dennis Kardon's ongoing series, *Jewish Noses* (fig. 4; plates 6 and 7). Kardon has here taken the dominant stereotypical feature for recognizing the otherness of the Jewish body in America and made academically modeled sculptural portraits of it. His models are art world personages, including other Jewish artists, curators, dealers, and collectors. He sculpts these pieces directly from the model and then meticulously paints them with lifelike veracity. These highly detailed works examine the societal constructions built upon body differences, a legacy of the physiognomic racist theories of the last century. Cultural critic and sociologist Sander Gilman reminds us that medical theories about the difference of the Jewish body moved from the notion of Jews as racially black, that is, having more pigmented skin, to an ethnic issue by which the Jewish body becomes different precisely because of such features as a Semitic nose. As Jews internalized these racist theories, any variant on supposedly "neutral," "Aryan"—read superior— noses became a troubling ethnic index to Jews themselves.[38]

By exhibiting these portrait "fragments" together as a group, and labeling the noses with the names of his art world sitters, Kardon parodies the earlier anthropological obsession with describing, collecting, and labeling cultural specimens in an attempt to fix "difference" among groups. Kardon reveals the ludicrousness of a practice which is itself based on nineteenth-century racist enterprise. The purposeful futility of Kardon's documentary fastidiousness and the inability of such an enterprise to furnish useful information recalls the Korean American artist Byron Kim's multicolored panels (fig. 3) that record, in excruciating detail, the specific shades of "brown," "yellow," and "white" pigmentation in his collection of painted swatches of the skin colors of his friends. Meanwhile, the quantity of Kardon's output—this sculptural project features forty-nine noses—recognizes the extensive participation of Jews in the New York art world. In effect, he has created a symbolic group portrait of a Jewish community within the art community, but one which has lost all social, religious, and ethnic coherence.

Kardon's noses were but the artist's first attempt to problematize his ethnic and religious identity. His more recent painting, *Lover's Quarrel* of 1994 (fig. 2), marks a shift from group identity to personal scrutiny. A double self-portrait, *Lover's Quarrel* shows Kardon from the back attached to his double as if they were Siamese twins. A scar exists at the join between the two nearly identical figures. One of the likenesses is wearing a baseball cap—the current popular male fashion accessory—the other a skullcap (a traditional Jewish head covering indicating religious observance and respect for God). These two selves, the secular and the religious, signal Kardon's continuing dilemma—a legacy of the assimilatory values which still affect many minority Americans—about whether to separate or integrate these two aspects of self.

Fig. 2. Dennis Kardon, Lover's Quarrel,

1994.

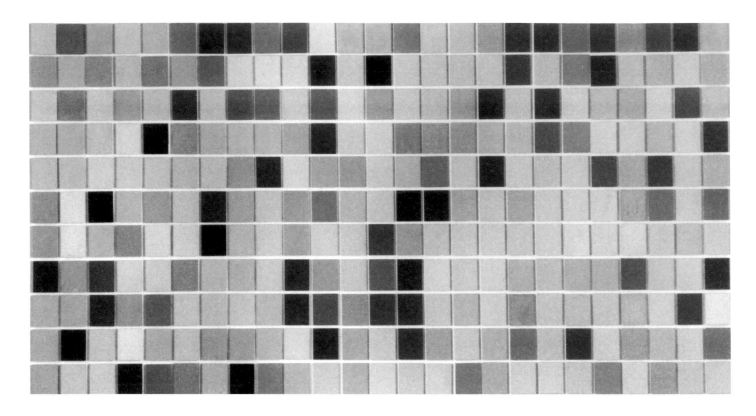

Fig. 3. Byron Kim, Synecdoche, *1992. Oil*

and wax on panel, 204, each 10" x 8".

Various private collections.

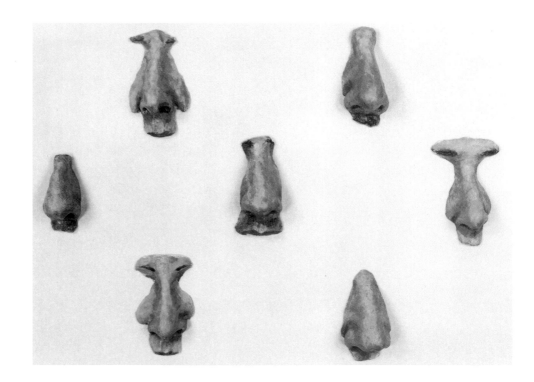

Fig. 4. Dennis Kardon, Detail, Jewish

Noses, *1993–1995.* LEFT TO RIGHT: TOP

ROW, *Helene Winer, Jay Gorney;* MIDDLE

ROW, *Josh Decter, Adam Bellow, Laurie*

Simmons; BOTTOM ROW, *Nan Goldin,*

David Deutsch.

NORMAN L. KLEEBLATT

Adam Rolston is also preoccupied with the "Jewish" nose (figs. 5–7). In contrast with Kardon, his interest is based on the Jewish reaction to this sign of difference. Rolston had earlier dealt with the construction of both male gay bodies and the racist theories that posited both Jews and gays as disease carriers. Thus he is sensitive to the prevalence of a stereotype that insists on the inferiority (and implicit danger) of "differences" among racial, gender, sexual, and ethnic groups. Given the pressure to conform within American society, the artist easily grasps how these "embarrassing" differences have left their psychological scars, especially given the wholesale marketing of homogeneity in America. Rolston's series of beautifully crafted drawings shows the surgical procedure of rhinoplasty, a cosmetic corrective, which has been particularly popular among Jews since the late nineteenth century.[39] Seen as a cure for the prominent "Jewish" nose, the surgery was particularly common in postwar America among Jews seeking to make their physical features conform with widely promoted standards of Anglo-Saxon beauty. The question of why and for whom Jews seek this cosmetic curative to ethnicity is complicated. One plastic surgeon who has analyzed the phenomenon comments: "[Jewish] Patients seeking rhinoplasty . . . frequently show a guilt-tinged, second-generation rejection of their ethnic background masked by excuses. . . . Often it is not so much the desire to abandon the ethnic group as it is to be viewed as individuals and to rid themselves of specific physical attributes associated with their particular group."[40]

But social commentary is not the only goal of Rolston's mission. The drawings themselves are rich in artistic strategies, including the reworking of earlier art sources and a calculated contrast between style and subject matter. Rolston, who, like Deborah Kass, has worked in a post- or neo-Warholesque mode, uses these drawings to reexamine the benign promotion of nose jobs in Andy Warhol's famous paintings *Before and After* of 1960 (fig. 8) and 1962. Warhol's two-part paintings of ethnic predicament and its surgical solution are typical of Pop Art's intentionally

Figs. 5–7. Adam Rolston, Untitled, *from the series "Nose Job," 1991.*

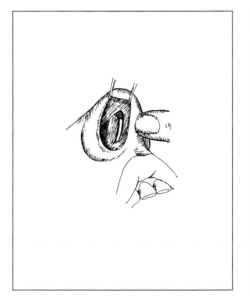

deadpan reflection of the simplistic aspects of American culture: the marketing of homogeneity during the 1950s and 1960s. Rolston adds critical scrutiny for the social issues of the 1980s and 1990s in his intensely beautiful drawings, showing the moments between the "before" and the "after" rather than Warhol's simpler juxtaposition. His use of finely wrought and delicate drawings offers a deliberate contrast with the not-so-subtle bodily violence underlying the surgical ordeal.

Among the indicators of the body of Jews, no aspect can be more obvious or more simplistic than the distinctiveness of Jewish names which had, in Europe, been assigned precisely to mark Jews' "difference." While rhinoplastic surgery was a painful procedure for removing ethnic physiological signs, a simple legal maneuver could convert Jewish-sounding appellations to ethnically neutral signifiers.

Ken Aptekar's exploitation of Old Master paintings playfully manipulates naming operations for Jews. These show, as Sander Gilman has observed, the possibility of "seeing objects [and words] as [both] reflection or distortion of self."[41] In addition to exploring ethnic erasure via name conversion, the artist simultaneously interrogates the purposeful exclusion of both Jewish representations and artists from the history of post-Renaissance art, a fact that his textual fantasies seek to redress. Aptekar's correctives, which focus on seventeenth-century Dutch and Flemish art, relate closely to the amends Hannah Wilke sought for Jewish women in the history of antiquity and to Deborah Kass's compensation for ethnic amnesia during the era of Pop Art.

Appropriating details of Dutch and Flemish Baroque canvases, Aptekar overlays his repainted pictures with glass, onto which he has etched phrases and stories, forcing the intersection of image and text, a method Aptekar associates with his interest in what he calls Jewish cognitive process. The intersection of these stories with the fragmented and appropriated "masterpiece" force a purposeful distortion of the original.[42]

Aptekar's textual overlays challenge the limits of seeing and the limits of interpretation.[43] For example, in the text for his 1994 painting *"In 1640 the artist may have changed the color of his hair"* (fig. 9), the artist fantasizes a Jewish appearance—hence identity—for Rembrandt. Like Hannah Wilke, Aptekar, as a Jew, humorously rewrites what he sees as an absence or at least an inadequacy, now forcing the masters of the Western canon and the imagery they created to include Jews in general and the artist in particular. His *"Albert.*

Fig. 8. Andy Warhol, Before and After, *1960. Synthetic polymer paint on canvas, 54" x 70".*

NORMAN L. KLEEBLATT

Fig. 9. Ken Aptekar, "In 1640 the artist may have changed the color of his hair." 1994.

Used to be Abraham." of 1995 (plate 1) takes a Dutch portrait, reverses it, and overlays it with a glass etched with the title words, which encourage the viewer to read the sitter's face as Jewish. By changing the seventeenth-century sitter's name, the artist implies not only that the sitter in the 1631 work, attributed to Isaac de Jouderville, is Jewish, but also that he has changed his name to mask his religious identity. Such imaginative reediting of history and art owes a debt to the strategies of feminist writers. Susan Suleiman reminds us that women writers frequently use such parody in the service of feminism, transforming patriarchal myth and reinventing it in the image of its female creators.[44] Aptekar manipulates parody and play to concoct Jewish myth, replacing the "Gentile" patriarchy with a Jewish one.

His 1995 painting *"Goldfinch. Used to be Goldfarb."* (plate 2), which uses the ornithological image in Karel Fabritius's 1654 painting *The Goldfinch*, operates somewhat differently. Here the name change implied in the textual overlay relates to the Anglicization of the German. The playful association of repainted images and fictive texts engenders further free association. Like Kardon, Aptekar's exercise reflects the lack of logic associated with the linguistic transformation of Germanic-sounding Jewish surnames into their "ethnically neutral" English versions.[45]

TRULY AMERICAN ★ ★ ★

. . . AND TRULY GOOD !

Her parents were the children of immigrants and wanted very much for her to be a true member of American society. They lived in a christian neighborhood where the anti-semitism was usually quite covert. During her early years she was unfavorably compared with the cherub-faced blonde down the street who was neat and clean and oh-so-well behaved. She went there for lunch occasionally: peanut butter sandwiches with butter and jam on white bread with the crusts removed, and campbell's tomato soup. Her overhand technique of holding a soup spoon was seen as crude, reflecting on the morals of "those (jewish) people" down the street.

Many years later she heard that the cherub-faced blonde had become a born-again christian.

She is four years old, living in a small town in Maine. Her family has nothing in common with the twelve other Jewish families in town. Everyone else belongs to one church or another. They are socially out of the loop.

On a street straight out of a Norman Rockwell painting she is being chased by the neighborhood kids. They yell "DIRTY LITTLE KIKE" and throw grapes at her.

She is running, crying, tripping over her feet, not understanding what she has done wrong. She runs past the white picket fences looking for home.

© 1994 BEVERLY NAIDUS

Figs. 10 and 11. Beverly Naidus, Details,

What Kinda Name Is That?, *1995.*

Beverly Naidus also combines word and image. Unlike Ken Aptekar's, her materials are deliberately humble and decidedly contemporary, being scavenged from popular culture. In her 1994 *What Kinda Name Is That?* (figs. 10 and 11), she uses photocopy manipulations to undercut the rhetoric that preaches a homogeneous American beauty. Naidus's work has always addressed the highly American and female preoccupation with consumerism, together with the sense of isolation and alienation that Jews and other ethnic and racial minorities experienced in this country. Naidus scours the well-known journals of the 1950s and 1960s for advertisements reminiscent of those she read growing up in the East Coast suburbs. These printed commercials promoted blond and slender beauty, an ethnic ideal that was precisely the antithesis of Naidus's own physiognomy.

As Aptekar uses glass overlays, Naidus uses the photocopy process to layer exaggerated stories onto the hygienic images of American postwar culture. In doing so, she underscores the unspoken humiliation that she was made to feel by being different from standard American issue. One of her fliers shows a perfectly manicured, coiffed, and stylishly clothed model who encounters Naidus's alter ego in a "clean and perfumed suburb." The Naidus alter ego is made to feel "dark, hairy armpitted, smelly"—in a word, ashamed of her difference.

Naidus shares the embarrassment of physically different features with other ethnic groups, particularly Latina women, with whom she empathizes. Although discussions of skin color and hair texture differences by African Americans and Latinos are more sharply focused (and their differences are more visibly conspicuous),[46] Naidus's dilemma as a white ethnic who looks different was nevertheless highly personal and painful. The artist's *What Kinda Name Is That?* and her *One Size Does Not Fit All* exemplify her continuing meditations on assumptions about ideal American bodies. Kobena Mercer's observation that "[t]he question of how ideologies of 'the beautiful' have been defined by, for, and—for most of the time—against black people" can, with the example of Naidus's project, be expanded to include individuals from white ethnic minorities. For that matter, it might pertain to all individuals whose physical makeup strays from the dogmatic notions of the beautiful and the normal.[47]

In his internationally acclaimed *Maus: A Survivor's Tale* of 1976–1986, Art Spiegelman confronts the self-conscious presentation of body stereotypes in the service of personal narrative. He also addresses the problems of the generation gap between a foreign-born father and thoroughly Americanized son as well as the privileged place of the Holocaust for the American Jewish community. Spiegelman's depiction of Jews in the allegorical guise of mice is radical and paradoxical: while plunging the reader/viewer into Hitler's well-known diatribe about Jews as vermin, he also highlights an almost instinctive human tendency to caricature and stereotype. The Nazis themselves masquerade as cats—the Poles as pigs, the French as frogs—in this thinly veiled Orwellian parody. Spiegelman's self-conscious exploitation of visual stereotypes evolved from his interest in racist caricatures of African Americans, which pervaded the 1930s comic books he was studying.[48]

The artist depicts the results of interviews conducted over several years with

Fig. 12. Art Spiegelman, Preliminary sketch for Maus: A Survivor's Tale, *Vol. 2, Chapter 1, c. 1983–1986.*

his cantankerous father; the resulting images are devoid of either sentimentality or restraint. He perceives his father's experience at Auschwitz through his own American perspective and the popular American comic strip, all the while recalling and paralleling his feeling of outsiderness during adolescence.[49]

Spiegelman's format and narrative question the production, assumptions, and value of traditional art and monuments representing the Holocaust.[50] Recounting his parents' experience of Auschwitz, he implies that there are moral issues about his inheritance of that experience. He also confronts difficult questions germane to contemporary Jewry. His deceptively naive comic book style helps make contemporary issues both accessible and transparent.

Spiegelman reveals his family's problems with his Catholic-born, though now converted wife, Françoise, in Book II, Chapter I (fig. 12). Rather than challenge us with the immediate, problematic social test of intermarriage, Spiegelman engages us in his artistic dilemma: how will he represent his French wife, given the animal codes he uses? The frog appears as a natural stereotype for French in this no-holds-barred play on typecasting. But quickly he rationalizes the transference of his wife's frog identity to that of a "beautiful" (read Jewish) mouse. Ironically, Françoise's conversion to Judaism includes a facial reconstruction that gives her the physiognomic, albeit symbolic, features that some Jews have sought surgically to erase. The conversion takes place in a few pages and becomes a minor digression in the brisk shuttle between Queens and Auschwitz, father and son, history and memory.

Aside from the power, tenderness, and unabashed honesty of the story, Spiegelman's major accomplishment in *Maus* is his use of the comic book format as a vehicle for serious literary and artistic achievement. *Maus* is at once universal and specific, literature and art, high and low. Spiegelman has insisted on keeping

Fig. 13. Rona Pondick, Little Bathers,

1990–1991.

NORMAN L. KLEEBLATT

the so-called "low art" scale, format, and distribution method of comics, and has used the breadth of his subject to transform the "humble" into what has now been admitted into the realm of "high" literature and art.

Rona Pondick's mysterious body parts (fig. 13) and clothing fragments situate the viewer in precisely the same position as that of the *Maus* comic. Pondick's terrain is every bit as precarious a subject as the Holocaust, and sometimes more frightening because of the very amorphousness of its imagery. Her images of heads, breasts, shoes, baby bottles, and beds, while sexually loaded with psychoanalytic intimations, are massed as fragmentary parts that cannot but recall imagery of mass extermination.

Pondick's work is heir to the Surrealist tradition, in particular the work of Hans Bellmer, but is also indebted to Philip Guston's late work, especially such masterpieces as *Head and Bottle* of 1975. The influence of the latter must have been important for this artist, who came of professional age during the period of Guston's radical break with abstraction. Clear reference to children's sexuality and the fragility of gender construction are central to Pondick's work. She studied at Yale in the early 1970s, where the formal purity and nonreferentiality of minimalism were canonized. This experience forced the artist to see her own difference within what she experienced as an emotionally neutral "male, WASP world."[51]

Kafka too is an important figure for Pondick, not least because of the very Jewishness of his enterprise. The discomfort we feel in the juxtaposition of the humorous and the serious in Pondick's grotesque and spoofy body parts fits the standard Kafkaesque amalgam of comic and tragic, pride and embarrassment. Kafka's example foreshadows the need to problematize expressions of ethnic and gender identities through which Pondick asserts her Jewish self. In this, she challenges the authority of the formalist, ethnically neutral modernism she was taught at Yale. Her work fights what Andreas Huyssen has called the "cognitive rational understanding" of Nazism and the Holocaust as "incompatible with the emotional melodramatic representation of history as the story of a family."[52]

RE-PRESENTING POPULAR CULTURE

Many of the artists included here came of age during the highly commercial era of postwar America, a time also marked by American artistic hegemony. In the arena of popular culture, technological advances, particularly television, helped promote concepts of newness and consumption already ensconced within American prewar culture. Regarding "high" art, pure formal invention was championed in a trajectory of progressive movements which ran the stylistic gamut from the hot, so-called "subjective" Abstract Expressionism to the cooler, distanced credo of Pop and Minimal Art. Beginning in the 1950s, other movements and art forms, such as Fluxus and process art, performance and mail art, initiated a challenge to the ascendancy of this neat package of art historical progress. But these less easily commodifiable alternatives were generally invisible in both academe and the white cube of the gallery and museum space.

A duality was nevertheless established that pitted high culture against low:[53] a regard for originality in the domain of the former versus a fixation with an assumed egalitarian homogeneity in the mass marketing of the latter. Even the advent of Pop Art, which promised to obliterate the split between the aesthetic and the non-aesthetic,[54] actually validated the power of artistic genius to transform the popular into art. These two seemingly incompatible, even polarized realms did meet on one matter: the homogeneity of popular culture and the objective originality promoted in painting and sculpture were both founded on the erasure of personal, ethnic, and/or religious identities.

Like many artists involved with issues of personal identity who have worked hard to question and subvert canonical notions of authority, those in *Too Jewish?* interrogate the hegemony of an art world dominated by empowered (sometimes Jewish) "white" men. The sort of ethnic amnesia which ran through both mass media and "high" culture had become a prerequisite to power, at least in terms of self-representation. In its wake, postmodernism brought a more complex critique to popular culture, deploying the forms and strategies of advertising and media. As opposed to Pop Art's shattering distinctions between aesthetic and non-aesthetic, a number of contemporary artists began to play with the free-flowing circulation of high and low materials and models. By circulating among these once separate regions, they problematize the notion of distinct levels of artistic practice, challenging the very foundations of Western artistic production. They often deploy the tactics of either Marcel Duchamp or Andy Warhol, complicating the former's elevation of the mundane utilitarian to the realm of art and parodying Warhol's method of transforming representations of inexpensive commodities into precious images.

The deceptive simplicity of materials and images is one of the most crucial strategies the *Too Jewish?* artists use in debunking authority in this dilemma of representation. In so doing, they add a new, crucial element of ethnicity and cultural specificity to the mix. The artists purposely try to reconfigure the past in a way that challenges its assumed authority. Homi Bhabha has summarized the complexity of these seemingly simple ventures: "The enunciation of cultural differences problematizes the binary division of past and present, tradition and modernity, at the level of cultural representation and its authoritative address. It is the problem of how, in signifying the present, something comes to be represented, relocated and translated in the name of tradition, in the guise of pastness that is not necessarily a faithful sign of historical memory but a strategy representing authority in terms of the artifice of the archaic."[55] To this must be added Craig Owens's observation that in the new artistic order, most of the fundamental, and authoritative, distinctions have been lost. These include the artistic equivalents of the binarisms of the literary and political realm to which Bhabha refers: "original and copy, genuine and fake, function and ornament. Each term seems to contain its opposite, and this indeterminacy brings with it the impossibility of choice, or, rather, the absolute equivalence and hence interchangeability of choices."[56]

NORMAN L. KLEEBLATT

Deborah Kass and Adam Rolston both work in a neo- or post-Warholesque mode, employing the circulation and purposeful dislocation of images and artistic strategies that they at once celebrate and critique. Both replace the ethnically neutral personalities and products in their oeuvres with culturally specific ones. Their various series defy the neat separation between painting and conceptual art, Pop Art and appropriation. In blatantly choosing, even obsessing upon Jewish representations, they seek to expose the equivocal role of today's Jewish artists, their ambiguous status within the Jewish community, and the basic resistance to Jewish subjects (and identity) in an art world that would seem to champion most other ethnically specific imagery. Warhol's brilliance had been to break the class barrier with middle-class artifacts transformed into high art. Such Jewish artists as Kass and Rolston, like their African American counterpart Danny Tisdale,[57] use Warholesque appropriation to break the ethnic barrier. Both Kass and Rolston also merge their Jewish identity with their lesbian and gay identity.

Yet there are major differences between Kass's and Rolston's work. Technically, Kass adheres to the slick, silkscreened surfaces that were a signature of Warhol's production. Rolston, especially in his more recent series such as the one with matzah boxes, works the surface to achieve certain self-conscious, idiosyncratic painterly effects. Kass focuses on Jewish personalities, Rolston on Jewish products.

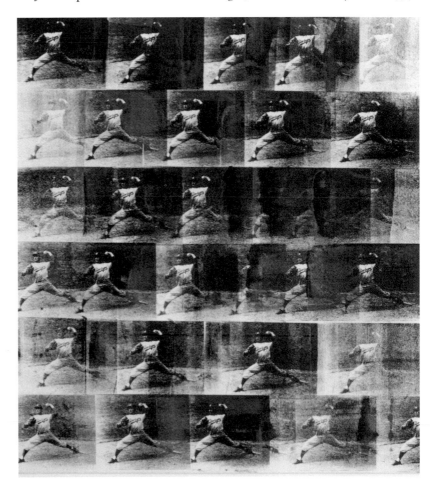

Fig. 14. Deborah Kass, Sandy Koufax, *1994.*

Kass's *Yentl* (fig. 1) and "Jewish Jackie" series (plates 8 and 9) pay homage to Warhol and to mass media. Her series on Gertrude Stein—humorously dubbed *Chairman Ma*, a Jewish feminist substitution for Warhol's *Chairman Mao*—is her homage to another lesbian, artist, and Jew, and an important early champion of the modernist enterprise. *Sandy Koufax* (fig. 14) is a celebrity portrait of the Jewish pitcher on the mound à la Warhol. (Koufax also happens to be related to Kass.) Through the image of the Jewish baseball hero, one is made to remember how vital such idols were to Jews in postwar America.[58] Visible and heroic, such sports champions as Koufax and Hank Greenberg broke the traditional (and stereotypical) image of the Jewish male as weak or feminine, forging an American version of Max Nordau's concept of a "muscle-Jew" and creating a fresh American Jewish identity wherein Jews assimilated into "tough, fighting men."[59]

Rolston's series of matzah boxes (for example, plate 32) focuses on the meanings inherent in the boxes' commercial labels and in the packaging and consumption of ethnicity in America. In contrast with the silkscreen methods of either Warhol or Kass, Rolston actually paints his monumental canvases, which depict the labels of Goodman's, Horowitz-Magareten, Manischewitz, and Streit's brand matzahs. His intentionally eccentric handling of paint sometimes mimics silkscreen but more often exposes the presence of both the artist's hand and his brush. Through such painterly manipulation, the artist, however, never loses sight of his goal of emphasizing the flatness of the picture plane. Rolston calls attention to the juxtaposition of Americanized logos which nevertheless market a distinctly ethnic product. He empties the boxes of their products by emphasizing the impenetrable surface of the pictures; the calculated effect is that this is only a play with representation. The boxes are also a metaphor for empty ethnic vessels. Rolston feels that for some Americans, the validation of ethnicity is simply marked by the purchase or consumption of ethnically specific products. Nevertheless, these neo–Pop Art extravaganzas assert Jewishness in the gallery space and indicate that the actual market is not as homogeneous and ethnically pure as Pop Art would have assumed.

Cary Leibowitz's monumental painting *I'm A Jew how 'bout U?!!* (plate 10) uses a deceptively childish-looking writing style to emblazon the eponymous phrase of the title across the sizable space of the baby-blue panel. In the panel, he conflates popular culture and high art using obvious sources from the current proliferation of "cute" variations on kitsch in the novelty market. Also evident are artistic sources that range from the writing-style abstractions of Cy Twombly to the word-based conceptual work of such artists as Lawrence Weiner and Joseph Kosuth. In its seeming shallowness, *I'm A Jew* . . . clearly parodies the profound and often oracular meanings put forward in word and text art. Its self-conscious acquiescence is a ploy that forces confrontation with a seemingly stupid rhetorical question that nevertheless refuses resolution—especially given the aesthetic context in which it is posed. Leibowitz is willing to proudly pronounce the unmentionable, the unassimilable. And his affirmative question negates the false self-effacement that has characterized many American Jews.

Under the provocative and purposely derogatory pseudonym Candyass, Leibowitz has created a distinctly gay artistic gloss on American popular culture as dominated by a white, heterosexual male power structure. His cutesy parodies, their confessional and dejected vision, offer a terse critique on modernism, its worship of male artist heroes, and its taboo against "Jewish" self-representation in the art world. It also inherently criticizes the high-tech appropriation products of such postmodern artists as Jeff Koons, Ashley Bikerton, Meyer Vaisman, and Haim Steinbach. A paradigm for the newly coined notions of "loser" or "slacker" artist, Leibowitz purposely castigates these postmodern products of macho genius with their slickly presented, technologically self-conscious, and chilly commentaries on the commodification of the art object.[60]

In late 1992, Leibowitz teamed up with Rhonda Lieberman, an artist and writer who was the first to thrust an ethnic Jewish feminism into the center of art

NORMAN L. KLEEBLATT

world discourse in the pages of *Artforum*. The two began to take an interest in things Jewish.[61] Both understood the descent of expensive European designer merchandise into the realm of American kitsch, and began to explore the association of those high-ticket items with the cultural stereotype of the Jewish American princess. Their controversial "fake" Chanel show, presented at Stux Gallery in December 1992, included a variety of transformed trademark Jewish foodstuffs such as Chanel matzah meal, in addition to other secular consumer items. One corner displayed fabricated and inventive, symbolic and functional Hanukkah holiday trappings, including such novelty appropriations as the "poor man's" tin Hanukkah lamp transformed into high fashion through its phony Chanel logo and a Hanukkah *geltbelt*—an invented ritual accessory (plate 11). The Chanel Hanukkah menorah was made from a fake Chanel bag (purchased from a street vendor) with nine of the designer's mass-produced lipsticks replacing the usual candleholders and candlesticks. The show was a searing indictment of American consumerism and conformism; it ridiculed the very notion of originality. And it dared to question the stereotype of the Jewish American princess—the mythological creature whose desires focus on high-priced designer objects that transform her into an image of a discreet and elegant, if ethnically *pareve* woman. Is this stereotype created by the outside culture or is it propagated through Jewish internal self-hatred?[62]

Rhonda Lieberman continued her investigation of the relationship between Chanel and the princess stereotype by flaunting images of famous Jewish female celebrities (figs. 15–17). Unlike Kass's monumental paeans to Jewish "heroes and heroines," Lieberman's parodic elegies to Barbra Streisand, Joan Rivers, and Sandra Bernhardt are modest and even functional. Her alternatives demonumentalize the images and recirculate them as commercial insignias on "fake" Chanel shopping bags. Lieberman also continued to probe what she sees as the ironic envy of Jews toward Christian aspects of American culture. For American Jews (and for Jews in most Western nations), Hanukkah has often become a con-

Figs. 15–17. Rhonda Lieberman, Pushy/Cushy/Tushy (Sandra Bernhard triptych from the series "Purse Pictures"), 1994.

frontation with Christmas. In fact, the American celebration of Hanukkah owes much to the appropriation of certain Americanized versions of the Christian tradition.[63] Lieberman brashly confronts the Christmas tree and the liberal appropriation of it by some American Jews with her Hanukkah bush—replete with images of Barbra Streisand emblazoned on six-pointed "Jewish" stars. Embarrassingly titled *Barbra Bush* (plate 12), the work was made for Barney's "Christmas" storefront windows (the store annually commissions artists to do its holiday windows). *Barbra Bush* playfully offered textual associations with slang codes for female genitalia and with the then First Lady of the United States. Simultaneously counterbalancing display merchandizing and art, Lieberman also uses commercial tactics derived from the highly political messages of feminist artists like Jenny Holzer and Barbara Kruger. She turns their more populist market into a luxury one, which she now infiltrates with ethnic paraphernalia.

Working in video, radio, and photography, Los Angeles media artist Ilene Segalove also observed the power of the mass media to reach more diverse audiences than could traditional art forms. A photographic text piece, *Jewish Boys* (plate 33), exemplifies her witty and accessible tales that recount the personal and paradoxical experiences of a Jewish woman growing up during the cultural upheavals of the 1960s and 1970s. Humorist, feminist, and social critic, Segalove mocks the solemnity of other contemporary conceptual artists. Her 1985 radio performance, *Hanukkah*, reenacted her childhood dilemma of participating in public school Christmas celebrations as a Jewish girl. In the audiotape, Segalove mimics her childhood voice, chanting Christmas carols while refusing to name either Christ or Jesus. Her touching omissions clearly show her awkwardness— the otherness she felt—in trying to maintain Jewish identity in a Christian-dominated society.

As a teenager growing up in the New York suburbs during the 1970s, Kenneth Goldsmith experienced anti-Semitic assaults which intensified his feeling of otherness. Looking for ethnically specific role models, he became enthralled with the counterculture of the previous decade, whose ranks included numerous Jews. In a recent series of works, he honors Jewish heroes of this epoch in American history such as Abbie Hoffman and Bob Dylan, seeking to identify with the ethnic aspect of their highly public personas. Goldsmith senses the conflicted religious identities of these icons of American culture and examines how the experience of "Jewishness" has affected their lives and work as well as his own. He employs his now signature strategy of manipulating and merging texts from a variety of sources. In *Bob Dylan* (plate 5), he conflates an image of the singer-songwriter, whose sense of Jewish identity has been ambivalent and conflicted over the years, with portraits of Allen Ginsberg, Abbie Hoffman, and himself, superimposed upon a collage ground of upside-down Hebrew letters. In his longing to relate to and even merge identities with these figures, Goldsmith sometimes scribbles notes of personal reflection across the face of these collages. The notes include homages to Dylan, radical political thought, and anti-Semitic invective both from the writings of T. S. Eliot and Ezra Pound and from his own suburban American community. The initially confusing effect of this work on the viewer mirrors the artist's experience of identity formation.

Like Rhonda Lieberman's modestly sized tribute to female Jewish entertainers, Neil Goldberg has created another small-scale, if ambivalent, homage to Jewish Borscht Belt comedians in his six-part panel of 1992 titled *Shecky* (plate 4). Goldberg's comedians, veterans of a previous generation and venerable symbols of Jewish schtick, are plastered on real matzah. Matzahs seem, by their very lack of either visual glamour or culinary flavor, to fuel the imagination of Jewish artists in ways that more canonical Jewish foods (e.g., chicken soup, bagels) have not. Goldberg's choice of male, Jewish comics also challenges a recent aversion to these once-famous men. Although generations of Jews had loyally patronized them, by the 1970s and '80s, they became stereotyped as Borscht Belt funnymen to be avoided by those seeking to assimilate. Jackie Mason, among those most closely affected by the new acculturated tastes of contemporary Jews, admitted that "people said [he was simply] too Jewish."[64]

Nurit Newman was also inspired by matzah for her *Complex Princess* installation (plates 14 and 15), in this case the pulverized form known as matzah meal, which she molds and casts, making wildly lavish and often ridiculous-looking crowns. Matzah meal, used as a substitute for flour or bread crumbs, is a highly symbolic gender-specific material, associated with traditional Jewish women's domestic functions. Newman's installation combines the suspended crowns of molded matzah meal adorned with rhinestones and tulle with a floor blanketed in hot-pink feathers. A television monitor at floor level presents a woman engaged in obsessive-compulsive behavior—picking at fingernail polish, piercing plastic bubble wrap, and playing with her shoes.

Newman here elevates the domestic service of the matzah meal into an illusion of luxury and overindulgence, inviting subliminal insertion of the word "Jewish" between the two words of the title. She is interrogating the complex construction of the Jewish princess in American postwar culture. The perplexing reality is that this stereotype was created by and traded among Jews, and has been marketed for mass secular consumption as well. *Complex Princess*, with its combination of homey matzah and decorative glitter, comments on the amazing role shift from the sacrificing "Jewish mother," another stereotype evolved from literature, film, and television, to the image of the Jewish princess as an insatiable, erotically neutral, and materialistic being—a shift that has taken place in the short space of one generation.[65] Like Rhonda Lieberman's, Newman's commentary in *Complex Princess* discloses that, despite the tragedies of the Holocaust, the Jew, even within his or her own circulating self-stereotype, is still associated with the notion of excess.[66]

We have often been reminded that it was a common habit for Jews, and other white European minorities, to assimilate by acquiring "civility" and middle-class values.[67] This is precisely the mechanism that Elaine Reichek scrutinizes. She has

Fig. 18 (left). Elaine Reichek, Detail,

A Postcolonial Kinderhood, *1994.*

Fig. 19 (right). Elaine Reichek, Detail,

A Postcolonial Kinderhood, *1994.*

long examined colonizing Western representations of non-Western cultures. In 1993 she translated her anthropological enterprise to the Jewish experience in postwar America, which was also her own. In *A Postcolonial Kinderhood* (figs. 18 and 19; plate 31) she "re-creates" her personal refuge in her parents' house, emphasizing their wholesale purchase of the American dream through the colonial-style trappings signifying American culture. Using a combination of store-bought and hand-made, she created a room that incorporates a colonial-style bed, washstand, rocking chair, floor lamp, and hooked rug to give a deceptively cozy, if ultimately tense, ambiance to her installation. Her aim for *A Postcolonial Kinderhood* is apparent from her statement: "The re-creation of my childhood bedroom explores the idea of decor as a means of Americanizing, of 'passing,' and of connecting people to a past they wished was their own."[68]

Reichek accomplishes her goal by incorporating quotations from family and friends about the dilemma of growing up Jewish in postwar America onto the diminutive samplers that were commonly made by young, and mostly Christian, girls. In a manner not dissimilar to the purposeful naiveté of Cary Leibowitz's *I'm A Jew how 'bout U?!!*, the inherent innocence of the samplers is undermined through the often embarrassing statements that appear on them. For example, a statement like "The parents of Jewish boys always love me. I'm the closest thing to a *shiksa* without being one"—adorned on an appropriated homespun, colonial-style embroidery and frame—makes the message confrontational and profound. Likewise, Reichek's linen towels carrying the monograms "J.E.W." confound the viewer through an ironic reuse of the civilized tradition of personalized embroidery. The appearance of the charged term in this diminutive, civilized, and domestic form heightens the dramatic sense of encounter. Obviously, the word "Jew" continues to

NORMAN L. KLEEBLATT

arouse hatred and fear. Reichek's blatant manipulation of the term reveals the inherent racism of a supposedly civilized culture as well as the still-nervous response to that designation, even among Jews themselves.

RE-INVENTING RITUAL

Religion is a relatively new aspect of identity-based art and writing. In its current application, it is predominantly the purview of marginalized Americans. As the discourse on identity has become more complex, dwelling on the multiplicity of and interstices between various identities, religious heritage has been recognized as a new and crucial element. For example, among many Latinos, the import of Catholicism and its hybridization with certain African and Native American religious traditions is inseparable from the complete understanding of diverse individual and group identities. Latino artists are now exploring these culturally specific blendings, with the work of Ana Mendieta serving as a forerunner.[69] Muslim and other Eastern

Fig. 20. Thomas Lanigan-Schmidt, Loving Kindness (Theotokos), 1978. Mixed media, 15" x 14½".

religious identities are also entering the identity web, though more often in literature than in art.[70] Catholic-born artists of European descent have also used their religion and its aesthetic and social traditions as inspiration. Thomas Lanigan-Schmidt (fig. 20), as early as the mid-1970s, was producing lavish reconstructions of the popular culture artifacts of his Catholic school childhood. Such artifacts were at once a critique of the commerciality of the culture and a recirculation of those images into a celebration of the religious and aesthetic traditions of his Central European Catholicism. More recently, certain Catholic-born artists have used both the subjects of Christianity and its aesthetic traditions as a terse critique on the rigidity of their faith, which recognizes the hegemonic rulings of one centralized and powerful leader. The controversial work of Andreas Serrano has, for example, often been read as a criticism of the faith, when actually it inherently asks for recognition of alternatives. Serrano purposely forces the viewer to hover between the world of blasphemy and spirituality, between corrupted aesthetic traditions and their recirculation into moving contemporary art.[71]

Jewish identity, however, is not always based on religious singularity, and indeed there are many different traditions and modes of observance inscribed in the current practice of a notably heterogeneous community. Much of the complexity of Jewish personal identity emerges from the tension between the notion of communal diversity for Jews and the need to recognize those not acknowledged. For some, Jewish identity can be either historic, cultural, or ethnic, but for the artists discussed here it is all of these things. To a number of Jewish artists, religion, including ambivalence toward certain aspects and modes of its traditional doctrine and practice, looms large as a source of inspiration and contention. In a new, multifaceted conceptual framework, some Jewish artists are rethinking their traditions in ways that render them more meaningful within the constant interplay of their other identities, including aesthetic, gender, and sexual.

Curiously, the *Too Jewish?* artists who treat religious aspects of Judaism and its aesthetic traditions have generally created work for the secular sphere of gallery or performance spaces. The challenges they confront are meant, nevertheless, to infiltrate sacred Jewish space or to influence tradition. Ironically, it is because of the religious theme or intent inherent in these works that many artists find their work "too Jewish" to exhibit in galleries, possibly even in Jewish-oriented spaces. However, the continuing attention to diversity within the gallery system has begun to reverse that earlier phenomenon.[72]

Archie Rand's installation of *The Chapter Paintings* (plates 17–30) is among the few works in this section that derive from an earlier religious project. Rand began his career as an abstract painter and drastically shifted direction after he was asked in 1974 to produce a mural for the B'nai Joseph synagogue in Brooklyn.[73] In preparation, he extensively studied Bible, Talmud, Jewish iconography, and Jewish law pertaining to the proscriptions against certain imagery in sacred spaces. Ultimately, he was forced to defend his work in a rabbinical court. Not surprisingly, the art world initially sought to separate Rand's secular from his religious production,

NORMAN L. KLEEBLATT

though in reality his work flowed freely between Jewish and secular, representation and abstraction. By now, Rand has come to be known as a master of Jewish iconography, an appellation that carries positive connotations in the world of highly specific Jewish culture but often negative ones within the art world.[74]

The Chapter Paintings is an installation comprising a painting on the theme of each of the fifty-four weekly divisions of the Torah. It merges quotations from limited Jewish iconographic sources with those from a variety of painting styles, such as Surrealism, Abstract Expressionism, and Pop. Rand combines literal symbols of the biblical passages that are contemporary and accessible to the reader with others that parodically conflate idea, image, and style. For example, the divided fields in his first painting, *Bereshith* (Genesis) (fig. 21), pay homage both to Jewish manuscript illumination and to Barnett Newman, whose serious, heroic, and often hidden kabbalistic meanings Rand admires. But by transforming Newman's abstraction and conflating it with concrete imagery whose sources are culturally specific, Rand also critiques the very notion of identity concealment that Newman's work symbolizes for him.[75] And by adding fake jewels to the corners of the canvases and classical columns as framing devices, Rand in fact produces the reverse of the high seriousness of the abstract masters whom he appropriates.

Fig. 21. Archie Rand, (1) Bereshith *from* The Chapter Paintings, *1989.*

It is the combination of and the play between the secular and the sacred, the representational and the abstract, between Jewish history and art history that Rand the artist finds challenging and meaningful. He strives in these works to offer living proof of a Jewish iconographic and aesthetic tradition. In essence, they represent his yearning for the Jewish equivalent of the Christian and art historical grandeur of Giotto's Arena Chapel. *The Chapter Paintings*, like most of Rand's oeuvre, manifests a high degree of self-consciousness.[76] Like many other "hyphenated" artists, Houston Conwill and Faith Ringgold, for example, Rand also uses playful visual narration to reinforce his religious and personal identity. Yet his sources are often more multivalent than those of many other hyphenated Americans. His goal is to fuse many different parts of American visual culture to produce painting that is analogous to the jazz improvisations of John Coltrane, with their amazing combinations of musical sources.[77]

Allan Wexler also came to study Jewish ritual through a commissioned art work, a *sukkah* he designed for the former sculpture court of The Jewish Museum in 1988.[78] Wexler reinterprets ritual art through postmodern design, at once breaking tradition and suggesting the infinite possibilities for particular kinds of applied art. The *sukkah* is a small temporary dining pavilion used by observant Jews during the fall harvest festival of Sukkot. Wexler's *Indoor Sukkah* (plate 35) provides a hand-crafted table and chairs whose legs are set into flats of live grass. The grass is made to grow indoors through the use of grow lights attached to the legs of the table and chairs, symbolically connecting its users to the outdoors. Skullcaps are cut directly out of the table covering to associate the white festival cloth with sacred headcovers that signify religious devotion.

Indoor Sukkah transforms a ritual based in the agricultural origins of ancient Judaism into an urban-based, yet environmentally sensitive structure. Working at the intersection of three artistic languages—architecture, craft, and conceptual art—Wexler compulsively fabricates prototypes to show the limitless possibilities for *sukkah* design. More recently, he has explored the theoretical notion of "*sukkah*ness," which examines the basic sanctification of eating. In this way, he ties the earth—the source of physical sustenance—to the sky—the symbol for spiritual nourishment.

Cary Leibowitz and Neil Goldberg also focus attention on the hypothetical re-design of Jewish ritual objects. In the aftermath of his and Rhonda Lieberman's Chanel Hanukkah project, Leibowitz created an edition of "Chanel" yarmulkes (fig. 22), which were essentially conceptual in intent. Self-consciously deploying the cool and calculated strategies of Minimal artists, who conceived their monumental works but refused a hand in their execution, Leibowitz ordered personal "designer" skullcaps in quantity from a producer of yarmulkes on New York's Lower East Side. In some ways the Leibowitz skullcaps might be said to operate between

Fig. 22. Cary Leibowitz, Untitled (jewelled yarmulkes)*, 1992.*

NORMAN L. KLEEBLATT

the convoluted and diametrically opposed areas of Minimalist strategy and Claes Oldenburg's soft remakes of popular culture icons. The yarmulkes are made of contrasting sections of black and white synthetic satin, gold braid, and adorned with dangling faux jewels and ornaments. Satirically stylish, their cheap materials in imitation of the Chanel signature look contrast sharply with the Minimalist enterprise of often large-scale industrial sculpture or the grand scale of the commodity commentaries of more recent art. Purposely complex in their wide range of recent art historical sources, they also operate somewhere between the newly coined movements of mannered conceptualism and contemporary folk art in their commentary on the commodification of Jewish culture and the commodification issues that pervaded the art world during the last several years.[79]

Aside from offering pronouncements on originality and the consumerism of contemporary society, these excessively decorated caps were meant to question gender roles both within Jewish tradition and in general. The highly decorated body of the Jewish woman has now been transferred onto the unadorned body of the Jewish man. Ironically, much as these yarmulkes are supposed to humble "mannered neo-conceptual commodity art," Leibowitz was surprised to find that they are actually being worn for Jewish rituals, thus being reappropriated right back into the culture whose roles and values they were meant to interrogate.

Neil Goldberg's *Workout Tallis* (fig. 23) exists as a commentary for Jewish tradition as well as a conceptual work in the "readymade" (well, almost) tradition. Yet this seemingly simple post-Duchampian manipulation of a standard-issue *tallit* and gymnastic hand grips forces complex religious and contemporary questions. Like the Catholic artist Serrano, Goldberg creates an unabashed clash of cultural signifiers in which the physical is boldly made to confront the spiritual. Obviously, his piece comments on the privileged place given to physical exercise and the development of the healthy body in contemporary society. Yet, except for the particularist culture of the observant, modern Jews pay less attention to the spiritual. Goldberg encourages equal time for body and soul. *Workout Tallis* also begins to call attention to the physicality of the act of prayer and the meeting of sacred and profane.

In response to both the AIDS crisis and to a Hasidic protest about the participation of lesbian and gay Jews at a gay rally that took place during Passover week of 1993, Goldberg was prompted to create two hinged matzahs memorials—an AIDS/Plague wall—both of which he has left *Untitled* (fig. 24). He was pro-

Fig. 23. Neil Goldberg, Workout Tallis, *1994.*

Fig. 24. Neil Goldberg, Untitled (hinged matzahs)*, 1992.*

foundly upset at the notion that Jews, who as a group had suffered so much as a reviled minority in their long history, would marginalize a portion of their own religious population, especially in sickness and death.

In April 1993, Goldberg and Alicia Svigals worked with a number of other artists, dancers, writers, and musicians on an ambitious performance at The Club at the La Mama E.T.C. Theater. The performers included dancer/choreographer David Dorfman and dancer Lisa Race, the musical group The Klezmatics, and writer/performer Richard Elovich. Debbie Levine and Co. dramatized excerpts from Sarah Schulman's *Empathy,* a novel that deals with the generational conflict in a dysfunctional Jewish family. Part contemporary performance, part alternative Seder, the evening was a coming together of klezmer music and Passover melodies, recitals of some holiday liturgy, reflections on the historical meaning of Passover, and meditations on growing up Jewish in America. Titled *The Third Seder* (fig. 25) and organized to insert the concerns of the Lower East Side artistic community into the liturgy of the Seder, it was scheduled for the night before the first Seder so that familial commitments would not keep the audience away.

The Seder form generally allows reinterpretation dictated by broader historical contexts, often substituting contemporary villains and aggressors for the historical Egyptian thugs.[80] So this alternative Seder posited AIDS as Jewish history's newest oppressor. The performance merged left-wing and gay and lesbian issues with ethnic schtick that was both humorous and poignant. Goldberg built the stage set, an elaborate and monumental wall of real matzah, backlit with flickering candles that made the matzah look translucent. His wall is a metaphor for the many walls central to Jewish history, including the Western Wall, as well as the "walls of the European ghettos and concentration camps, to the more abstract walls of cultural/religious isolation."[81]

Helene Aylon's *The Liberation of G-d* (plate 3) is a deliberately contemplative work about reading the Hebrew Bible from a feminist vantage point. Her project was first proposed over a decade ago when the issue of women's places within certain sects of Jewish religious tradition was more contentious.[82] Raised an Orthodox Jew, Aylon found that only through her art could she articulate her critique of Jewish male authority. *The Liberation of G-d* is realized as an installation for the *Too Jewish?* exhibition.

Consonant with much feminist art, Aylon's work has eluded simple categorization as process art, conceptual art, performance, or an eco-feminist version of earth art. Her work's continual preoccupation with impermanence and change is perhaps best seen in her series of paintings circa 1975 that change over time.

This group of works, in which she applies various oils and pigments to begin a process of "growth" and alteration, counters the notion of permanence or immutability so central to the traditional notion of Western art. It is, in particular, process and performance that intersect in *The Liberation of G-d*. The work incorporates Hebrew Bibles, overlaid with translucent paper on which Aylon highlighted the "offending" passages that speak to and for a patriarchy. Using repetitive, time-consuming techniques of such performance/process artists as Linda Montano, Aylon is able to diffuse her anger and use it productively through the contemplation of text and her "corrective" notations. She assumes the "male" role of Torah student and scholar, at the same time creating a personal place for herself and all women in this historic text. Like other feminist artists who insert themselves, either through image (Cindy Sherman) or text (Jenny Holzer), into representations of male authority, Aylon posits feminist concerns onto the ur-text of the Judeo-Christian tradition.

On the other hand, the spirit of Aylon's installation derives from the age-old rabbinic tradition of midrash: rereading, questioning, and reinterpreting the Bible, thereby ensuring its relevance to contemporary life. While the text cannot be altered, interpretations and emphases can.[83] Aylon's longtime fascination with change is closely allied with the process of midrash, and the manipulation of the immutable text through interpretation reflects Aylon's preoccupation with change itself.

In probing the Jewish aspect of their subjectivity, the artists in *Too Jewish?* open themselves to complex identities. They explore the specific and various ethnic, cultural, and religious aspects of their Jewishness within the already established sexual, gender, and political diversities in contemporary discourse. Such investigations of difference interrupt the older strategies of assimilation and become necessary for the general realignment of Jews outside the monolithic power structures of American society. Heirs to a history of social and political struggles similar to those of other racial, ethnic, sexual, and gender groups, these Jewish artists nevertheless refuse to define themselves as victims. Rather, they insist on recognizing and affirming, even celebrating, their difference as a means to understand the differences of others.

We are left with some obvious questions: Where will the artists and the community go from here? Will these artists' voices bring the Jewish community out of a certain complacency and permit it to accept an increasing degree of internal diversity? Will their affirmative notions of identity help Jews put an end to their historic embarrassment about their difference? And will the entrance of "Jewish" into the multicultural equation forge stronger alliances in the ongoing dialogues on difference in the United States? There are no easy or obvious answers to questions about the future, but, as the artists' work has already suggested, these issues are important to ponder.

NOTES

1. Toni Morrison, "Unspeakable Things Unspoken: The Afro-American Presence in American Literature," *Michigan Quarterly Review* 28 (Winter 1989): 1–34.
2. David Biale, "Jewish Identity in the 1990s," *Tikkun* 6 (November 1991): 60.
3. For a selected list of exhibitions, see Abigail Solomon-Godeau and Constance Lewallen, *Mistaken Identities*, University Art Museum, University of California at Santa Barbara (Seattle: University of Washington Press, 1993), 79. To this list must be added the more recent exhibitions *Bad Girls*, organized by Marcia Tucker and Marcia Tanner for The New Museum of Contemporary Art and the UCLA Wight Galleries; and *Black Male* at The Whitney Museum of American Art. The 1993 Whitney Bienniel was also strongly focused on identity politics and issue-based art. *Sense and Sensibility* at The Museum of Modern Art, while it cast women's art under the rubric of a stylistic canon of Minimalism, might nevertheless be said to have emerged from the art world's interest in diversity.
   Lucy Lippard's book *Mixed Blessings: New Art in a Multicultural America* (New York: Pantheon, 1990) began to define the movement predominantly from the point of view of race. As Johanna Drucker has observed in her review of the book, Lippard did not consider white ethnic minorities. Drucker's article appeared in *Art Journal* 50 (Winter 1991): 109–111.
4. See, for example, the two last chapters in the third edition of Edward Lucie-Smith's popular book *Movements in Art Since 1945* (London and New York: Thames and Hudson, 1995), newly subtitled *Issues and Concepts* in deference to the postmodern and critical writings about modernism in recent years. The last two chapters are titled "Questioning the Modernist Canon from the 'Margins'" and "Issue-based Art," respectively. I thank Ann Gibson for leading me to this recently revised survey.
5. Cornel West, "The New Politics of Difference," *October* 53 (Summer 1990): 109.
6. Susan Rubin Suleiman, *Subversive Intent: Gender, Politics, and the Avant-Garde* (Cambridge, Mass.: Harvard University Press, 1990), xv.

7. Foreword by Fredric Jameson to Jean-François Lyotard, *The Postmodern Condition: A Report on Knowledge*, trans. Geoff Bennington and Brian Massumi (Minneapolis: University of Minnesota Press, 1984), xviii and xix.

8. Craig Owens, "The Discourse of Others: Feminists and Postmodernism," in *Beyond Recognition: Representation, Power, and Culture*, ed. Scott Bryson, Barbara Kruger, Lynne Tillman, and Jane Weinstock (Berkeley and Los Angeles: University of California Press, 1992), 166–190.

9. Andreas Huyssen, *After the Great Divide: Modernism, Mass Culture, Postmodernism* (Bloomington and Indianapolis: Indiana University Press, 1986), 198.

10. Eleanor Heartney, review of Lucy Lippard's *Mixed Blessings, Art in America* 80 (September 1992): 39.

11. For example, Elaine Reichek's extensive oeuvre about the representation of Native Americans and the indigenous peoples of the South Pacific incorporates both a critique of Western representation of these colonized peoples and a feminist critique of modernist art materials and display. One Jewish artist was represented in the exhibition *Counterweight* organized by Sondra Hale and Joan Hugo for the Santa Barbara Contemporary Arts Forum from November 7, 1992, through January 23, 1993; the artist's inclusion may have been because she was the child of Holocaust survivors. Maurice Berger's 1993 exhibition *Ciphers of Identity* was perhaps the first to include the self-representation of a Jewish artist.

12. Matthew Baigell, "From Hester Street to Fifty-seventh Street," in *Painting a Place in America: Jewish Artists in New York, 1900–1945*, ed. Norman L. Kleeblatt and Susan Chevlowe (Bloomington and Indianapolis: Indiana University Press, 1991), 28–71.

13. Margaret Olin's essay in this catalogue provides an account of the critic Clement Greenberg and his ambivalent relationship to his Jewish identity. The classic study for the American dominance of postwar international culture is Serge Guilbaut's *How New York Stole the Idea of Modern Art* (Chicago: University of Chicago Press, 1983).

14. Edward S. Shapiro, "Jewishness and the New York Intellectuals," *Judaism* 38 (Summer 1989): 282–292. Also Shelley Fisher Fishkin, review of *Jews in the American Academy 1900-1940: The Dynamics of Jewish Assimilation, Journal of American History* 79 (September 1992): 693.

15. West, "The New Politics of Difference," 109.

16. This well-known and much discussed observation is also included in Ronald Takaki's chapters on Jews in his recent general multicultural history, *A Different Mirror: A History of Multicultural America* (Boston: Little, Brown, 1993), 298–310. For a more critical notion of the complex attitudes about assimilation in postwar America see Barry Rubin, *Assimilation and Its Discontents* (New York: Random House, 1995), 87–114.

17. Michael Korda, "The Publishing World: Wasn't She Great?" *The New Yorker*, August 14, 1995, 66.

18. I am borrowing Leo Bersani's model of the highly visible gay community in the era of the AIDS epidemic, which, to Bersani's thinking, has caused an eradication of gay individuality. Here the analogy would be to Jews in the post-Holocaust world who found themselves with new collective strength as they sought shelter from individual cultural association, in part because of the strict conformity during and in the wake of McCarthyism. Leo Bersani, *Homos* (Cambridge, Mass.: Harvard University Press, 1995), 31–35.

19. Michael Lerner, "Jews Are Not White," *The Village Voice*, May 18, 1993, 33–34.

20. I thank Riv-Ellen Prell for her insights into these issues from her vantage point on postwar Jewish writers and critics.

21. The African American artist Renée Green observed: "It's still a struggle for power between various groups within ethnic groups about what's being said and who's saying what, who's representing whom? What is a community anyway? What is a black community? What is a Latino community? I have trouble with these things as monolithic fixed categories." As quoted in Homi K. Bhabha, "Beyond the Pale: Art in the Age of Multicultural Translation," in *Biennial Exhibition* (New York: Whitney Museum of American Art in association with Harry N. Abrams, 1993), 65.

22. Homi K. Bhabha, *The Location of Culture* (London and New York: Routledge, 1994), 2.

23. Henry Louis Gates, Jr., "Multicultural Madness," *Tikkun* 6 (November 1991): 56–58.

24. Kwame Anthony Appiah and Henry Louis Gates, Jr., "Multiplying Identities," *Critical Inquiry* 18 (Summer 1992): 625. See also Audre Lorde, "Age, Race, Class, and Sex: Women Redefining Difference," in *Out There: Marginalization in Contemporary Cultures*, ed. Russell Ferguson, Martha Gever, Trinh T. Minh-ha, and Cornel West (Cambridge, Mass.: MIT Press, 1990).

25. See Susan Tumarkin Goodman, *Jewish Themes/Contemporary American Art*, The Jewish Museum, New York, 1982 and *Jewish Themes/Contemporary American Art II*, The Jewish Museum, New York, 1986.

26. Rubin, *Assimilation and Its Discontents*; also Philip Roth, "Some New Jewish Stereotypes," *Reading Myself and Others* (New York: Farrar, Straus and Giroux, 1975), 137–143. This is not to suggest that earlier Jewish writers were neither concerned with their Jewish identity nor willing to confront the problems of Americanization. Abraham Cahan, Henry Roth, and Anna (Anzia) Yezierska are examples of Jewish authors who dealt with this conflict in their writing. What I am suggesting is that Roth was the first to question the assimilatory strategies of Jews in America using irony, paradox, and humor comparable to approaches of the artists in *Too Jewish?* I thank Jack Salzman for pointing out this historical fact and for discussing with me the similarities and differences between Philip Roth and his Jewish American precursors.

27. Roth, "Some New Jewish Stereotypes," 137–143.

28. See article in this catalogue by Maurice Berger, "The Mouse That Never Roars," 93–107.

29. Chicago Cultural Studies Group, "Critical Multiculturalism," *Critical Inquiry* 18 (Spring 1992): 546.

30. The earliest and most important resource in this area is the work of Sander L. Gilman, whose essay "The Jew's Body" can be found in this volume. His book of the same name is an important reference. *The Jew's Body* (New York and London: Routledge, 1991). Also significant are Daniel Boyarin's *Carnal Israel: Reading Sex in Talmudic Culture* (Berkeley and Los Angeles: University of California Press, 1993) and Howard Eilberg-Schwartz's *People of the Body: Jews and Judaism from an Embodied Perspective* (Albany: SUNY Press, 1992).

31. Joanna Freuh, *Hannah Wilke* (Columbia: University of Missouri Press, 1989), 15, 73.

32. Ibid., 33, 35.

33. The pioneering study in this area is Laura Mulvey, *Visual and Other Pleasures* (Bloomington and Indianapolis: Indiana University Press, 1989).

34. Sartre's observation is applied art historically in Carol Ockman's "Two Large Eyebrows à l'Orientale: Ethnic Stereotypes in Ingres' *Baronne de Rothschild*," *Art History* 14 (December 1991): 525.

35. Maurice Berger, "Seeing Myself, Seeing Myself," unpublished text for a catalogue to the exhibition *Slittamenti*, organized by Christian Leigh for the 1993 Venice Biennale.

36. Marjorie Garber, *Vested Interests: Cross Dressing and Cultural Anxiety* (New York: Harper Perennial, 1993), 77–79.

37. Ibid., 79.

38. Gilman, *The Jew's Body*, 169–233.

39. Ibid.

40. Ibid., 193.

41. Sander L. Gilman, *Difference and Pathology: Stereotypes of Sexuality, Race, and Madness* (Ithaca, N.Y.: Cornell University Press, 1985), 23.

42. Ken Aptekar, facsimile transmission to author, September 22, 1995.

43. Lisa G. Corrin, "Contemporary Artists Go for Baroque," in *Going for Baroque: Eighteen Artists Fascinated by the Baroque and Rococo*, ed. Lisa Corrin and Joan Eath Spicer (Baltimore: The Contemporary and The Walters, 1995), 21–22.

44. Suleiman, *Subversive Intent*, 142.

45. For a short description of the routine change of names in the pursuit of assimilation see

NORMAN L. KLEEBLATT

Irving Howe, *World of Our Fathers* (New York: Schocken, 1989; illustrated ed. Harcourt Brace, 1989), 1288.

46. See, for example, Kobena Mercer, "Black Hair/Style Politics," 247–264 and "Complexion," 365–380 in *Out There: Marginalization and Contemporary Culture*, ed. Ferguson et al. Also Ronald E. Hall, "The 'Bleaching Syndrome': Implications of Light Skin for Hispanic American Assimilation," *Hispanic Journal of Behavioral Sciences* 16 (August 1994): 307–314.

47. Mercer, "Black Hair/Style Politics," 247.

48. Jonathan Rosen, "Spiegelman: The Man Behind *Maus*," *The Forward*, January 17, 1992, 9. Also "Pour Mémoire," an interview with Art Spiegelman by Christian Fevret and Serge Kaganski, *Les Inrrockuptibles*, no. 42 (January 1993): 101–107.

49. "Pour Mémoire."

50. Andrew Weinstein, "Art after Auschwitz," in *Boulevard* 9 (1994): 187–196. Weinstein compares the intentions and complexities of Claude Landsman's *Shoah* and Steve Reich's *Different Trains* with Spiegelman's project. For Holocaust monuments that dare to speak of the impermanence of history and the possible artificiality of the reverence for the Holocaust, see James E. Young, "The Counter-Monument: Memory Against Itself in Germany Today," *Critical Inquiry* 18 (Winter 1992): 267–296.

51. Joan Porat, "Pondick Sculptures at CAM," *The American Israelite*, June 15, 1995, B-6.

52. Huyssen, *After the Great Divide*, 95.

53. Clement Greenberg, "Avant-Garde and Kitsch," in *Clement Greenberg: The Collected Essays and Criticism*, Vol. 1: *Perceptions and Judgments, 1939–1944*, ed. John O'Brian (Chicago: University of Chicago Press, 1986).

54. Huyssen, *After the Great Divide*, 143.

55. Bhabha, *The Location of Culture*, 35.

56. Owens, "The Discourse of the Other: Feminists and Postmodernism," 77.

57. Thelma Golden, "My Brother," *Black Male: Representations of Masculinity in Contemporary American Art* (New York: Whitney Museum of American Art, 1994), 37.

58. David Mamet, "The Decoration of Jewish Houses," in *Some Freaks* (New York: Viking Press, 1989), 7–14.

59. Stephen H. Norwood, "My Son the Slugger: Sport and the American Jew," *Reviews in American History* 21 (1993): 465–470. For a discussion of the scientific notion of the physical deficiency of Jewish men and their compensatory notions to overcome that weakness, see Gilman, *The Jew's Body*, 52–55.

60. For a further extrapolation of these terms, see Rhonda Lieberman, "The Loser Thing," *Artforum* 31 (September 1992): 78–92 and Jack Bankowsky, "Slackers," *Artforum* 30 (November 1991): 96–100.

61. For writings on the subject, see Rhonda Lieberman's three "Glamour Wounds" columns in *Artforum*: "Glamorous Jewesses" (January 1993); "Miami Fantasia, Part I: The Fountainbleau" (February 1993); and "Miami Fantasia, Part II: Rhonda Lieberman on the Jew Beat Again" (March 1993). Her columns have continued to dwell on Jewish issues and her article on "Jewish Barbie," which appeared in two installments in *Artforum* (March and April 1995), is reprinted in this book.

62. The show became quite controversial as Chanel's attorneys tried to shut it down for trademark infringement. Leibowitz and Lieberman eventually won their point that this was an art show, and as such protected by the First Amendment. See Carol Vogel, *The New York Times*, December 18, 1992, and *Art in America* 79 (February 1993): 128. On the anthropological construction of the Jewish princess, see the essay by Riv-Ellen Prell in this volume.

63. Jenna Weisman Joselit and Susan Braunstein, *Getting Comfortable in New York: The American Jewish Home, 1880–1950* (New York: The Jewish Museum, 1990), 61–64.

64. Quoted in Gilman, *The Jew's Body*, 26–27.

65. See the essay by Riv-Ellen Prell in this volume, 74–92.

66. Linda Nochlin, "Starting with the Self: Jewish Identity and Its Representation," in *The*

Jew in the Text: Modernity and the Construction of Identity, ed. Linda Nochlin and Tamar Garb (London: Thames and Hudson, 1995), 14–15.

67. Takaki, *A Different Mirror*, 298. For a more complex and theoretical argument about the ambivalence of Jews about the so-called "civility" of their newfound assimilation, see John Murray Cuddihy, *The Ordeal of Civility: Freud, Marx, Lévi-Strauss, and the Jewish Struggle with Modernity*, 2d ed. (Boston: Beacon Press, 1987).

68. The Jewish Museum, *A Postcolonial Kinderhood: An Installation by Elaine Reichek*, exhibition brochure with text by Emily Whittemore, 1994.

69. Lippard, *Mixed Blessings*, 67, 86.

70. Appiah and Gates, "Multiplying Identities," 628.

71. Wendy Steiner, "Below Skin-deep," in *Andreas Serrano: Works 1983–1993*, ed. Patrick T. Murphy (Philadelphia: Institute for Contemporary Art, 1994), 11–16.

72. For example, The Montclair Art Museum displayed Archie Rand's *The Bible* series during the Christmas season as a Jewish pendant to a previously planned exhibition of the Christian iconography of African American artist Allan R. Crite. Ironically, the critic for *The New York Times* referred to Rand's paintings using the Christian term Old Testament (New Jersey section, January 9, 1994).

73. Ross Feld, "On the Hook: The Work of Archie Rand," *Arts* 52 (December 1977): 136–139; and John Ashberry, "A Joyful Noise," *New York*, June 5, 1978, 91.

74. Robin Cembalest, "Taking an Air Gun to the Eyes of Jesus," *The Forward*, May 6, 1994, "Arts and Letters," pp. 1ff.

75. Some of these ideas are already apparent in John Yau's essay "*The Letter Paintings*, Then and Now," which was commissioned for the exhibition of Rand's eponymous works at Exit Art in New York in 1991. This essay has never been published. I thank Archie Rand for providing a copy of it.

76. Dan Cameron, "Possible Painting," essay in the catalogue of the exhibition of Archie Rand's paintings at the Scott Hansen Gallery, New York, 1990.

77. Various conversations with the artist; telephone confirmation, October 12, 1995.

78. Wexler was commissioned in 1988 by The Jewish Museum to create a *sukkah* for its then sculpture court. His commission was not predicated on any former religious work, but rather on the basis of the artist/architect's reputation for his attention to temporary structures. The *sukkah,* used by observant Jews for one week annually, is precisely such a structure.

79. Tricia Collins and Richard Milazzo, "From Kant to Kitsch and Back Again," *Tema Celeste* (January–February 1991): 76–77.

80. El Lissitzky's *Had Gadya*, 1919, is an example. The artist saw the release of the Jews from Egyptian bondage as an allegory for the Bolshevik victory of the same year. See C. Abramsky, "El Lissitzky as Jewish Illustrator and Typographer," *Studio International* 172 (October 1966): 182–185.

81. Neil Goldberg, letter to Diane Saltzman, February 9, 1993.

82. Women were first permitted to be ordained as rabbis in the Conservative movement in 1985.

83. Letter to author from Rabbi Burton L. Visotzky, April 11, 1992. For a discussion of midrash, see the book by Visotzky, *Reading the Book: Making the Bible a Timeless Text* (Garden City, N.Y.: Doubleday/Anchor, 1991). Also important in this context is Geoffrey H. Hartman, "The Struggle for the Text," in *Midrash and Literature*, ed. Geoffrey H. Hartman and Sanford Budick (New Haven: Yale University Press, 1986), 3–18.

NORMAN L. KLEEBLATT

MARGARET OLIN

C[LEMENT] HARDESH [GREENBERG] AND COMPANY

FORMAL CRITICISM AND JEWISH IDENTITY

FOLLOWING HER RESEARCH ON THE NATIONALISM AND PREJUDICE THAT PER-
MEATE MUCH OF THE WRITING OF ART HISTORY AND CRITICISM IN THE TWEN-
TIETH CENTURY, THE AUTHOR CONSIDERS THE WORK OF JEWISH ART
HISTORIAN/CRITIC CLEMENT GREENBERG, WHOSE FORMALIST ART THEORY
DENIED THE SUBJECTIVE IN ART, IN EFFECT ERASING ANY ASPECT OF THE
ARTIST'S PERSONAL IDENTITY FROM IT. SHE CONSIDERS THAT THIS STANCE
WAS, INDEED, AN ASSIMILATIONIST TACTIC, AND THAT THE AMBIVALENCE TO-
WARD "JEWISH ART" THAT IS INTRINSIC TO THE ART CRITICISM OF GREEN-
BERG AND HIS CIRCLE MAY HAVE BEEN A REACTION TO THE ANTI-SEMITISM
THAT HAS BEEN ENDEMIC TO MODERN ART THEORY.

When asked to speak on the topic "Is There a Jewish Art?" at The Jewish Museum in 1966, the art critic Harold Rosenberg had trouble coming up with something to say. Little more came to mind than his grandmother's cooking, whose
highlights were virtuoso noodle-cutting and *challah* cleverly fashioned in the
shape of a bird.[1] As tangible (edible?) evidence of Jewish artistry, these starchy
works did not amount to much. For one thing, his grandmother's best cooking
days were probably over even before Willem de Kooning's best painting days
began, making Jewish art seem dated. For another, if we leave aside the noodles,
her "bird bread" was solidly representational, while modern art was moving in
nonrepresentational directions. An identifiable style was Rosenberg's criterion for
the nonculinary visual arts, and although a number of important American
artists of his day were Jewish (he listed several), they created as individuals, not as
Jews, and contributed to American, not Jewish art.[2]

Clement Greenberg, Rosenberg's great rival for the position of spokesperson
for the Abstract Expressionists, never dared tackle the question of Jewish art directly. He did, however, touch on it occasionally, and the few remarks he made
exhibited discomfort with the topic. For example, he sensed an affinity to the
"Old Testament" in the apocalyptic landscapes of the Israeli painter Mordecai
Ardon, but was unable to define or explain it. "Far be it for me to see an eternal
Jewish soul any more than an eternal Anglo-Saxon one," he sputters, "but. . . ."[3]

MARGARET OLIN *is an associate professor in the Department of Art History, Theory, and Criticism, The
School of the Art Institute of Chicago.*

Fig. 1. Silver brooch from the graves at

Dürkheim. (From Hubert Janitschek,

Geschichte der deutschen Malerei *[Berlin:*

G. Grote'sche Verlagsbuchhandlung, 1890].)

He rarely mentions an American Jewish artist's religion, but when he compares the American painter Arnold Friedman stylistically to Ardon, he adds that he is "also a Jew," as though he means gingerly to open the possibility that Jewish artists have stylistic similarities.[4] Otherwise, Greenberg's vast output contains few references to Judaism in the visual arts.

Rosenberg and Greenberg both wrote cogently about Jewish identity in other areas of endeavor, particularly literature.[5] Their reticence concerning Jewish identity in the visual arts, however, is not surprising, given that most of us probably assume that Rosenberg was right: assimilated Jews express themselves in the visual arts as individuals, not "as Jews." Few of the Jewish artists championed by Rosenberg and Greenberg advertised their religious identity.[6] Moreover, if Jewish art is seldom discussed, Jewish law itself is to blame: the commandment against the making of graven images ensures that there is not much to talk about. Thus, the silence about Jewish identity in the discourse of art criticism appears natural.

If Rosenberg's and Greenberg's reticence on the topic had been only personal, the omission might not be worth remarking, in spite of the significance of their contributions to high modernism. But the refusal of Greenberg and Rosenberg to discuss Jewish art is nevertheless significant. Their few remarks represent alternative positions in a discourse prepared and conditioned in the history of their discipline. Even if they had made a concerted effort to consider Jewish identity within the purview of art criticism, they would have had major obstacles to surmount. Discourse on Jewish art was a component of the theoretical and historical map of the discipline of art history, and that map made anti-Semitism in the discussion of the visual arts hard to avoid. Greenberg's and Rosenberg's reluctance to discuss Jewish art therefore represents not only a footnote to a body of influential criticism, but also a component of the structure of a discipline and the position within it of ethnic minorities. To understand how contemporary Jews were regarded in American criticism of the mid-twentieth century, then, it is necessary to tour this historical terrain as it was mapped one hundred years earlier in Europe.

THE NATION WITHOUT ART

The modern discipline of art history began in the early nineteenth century. It evolved from, and with, nationalism. Its entailment with nationalism imbued it with a pattern of aims and categories it shared with anti-Semitism. Modern anti-Semitism was part of a structure of racism that helped give nationhood a basis in biology, while narratives of art history chronicled a people's emerging awareness

MARGARET OLIN

of nationhood, giving the eventual political legitimization of nationhood the look of inevitability.[7] The two strands united because cultural phenomena were among the diverse, conflicting criteria by which nineteenth-century scholars classified people into races or nations.[8]

In Germany, the native country of art theory and scholarship, nationalism and art history were early intertwined, beginning in the eighteenth century, when G. E. Herder began to use language as a criterion to identify a shared cultural heritage that makes up a people in the sense of modern nationhood. J. J. Winckelmann had already inaugurated modern art historical scholarship by tying Greek art to Greek climate, culture, and form of government.[9] By the mid-nineteenth century, the visual was thoroughly bound up in the national. Beginning with Romanticism, France and Germany competed for the right to call Gothic art their own.[10] Techniques and media were cultivated as national treasures.[11] Institutional art history grew up in the midst of such phenomena, as scholars in civil service, appointed to posts in museums and universities directly by the governments of Germany, Austria, and Switzerland, provided the public with scholarship to support national claims.[12]

These scholars did not regard a nation as a contingent phenomenon but as the unchanging element that furnished history with coherence. This function made the investigation of origins central to nationalistic narratives. A "national" art must be grounded in primal traits identifiable in their pure form in early handicraft and ornament.[13] Scholars dated official German nationhood to the Treaty of Verdun in 843 rather than 1871, and searched "back to the darkness of the tribal past" for "the soft and gradually perceptible stirrings of the artistic spirit of the Germanic tribes" who awakened and developed a consciousness of German identity even before the ninth century.[14] A Swedish scholar attributed the growth of prehistoric archaeology to government support for "the urge of the people for self-recognition and their love for the monuments of their prehistory."[15]

The language of nationalism, however, could not consist in the name of just one nation.[16] Nationalists had to compare or contrast their own nationalities to a network of alternative ones. To define Gothic as German was to deny that it was French. To define the German spirit as like the Hellenic required a definition of both peoples. Industrious, practical Romans and beauty-loving Greeks were crucial to the construction of Germanic spiritual depth. The importance of ethnic Others to the shaping of national identity meant that a consciousness of French or German identity could emerge through studies of the art of ancient Rome, Baroque Italy, the Levant, or India. Jews were one element in this vast complex.

An art history for which nationalists set the terms of the discourse, in which the contributions of countries, peoples, and races or the place of a work in a unified evolutionary development headed the scholarly agenda, would seem to have little room for Jewish art. Because, like gender minorities, Jews had no single community and geographical location, there was no established narrative into which "Jewish art history" could fit, and only a limited market for histories of

Jewish monuments or the professors who studied them. The biblical underpinnings of nineteenth-century surveys, however, made an explicit Jewish appearance obligatory, albeit brief and confined to what could be culled from the Hebrew Bible. Even here, the cherub-bedecked Ark of the Tabernacle was given short shrift compared to the architectural projects of Solomon.[17] Since these monuments do not survive, most scholars professed ignorance of Jewish artistic origins, but this did not keep them from drawing wide-ranging conclusions about the Jewish artistic character. The French archaeologists Georges Perrot and Charles Chipiez meticulously reconstructed the temples of Solomon and even Ezekiel in fanciful detail, concluding that Jews were the "least artistic of the great peoples of antiquity."[18] According to Elie Faure, while "their whole effort was employed in raising a single edifice, the house of a terrible and solitary god," it proved unworthy of "that Jewish genius, so grandly synthetical, but closed and jealous . . . whose voice of iron has traversed the ages."[19]

Others, citing the participation of Phoenician artists in the building of the Temple, concluded that Jews had no art at all. Wilhelm Lübke wrote in his survey in 1888 that "Jews, having no artistic sensibility of their own, borrowed architectural forms on an eclectic principle from the nations dwelling around them."[20] The remark sounds innocent from a postmodern standpoint, but for Lübke to characterize Jews as a people who borrowed from others the art they could not create on their own lent a historical basis to the anti-Semitic stereotype of Jews as chameleonlike parasites. With reference to such ancient forebears, Max Liebermann's love of French art could be explained as owing to the chameleon quality

Fig. 2. Outer Sanctuary, Temple of Israel (after Ezechiel), southern portal, seen from the southwest. Reconstruction by Charles Chipiez. (From Georges Perrot and Charles Chipiez, Histoire de l'art dans l'antiquité, *Vol. 5:* Judée, Sardaigne, Syrie, Cappadoce *[Paris: Librairie Hachette, 1887], pl. 4.)*

MARGARET OLIN

Fig. 3. Max Liebermann, In den Dünen.

(Drawing from Die Graphischen Künsten

[1902].)

of the Jew rather than to an affinity for the Gauls.[21] Such insinuations may have encouraged Heinrich Wölfflin explicitly to stress Liebermann's identity as a Berliner in a 1927 review in a Berlin journal.[22]

Jews were not only a people without art, however. The commandment forbidding graven images was used to portray them, more insidiously, as a people *against* art. In an inspired early essay, Hegel painted a brilliant picture of the Jews as representations of pure isolating negativity. The spiritual emptiness of the Jews reflected emptiness in all their creations: their sanctuary was an "empty room," their day dedicated to God an "empty time," their God invisible.[23] "They despise the image because it does not manage them, and they have no inkling of its deification in the enjoyment of beauty or in a lover's intuition."[24] The intolerant Hebrew God whose jealousy doomed Jewish art made His way into art historical treatises as well. Herbert Read invokes Him to explain the lack of Jewish art, for example, in his *Art and Society.*[25]

This extreme negativity distinguished Jews even from other "Semites" or "Orientals" who at least possessed a decorative tradition. At best Jews were written out of art history as a people defined by lack: lack of history, land, and art.[26] As an anti-artistic people, however, Jews grew into a threatening anti-nationality, and could reenter art history as the villain.[27] Just as Richard Wagner did not pity Jews for an alleged lack of musical ability, but feared them as a threat to Western music, so anti-Semitic art theorists could portray Semitic anti-art as a diabolical force, giving anti-Semitism a voice in art history.[28]

Avowed anti-Semitism was not the most significant problem posed by the role of Jewish anti-art in the structure of art history. This structure remained intact even where anti-Semitism was not a factor, forcing unavoidable examples of Jewish art to conform to rhetoric not designed to accept them. These conditions prevail even now. While Islamic art, tied to distinctive geographical centers, is beginning to find coverage in art historical surveys, Jewish monuments, where they are mentioned, are integrated into canonical, non-Jewish artistic developments.[29] More often, because Jewish art is factored out of art history, discussions of it are confined to specialized, self-consciously marginalized texts.[30] In order to bring explicitly Jewish monuments into mainstream scholarship, even specialists often find it necessary to baptize them. The historical value of the pictorial program of the third-century synagogue at Dura-Europos, for example, has been justified with reference to later Christian developments.[31]

The discourse that represented Jews as nonvisual, and for which the only genuine criterion for art was national, extended beyond the confines of academia. It affected art critics, museum officials, and gallery owners. Champions of contemporary Jewish artists such as Max Liebermann had to cope with their own

Fig. 4. Dura-Europos, synagogue wall fresco, detail: Elijah revives the widow's child. (From replica made by Evergreene Painting Studios, Inc.)

misgivings about the art of the ancient Israelites. The organizers of the first exhibition of Jewish artists in Berlin in 1907, featuring Maurycy Gottlieb, Artur Markowicz, Josef Oppenheimer, Camille Pissarro, and Lesser Ury, began the catalogue by assuming that Jewish tradition was hostile to the visual arts.[32]

Martin Buber pioneered the rehabilitation of the Second Commandment in his introduction to a book celebrating the art of well-known Jewish artists such as Liebermann and Josef Israels along with lesser-known artists identified with Jewish subjects. Like anti-Semites, he attributed the nonvisuality of Jews to "racial characteristics." His reference was not to "blood," but to the climate, conditions, and social structure of early Jewish life. Yet the results were grim all the same. The Jews' inability to visualize constricted their *Weltanschauung* to "I-relationships," or function, making it impossible for them to see the beauty of forms, like the Greeks, or, like the Hindus, the spirituality in the objects around them. In the Diaspora, the restriction of Jews to occupations such as money-lending stifled emerging visual as well as spiritual urges. "This is when religious law became all-powerful. The human body is despicable. Beauty is an unknown value. Seeing is a sin. Art is a sin. . . . Everything creative is smothered at its first appearance."[33]

Fig. 5. Max Liebermann, Juedischer Kuenstler, *ed. Martin Buber (Berlin: Juedischer Verlag, 1903).*

To a non-Jewish reader, such judgments may appear damning. Buber's readership, however, was Jewish, since his book appeared under Zionist auspices. The encouragement of Jewish art was important to Zionism, under whose aegis an art academy was founded in Palestine, named after Bezal'el, the maker of the cherub-bedecked ornaments of the Tabernacle, ignored by surveys of art history.[34] Buber saw recent promising developments in Jewish art as part of a restructuring of the Jewish faith that had begun with Hasidism in the eighteenth century and continued with emancipation. His concept of the spiritualization of Jewish relational tendencies later led him to the dialogism of his *I and Thou.*[35] In his view, the construction of a specifically Jewish art would contribute significantly to a dawning modern age, "whose essence seems to be the dissolution of substance into relationships and its transfiguration into spiritual values."[36] A nonvisual people could contribute to art in an immaterial age.

Although Rosenberg probably never read Buber's essay, he made a similar argument at the end of his talk at The Jewish Museum. Unwilling to let the Jews in his audience go away empty-handed, Rosenberg turned the prohibition against images in the Second Commandment into an artistic manifesto—for anti-art. "Jewish art then," he said, "may exist in the negative sense of creating objects in the mind and banning physical works of art."[37] He also identified an "Old Testament" provenance for found art. Jews held the "idea that if you inhabit a sacred world you find art rather than make it."[38] In claiming the ancient Jews as forerunners of the found and conceptual art movements of the 1960s, he can be seen as updating Buber's argument for a contemporary, secular art world that regarded art as intellectual rather than as spiritual, and to whom an anti-artistic stance was perfectly acceptable. Both Buber and Rosenberg, then, sought to work within rather than challenge the notion that the Second Commandment banned art.[39]

PURITY IN ART AND RACE

Fig. 6. Marc Chagall, Yellow Crucifixion, 1943.

Clement Greenberg's attempt to confront Jewish art, even though less explicit, was more complex and problematic than that of Rosenberg. While Rosenberg, in his commitment to anti-art ideas of the 1960s, could subvert anti-Semitic rhetoric, Greenberg could only account for Jewish art within an established art historical framework, that of formal analysis as conceived and established by scholars in the late nineteenth and early twentieth centuries.

Jean-Paul Sartre, in his work *Anti-Semite and Jew*, offers a tool for understanding the function of formalism in relation to ethnicity.[40] According to his paradigm, the myth of universal humanity and the practice of "abstraction" enabled Jews to deny the reality of their own oppression.[41] Formalism in art had this potential as well because, like the symbolist movement in art and literature, it was a response to a crisis of artistic representation. It attempted not, as is sometimes assumed, to abolish or denigrate subject matter in art (it was never against content), but to provide for art a more unassailable basis. It placed formal considerations above subject matter in order to discover universal truths beyond academic conventions, and denied difference in order to search for common denominators.[42] Formalism's potential support for the idea of universal humanity led Jews and other anti-nationalists to embrace it, just as they later embraced the International Style and abstract art.

Formalism, within Sartre's framework, can be seen as a kind of denial. Unlike Marxism, which Sartre thought would remedy anti-Semitism by

MARGARET OLIN

changing the social structures that led to it, the formalist internationale offered a comfortable refuge, making art appear applicable to the whole of humankind, a pure realm of visuality not associated with specific racial, ethnic, or political agendas. Or religious ones. Art offered Christians as well as Jews a secular religion to replace faith lost in the Enlightenment. For Jews, however, the denial of iconography allowed them in addition to worship at Renaissance altarpieces without the necessity of a formal conversion. Even better, it opened nonreligious art to devotional purposes, making it possible to deploy a rich spiritual vocabulary in praise of abstract paintings, a form of criticism often embraced by secular Jews.[43]

Although formalism helped Greenberg and others handle Christian art and even Surrealism, whose iconography he disliked, it let him down in the face of Jewish art. Formalism, for example, forced Greenberg to resort to an "eternal Jewish soul" when seeking to explain the relation between Ardon's "apocalyptic landscapes" and the "Old Testament" because it forbade any explanation based on traditions of biblical landscape or imagery, which might conceivably have helped him (2:216). Even Rosenberg, we recall, was enough of a formalist to insist on style as the only reliable criterion of Jewish art.[44] Similarly, Greenberg's discussion of Marc Chagall's origin far from Paris emphasized differences in painting traditions, but not cultural differences (2:81–85). His rhetoric posed "visual logic" against a "murky, indeterminate *fond*," and set a picture that "happens to repeat Chagall's previous success with royal blue" against "the large and unresolved Crucifixion with its yellowish malaise" (1:165). But the essay ignores the subject matter of these works, which are replete with references to Jewish experience.[45]

The reference to Ardon's "eternal Jewish soul," even though Greenberg rejects it, illuminates the way in which formalism, Greenberg's route to universalism, could fuel anti-Semitism. Formalism grounded representation in the universality of nature, rather than in the arbitrariness of conventional codes. Greenberg contributed to the "naturalization" of formalism in such essays as "The Role of Nature in Modern Painting" of 1949 (2:271–275).[46] He also understood art on the biological basis of the senses, and appropriated from earlier formalists the perceptual rhetoric of "optical" and "tactile."[47] Biology, in the mode of perceptual psychology, naturalized formalism, just as, in the mode of racism, it naturalized nationhood. Formalism, despite—or because of—its aspiration to universality, could be used comfortably with the nationalistic structure of art history.

Because biologic formalism erects standards and identifies deviations, racism was always an option. The insights of Gestalt psychology, for example, which postulated a biophysical relationship between human response to form and internal molecular organization, could also be used to bolster racial stereotypes. Rudolf Arnheim came close on occasion to turning Gestalt into a new phrenology, suggesting that the external forms of "criminals and homosexuals" were related to the internal molecular organization that made them "deviants." To bolster his call for an examination of the relation between the "spirit" of national groups and the configuration of their gestures, he cited a study of Jewish and Italian communities in Brooklyn.[48]

Fig. 7. Ghetto Jew: Confined gestural radius, movement from elbow. Sketch by Stuyvesant van Veen. (From David Efron, Gesture, Race, and Culture, Approaches to Semiotics, *no. 9, ed. Thomas A. Sebeok [1941; rpt. The Hague and Paris: Mouton, 1972].)*

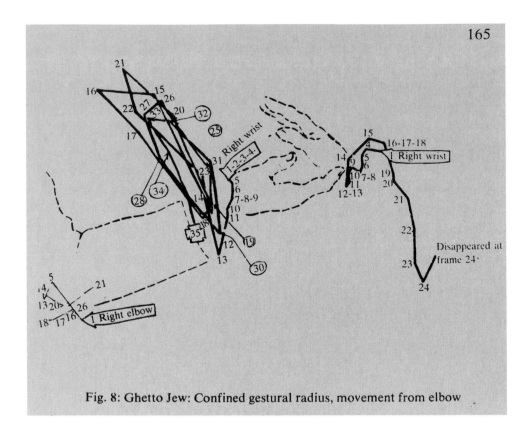

Fig. 8: Ghetto Jew: Confined gestural radius, movement from elbow

Arnheim was not the only formalist critic whose universalism was sabotaged. Bernard Berenson, whose criticism Greenberg admired, espoused his own universalism in 1938, partly in response to the Nazi threat. He condemned the search for influence because it "is seldom free of nationalistic prejudices." "My tendencies toward universalism and timelessness," he wrote, "have disinclined me to dwell on differences that seem slight compared with wide and deep resemblances, and have induced me to look for the same human quality in every individual." Yet he laid a trap for himself when he continued, "and furthermore to erect the same qualities into ultimate standards and to appraise societies as well as individuals by the extent to which they have possessed these qualities."[49] Thus, like George Orwell's *Animal Farm*, which found some animals more equal than others, he found some societies more universally human than others.

These remarks, in his *Aesthetics and History in the Visual Arts*, appear in an explicitly anti-Semitic discussion of Jewish art.[50] Following the traditional formulas, Berenson consigns Jews to a dismal artistic existence: in some passages they lack a national art; in others they lack art altogether. He appears to forget his own rejection of the cult of originality when he condemns Jews as imitators:

Neither they themselves nor their forebears possessed any kind of plastic or even mechanical ability. . . . As a matter of fact Israel through the ages has manifested nothing essentially national in the plastic arts, neither in antiquity, nor through the Middle Ages, nor to-day. The coinage of their

Maccabean period is the poorest Hellenistic. . . . In later periods Jews imitated the art of the peoples among whom they were scattered, to the pitiful extent that they made use of art at all. Even in recent years when Jews emancipated from the ghetto have taken to painting and sculpture and architecture, they have proved neither original nor in the least Jewish. I defy anyone to point out in the work of Liebermann, Pissarro, Rothenstein, Modigliani, Messel, Antokolskij, Epstein, Chagall, or Soutine, anything excepting subject matter that is specifically Jewish.[51]

The assimilated nature of Pissarro's art may be hard to refute, but Berenson's remarkable leap from Maccabean coinage to the avant-garde movements of his own youth suggests that for him the problem is racial.[52] He himself entertains this possibility: "The Jews like their Ishmaelite cousins the Arabs, and indeed perhaps like all pure Semites (if such there be), have displayed little talent for the visual, and almost none for the figure arts."[53]

Along with biologism came the fear of miscegenation. Hybridity was a problem for formalist methodologies because the formalists' aspiration for universality did not admit difference. In the 1930s and '40s, when Greenberg was earning his wings, the longing for purity that pervaded modernism often found expression in the abhorrence of "hybrid" styles and mixed genres. Berenson, for example, quotes with approval the remark by the (refugee Jewish) Islamist Ernst Herzfeld that "hybrid" Persian arts appropriating misunderstood Greek form could have historical but not aesthetic interest.[54] Colonial expressions now celebrated as examples of the "hybrid" were viewed with disdain.[55] The very methods of art history were nationalistic.

Greenberg's early essay "Towards a Newer Laocoön" (1940) demonstrates how a biological view of art accords with a fear of hybridity. In the essay, Greenberg personified art, importing into it the class struggles that concerned him as a socialist: literature was "dominant," visual art "subservient." When arts become subservient, "they are forced to deny their own nature in an effort to attain the effects of the dominant art" (1:24). Dominance and subservience are part of Marxist discourse, but the "nature" of these arts is not. The notion that the arts have a nature comes from formal theory, which divides arts according to the senses to which they appeal. Greenberg's emphasis on the "medium" is not simply an expression of his historical materialism; it is at the quasi-biological basis of art.

Acceptance of the physicality of the medium was a ruling metaphor throughout Greenberg's writings, backed by metaphors of the body and of medicine. In "Towards a Newer Laocoön," the Romantic artist is said to be "ashamed to admit that he had actually painted his picture instead of dreaming it forth" (1:29). The phrasing suggests shame about the body. Elsewhere, health is at issue: "The extreme eclecticism now prevailing in art is unhealthy, and it should be counteracted, even at the risk of dogmatism and intolerance" (1:213). Middlebrow culture posed a danger to the body of art as well: "[it] attacks distinctions as such and insinuates itself everywhere, devaluating the precious, infecting the healthy, corrupting the honest, stultifying the wise" (2:257). The metaphors in this constellation do not merely personify art by embodying it, they protect its virtue against cross-breeding. Universalism in art did not extinguish racism by repressing it; it displaced it into another realm.

Greenberg's formalism, like that of the pioneers of formalism, was not ahistorical. Like his predecessors, he accepted a universalist notion of history, according to which one current (Greenberg called it a "mainstream") flows at any given time.[56] This totalistic sense of history may also have been informed by Marxism, but the sense of the unity of a culture was more Hegelian than Marxian. Greenberg's view of Dutch art, for example, was based on a totalistic notion of the seventeenth century, in which space and light were explored through many areas of culture, an idea common among early twentieth-century thinkers (2:8, 32). Like them, he related arts to scientific advancement. "A substantial art," he wrote, "requires balance and enough thought to put it in accord with the most advanced view of the world obtaining at the time" (2:167).[57] Greenberg's lineage of "advanced views," from medieval religion through abstract thought (idealism), was borrowed from nineteenth-century histories. In his day, according to Greenberg, the most advanced thought was positivism, by which he meant a nineteenth-century intellectual movement that stressed empiricism rather than idealism or rationalism (2:316; 2:160–170).[58] The corollary of these totalistic views is that there was no room for multiple standards in art writing, even where there was a stake in unity in diversity.[59] The public should not only recognize advanced painting, he wrote, but also reject other kinds (2:195).

Not only did Greenberg share with his forebears a universal, progressive conception of history, he also accepted their concern for national character. Several times he characterized Klee's nature as "Nordic," and Picasso's as "Mediterranean," although Picasso unsuccessfully denied his own nature by trying to paint like the French (2:297–299). Greenberg also took pains to determine what was uniquely American in American art. When he proclaimed the victory of New York over Paris, announcing that "the main premises of Western art have at last migrated to the United States, along with the center of gravity of industrial production and political power," and that "the immediate future of Western Art . . . depends on what is done in this country," his exultation was purely patriotic (2:215, 193). For the triumph belongs not just to a small group of painters, but to the spirit of a people.

C. HARDESH: PAINTING MAKES *TESHUVAH*

The triumph did not belong to the "Jewish spirit," however. When Greenberg proclaimed New York the new artistic center, he did not mention that many of the artists that had made it so, Barnett Newman, for example, or Adolph Gottlieb, were Jewish. Their "nationality" was definitively American. In this, Greenberg followed a typical post-Holocaust scenario, in which Jews sought to demonstrate their American identity.[60] Yet the stance also accorded with Greenberg's commitment to a single artistic direction, and a single center in which such direction evolves at a given moment. Any difference from the general population, according to this account, was in danger of falling into the category of the hybrid. Like other minority identities, Judaism enters into Greenberg's criticism primarily to explain provinciality. He usually identified provinciality, whatever an artist's origins, with an understanding of cubism mediated by German expressionism. Thus the Russian Kandinsky, transplanted into Germany, is "provincial" in the same way as are the Israeli artist Mordecai Ardon and the American Jewish artist Arnold Friedman. Greenberg's ambivalence shows in his assessment of Chagall. He admired Chagall as a "hero" for mastering Parisian art despite his origins in an Eastern European Jewish enclave. But in contradiction to this seeming admiration of hybridity, he worried that Chagall "represented something impure" that made it difficult for his art to become "eligible to take its place in the social order called beauty" (2:84). Even if Greenberg had believed in the existence of Jewish art, therefore, the value of such art would have been limited. Lacking a national center, it could only relate to the mainstream as a hybrid.

Greenberg allowed his concern for Jewish identity to appear openly in discussions of literature and current events. There, his conflicts are apparent. He disliked the use, by "chauvinist" Israeli Jews, of "Western European standards," which led to the disdain for Eastern European refugees and the ideal of Jews as blond and blue-eyed as any Hitler Youth. However, his grandiose counter-conjecture—"it is possible that by 'world-historical' standards the European Jew represents a higher type of human being than any yet achieved in history"—does not suggest multiple standards (2:107). Moreover, although he says "there is much to argue for its possibility," he does not take his counter-conjecture further. In his first discussion of Jewish issues, he seeks to dissociate "ghetto Jews" from "Orientals," but not because either category is a stereotype. Rather, "the ghetto Jew [was] 'Oriental' perhaps in his poverty and in the denseness of the atmosphere in which he lived but not in his realism and in his abhorrence of hypocrisy" (1:156). In the attribution to Orientals of hypocrisy and lack of realism (often called, disparagingly, "fantasy"), we would now recognize the familiar rhetoric of Orientalism.[61]

Occasionally, Greenberg appears to regret the loss of what he regarded as traditional Jewish ways. His review of Peggy Guggenheim's book *Out of This Century*, which he signed "Hardesh," the Hebrew for "Green Mountain ('Berg' means 'mountain' in German)," is a lament for the "martyrs of bohemia." Guggenheim's "martyrdom" was due to her unquestioned acceptance of bohemia, which allowed her to be victimized by it. Her fall was, however, directly linked to her Jewish origins. She tried to escape

moneyed, bourgeois, claustrophobic stuffiness. And it was for fear of being recaptured and returned to it somehow—the unconscious conviction that she would be, simply because Jews are forced to remain bourgeois in spite of themselves—that she threw herself so unreservedly into bohemia and has dwelt in it so unqualifiedly, recklessly, and gullibly. (2:98)

Bohemia is hard on Jews:

In the list of martyrs of bohemia, Jewish names stand out, the names of gifted Jews, too, not merely aberrated ones—beginning with Simeon Solomon in Pre-Raphaelite England and continuing through Modigliani, Pascin, and even Soutine, in Paris. In proportion to the size of the Jewish contingent in bohemia—which is smaller than one would expect—the martyrs are too many, and examples like Miss Guggenheim's too frequent. (2:99)

The cause of her downfall, Hardesh speculates, is her abandonment not of modern bourgeois ways, but of traditional Jewish ones. "As a Jew I am disturbed in a particular way by this account of the life of another Jew. Is this how naked and helpless we Jews become once we abandon our 'system' completely and surrender ourselves to a world so utterly Gentile in its lack of prescriptions and prohibitions as bohemia really is?" (2:98–99)

The story, as related by Greenberg, is a tragedy of assimilation, with the twist that the heroine is a member of the mainstream bourgeoisie and the group to which she wishes to assimilate is on the fringe of society. He investigates the topic of assimilation further in the essay "Under Forty," about American Jews and literature. Like Sartre, he ascribes the tendency of Jews to abstract, to conceptualize, and to marvel at the "sensuous and sentimental data of experience" to their status as wanderers and outsiders, a typically capitalist plight, which Jews exemplify to an extreme. Writing serves as a means of access to the general culture. While the non-writing Jew is integrated into American life, accepting "suffocatingly middle-class" ways, but having nothing to write about, writers have a code that protects them from the "ravages of bohemianism" that engulfed Peggy Guggenheim. But their code is too middle-class to be used to criticize society. Thus in his essays on literature, Greenberg recognizes Judaism as an identity worked out within and against a dominant culture. The Jewish experience turns out to embody the universally modern experience of isolation and alienation in intensified form because of Judaism's special historical circumstances.

Group identity frightened many in the 1950s and '60s, years as much of defiant individualism as of group solidarity. It may, however, have frightened Jews more than most. There is an urgency, for example, in Rosenberg's passionate defense of assimilation in the name of individualism before a group of Jewish engineering students.[62] Similarly, Greenberg explicitly favored individual actions against anti-Semitism, maintaining that communal actions fueled "rabid nationalism" (3:53). Given their energetic embrace of American identity, however, Greenberg's and

Rosenberg's use of the rhetoric of individuality to justify the rejection of an explicit Jewish identity may conceal a fear of identifying openly as a Jew.

Fear of espousing Jewish identity may have been justified. While he did not seek connections between the New York abstractionists and their Jewish culture, Greenberg's detailed account of the relation of the writer Franz Kafka to his Jewish culture gave rise to an acerbic exchange. The presence of Jewish content in Kafka, argued prominent literary critic F. R. Leavis, made Greenberg overvalue Kafka's achievement. Greenberg understandably took offense at this insinuation that Kafka's relation to Talmudic law can be of interest only to Jews. Kafka's "Halachic logic," he wrote, makes him no more parochial than Christian cosmology makes Dante. Yet Greenberg perhaps felt vulnerable to the accusation of "Jewish egocentricity," for even as he defends Kafka, the man who signed himself "C. Hardesh" a few years earlier confesses that "I am not, in my ignorance of Hebrew and many other things, that familiar with Jewish tradition anyhow" (3:213).[63] In an essay about "self-hating Jews," he was honest enough to begin by counting himself among them (3:45).

If Hardesh's essay is a tragedy of assimilation, "Towards a Newer Laocoön" could be viewed as a tale of *teshuvah*, an expression for the religious return to Judaism.[64] It registers anxieties that cannot be spoken of explicitly. In reference to the infiltration of literature into art, Greenberg writes that the arts can only be "mishandled in this way when they have reached such a degree of technical facility as to enable them to pretend to conceal their own mediums" (1:24). Like Jews, whom anti-Semites characterize as chameleonlike in their ability to assimilate, arts, too, have the urge to assimilate into the dominant form and the potential to acquire the skill to do so. Yet, like Peggy Guggenheim in the face of bohemianism, it is dangerous for the arts to deny their own natures. The biological understanding of painting that Greenberg inherited from Europe, along with its racial underpinnings and the "school of Paris" itself, has been applied to the issue of identity. The search for identity embroils both painter and painting. It is as important for a painting to be "all painting; none of it . . . publicity, mode or literature" as for a painter to be "his true self" (2:14, 18).[65]

Greenberg's few remarks about Judaism represent the pathos of his enterprise, a pathos at the heart of modernism. In Greenberg's view, modernist art strove for a unity it thought unobtainable in life; the greater the diversity it reconciled, the greater the art. Piet Mondrian achieved such unity. But Greenberg saw expressionism as exploiting tension rather than resolving it to effect unity.[66] Thus expressionism, the artistic practice of Jewish and other provincial artists, was about the longing for unity rather than its achievement. Like other modernists, Greenberg could not celebrate unresolved diversity.

Just as Kafka's Jewishness expresses a universally modernist crisis in extreme form, Greenberg's relation to Judaism exemplifies in its extreme the contradictions and strain in his conception of the relation between art and politics, even between art and life. Unlike Sartre's apolitical Jews, Greenberg was committed to political engagement both within and beyond the boundaries of his discipline.[67] Yet formalism necessarily saw art as isolated from life; for universal forms took precedence over the necessarily particularistic subject matter of life. As we have seen, however, formalism had its own politics, since its universal standards were founded on those of white, Gentile Europe. Within formalism, it was impossible to do justice either to Jewish identity or to political responsibility. The difficulty of reconciling an art conceived as necessarily isolated with a life committed to political, religious, or ethnic issues, was, in fact, a defining tension throughout modernism.[68]

Greenberg's attraction to formalism corresponded to his attraction to traditional Judaism: the separation between art and life that he struggled to maintain was one he thought he saw in traditional Judaism as well.[69] In the Old World, he wrote, what really mattered, the spiritual, had to be strictly separated from life and particularly from power (2:183–184). In this conceptual scheme, Judaism constitutes a relation, albeit negative, to politics. It might be called a formalist politics. Whether rooted in the Eastern European ghetto or assimilated in Prague, Judaism is an escape, like formalism, from the politics, and the history, of the Gentiles.

After raising the possibility that by "world historical standards" Jews might be the highest form humanity has yet evolved, Greenberg continued: "No one, I say further, has any right to discuss the 'Jewish question' seriously unless he is willing to consider other standards than those of Western Europe." The remark was more insightful than he thought. By his own criteria, Greenberg was ineligible to discuss the Jewish question in art.

NOTES

1. Harold Rosenberg, "Is There a Jewish Art?" (1966), in *Discovering the Present: Three Decades in Art, Culture, and Politics* (Chicago: University of Chicago Press, 1973), 223–231.

2. Ibid., 231.

3. Clement Greenberg, *The Collected Essays and Criticism,* Vol. 2: *Arrogant Purpose, 1945–1949* (Chicago: University of Chicago Press, 1986), 216. Further references to this and the other three volumes in the series of collected writings will be in the text.

4. Ibid.

5. Some of these will be discussed below. Clement Greenberg's best-known essay is "Kafka's Jewishness," which he included in the collection of essays *Art and Culture: Critical Essays* (Boston: Beacon Press, 1961), 266–273. Harold Rosenberg seems to have taken the subject of Judaism more seriously than Greenberg. *Discovering the Present* contains a section devoted to the subject, 223–287.

6. Even when Barnett Newman used explicitly Jewish subject matter, Rosenberg took pains to dissociate him from it, carefully distinguishing Newman's interest in the kabbalah and his design for a synagogue from an identification with Judaism, although he does refer to the Jews as Newman's "tribe." Harold Rosenberg, *Barnett Newman* (New York: Harry N. Abrams, 1978), 27, 79.

7. On the role of institutions in forming "official nationalisms," see Benedict Anderson,

Imagined Communities: Reflections on the Origin and Spread of Nationalism (London and New York: Verso, 1983), esp. 80–103; on narratives of nationalism, see Homi K. Bhabha, *The Location of Culture* (London and New York: Routledge, 1994), 139–170. On the relation between racism and nationalism, see Etienne Balibar, "Racism and Nationalism," in *Race, Nation, Class: Ambiguous Identities*, ed. Etienne Balibar and Immanuel Wallerstein, trans. Chris Turner (London and New York: Verso, 1991), 37–67. On the historical distinction between racist and religious anti-Semitism, see Robert Wistrich, *Anti-Semitism: The Longest Hatred* (London: Thames Methuen, 1991), 3–53.

8. George W. Stocking, Jr., "The Turn-of-the-Century Concept of Race," *Modernism/Modernity* 1 (1994): 4–16.

9. Johann Gottfried Herder, *Philosophie der Geschichte zur Bildung der Menschheit* (1774), in *Johann Gottfried Herder Schriften*, ed. Karl Otto Conrady (Munich: Rowolt, 1968), 64–139; Johann Joachim Winckelmann, *Gedanken über die Nachahmung der griechischen Werke in der Malerei und Bildhauerkunst* (1755) (Stuttgart: Reclam, 1969).

10. Paul Frankl, *The Gothic: Literary Sources and Interpretation through Eight Centuries* (Princeton: Princeton University Press, 1960), 417 and passim; and Mitchell Schwarzer, *German Architectural Theory and the Search for Modern Identity* (Cambridge: Cambridge University Press, 1995), 128–166.

11. Wood, for example, was a German medium, and the use of Latin or German typeface (Fraktur) or their respective handwritten forms became associated with political stances. See, for example, report of a lecture delivered by Engelbert Mühlbacher on 25 January 1883, on "Die Entwicklung der Schrift," *Mitteilungen des k.k. österreichischen Museums für Kunst und Industrie* 18 (April 1883): 374–375.

12. The first chair in the field was established in Berlin in 1844. By 1871, when German unity was achieved, art history was established in many German and Austrian universities. On early art historians in Germany and elsewhere, see Udo Kulterman, *Geschichte der Kunstgeschichte: Der Weg einer Wissenschaft* (Munich: Prestel, 1990); Wilhelm Waetzoldt, *Deutsche Kunsthistoriker*, 2 vols. (Berlin: Wissenschaftsverlag Volker Spiess, 1986).

13. Balibar, "The Nation Form: History and Ideology," in *Race, Nation, Class*, 86–106.

14. Hubert Janitschek, *Geschichte der deutschen Malerei* (Berlin: G. Grote'sche Verlagsbuchhandlung, 1890), 3–4.

15. Sophus Müller, *Nordische Altertumskunde nach Funden und Denkmälern aus Dänemark und Schleswig*, trans. Otto Luitpold Jiriczek (Strassburg: Karl J. Trübner, 1898), 2:308.

16. Early in the century, the linguist Ferdinand de Saussure first argued that in language, meanings are created in conjunction with contrasting meanings. *Course in General Linguistics*, ed. Charles Bally and Albert Sechehaye, trans. Wade Baskin (New York: McGraw-Hill, 1959).

17. The Tabernacle was, however, described in the first major attempt at universal art history, Franz Kugler, *Handbuch der Kunstgeschichte* (Stuttgart: Ebner u. Seubert, 1842), 77–78.

18. Georges Perrot and Charles Chipiez, *Histoire de l'art dans l'antiquité*, Vol. 5: *Judée, Sardaigne, Syrie, Cappadoce* (Paris: Librairie Hachette, 1887), 475.

19. Elie Faure, *History of Art: Ancient Art*, trans. Walter Pach (New York and London: Harper and Brothers, 1921), 104–105.

20. Wilhelm Lübke, *Outlines of the History of Art*, ed. Clarence Cook, 2 vols. (New York: Dodd, Mead, 1888), 1:86. The book was first published in German in 1860. For a discussion of the ideological implications of the entailment of Phoenicians and Jews in nineteenth-century scholarship, see Martin Bernal, *Black Athena: The Afroasiatic Roots of Classical Civilization*, Vol 1: *The Fabrication of Ancient Greece, 1785–1985* (New Brunswick, N.J.: Rutgers University Press, 1987), 337–399.

21. Liebermann was subject to anti-Semitic remarks that described him as an "Oriental." See, for example, Josef Strzygowski, *Die bildende Kunst der Gegenwart: Ein Büchlein für Jedermann* (Leipzig: Quelle und Meyer, 1907), 270. But because of his love for French Impressionism, he was also denied a German pedigree by positive reviewers. Alois Riegl,

for instance, wrote that Liebermann "ebensogut Franzose sein könnte" ("could as well be French"). Review of *Die deutsche Kunst des neunzehnten Jahrhunderts: Ihre Ziele und Thaten*, by Cornelius Gurlitt, *Die Mitteilungen der Gesellschaft für vervielfältigende Kunst*, supp. to *Graphischen Künsten* 23 (1900): 3.

22. Heinrich Wölfflin, "Max Liebermann" (1927), in *Kleine Schriften* (1886–1933), ed. Joseph Gantner (Basel: Benno Schwabe, 1946), 139–140. Wölfflin helped Liebermann get an honorary degree from Berlin University, and was careful to recommend Jewish colleagues and students for jobs they could actually get. Joan Hart kindly communicated this information to me.

23. G.W.F. Hegel, *Early Theological Writings*, trans. T. M. Knox (Philadelphia: University of Pennsylvania Press, 1948), 182–205.

24. Ibid., 192.

25. Herbert Read, *Art and Society* (New York: Macmillan, 1937), 99. Wistrich traces this attitude to Voltaire (*Anti-Semitism*, 48–49).

26. Ahistorical timelessness is often attributed to non-European "Others." For a relevant argument see Johannes Fabian, *Time and the Other: How Anthropology Makes Its Object* (New York: Columbia University Press, 1983). According to Ernst Renan, the "Semitic" race had "no mythology, no epic, no science, no philosophy, no fiction, no plastic arts, no civic life: there is no complexity, nor nuance; an exclusive sense of uniformity." Quoted in Wistrich, *Anti-Semitism*, 47.

27. Jews took this role, for example, throughout the writing of Josef Strzygowski, an art historian whose early work contributed significantly to the opening up of art historical boundaries, and secured the Middle East, Asia Minor, and India a place on the art historical map. Even these works, however, are structured along explicitly anti-Semitic lines. See M. Olin, "Alois Riegl: The Late Roman Empire in the Late Habsburg Empire," *Austrian Studies* 5 (1994): 107–120.

28. Richard Wagner, "Das Judentum in der Musik" (1850), *Gesammelte Schriften und Dichtungen* (Leipzig: E. W. Fritsch, 1887–1888), 5:66–85.

29. For example, in the popular survey by H. W. Janson, the frescos of the synagogue at Dura-Europos appear under the rubric of Roman art (H. W. Janson, *History of Art*, 4th ed., rev. Anthony F. Janson [New York: Harry N. Abrams, 1991], 252–253), while the books by Frederick Hartt and Hugh Honour and John Fleming place them under Early Christian art (Frederick Hartt, *Art: A History of Painting, Sculpture, Architecture*, 3d ed. [Englewood Cliffs, N.J.: Prentice-Hall; New York: Harry N. Abrams, 1989], 292; and Hugh Honour and John Fleming, *The Visual Arts: A History*, 3d ed. [New York: Harry N. Abrams, 1991], 261–262). All the authors, but particularly Honour and Fleming, seem to find anomalous the fact that Jews used figured decorations.

30. Indeed, when Carol Krinsky published her work on synagogues in Europe, she wrote at length in her introduction about the increased "willingness to admit ethnic studies," and the appreciation of diversity that made the book possible, but placed it nevertheless on the margin by pleading that a "study of cultural context also helps us to understand the special qualities of the masterful creation." Carol Krinsky, *Synagogues of Europe: Architecture, History, Meaning* (New York: Architectural History Foundation; Cambridge, Mass.: MIT Press, 1985), 1.

31. See Anabelle Jane Wharton, "Good and Bad Images from the Synagogue of Dura-Europos: Contexts, Subtexts, Intertexts," *Art History* 17 (March 1994): 1–25.

32. Richard I. Cohen, "An Introductory Essay: Viewing the Past," in *Art and Its Uses: The Visual Image and Modern Jewish Society*, Studies in Contemporary Jewry 6 (1990), 5. On Zionist debates on role of Jewish art, see Michael Berkowitz, "Art in Zionist Popular Culture and Jewish National Self-Consciousness," in ibid., 9–42.

33. Martin Buber, introduction to *Juedischer Kuenstler*, ed. Martin Buber (Berlin: Juedischer Verlag, 1903), n.p.

34. Exodus (31:1) relates that God filled Bezal'el with the spirit of the Lord, as well as wisdom and understanding and skill in all manner of workmanship.

35. Martin Buber, *Ich und Du* (Leipzig: Insel-Verlag, 1923).

36. Buber, introduction to *Juedischer Kuenstler*.

37. Rosenberg, *Discovering the Present*, 230.

38. Ibid.

39. An argument making Jewish Halachah (Law) a forerunner of the modernist aesthetics of abstraction and distortion was made by Steven Schwarzschild, "The Legal Foundation of Jewish Aesthetics" (1975), in *The Pursuit of the Ideal: Jewish Writings of Steven Schwarzschild*, ed. Menachem Kellner (Albany: SUNY Press, 1990), 109–116. I owe this reference to Rabbi Arnold Jacob Wolf. Attempts to challenge the notion that the Second Commandment forbade art began in the late nineteenth century.

40. Jean-Paul Sartre, *Anti-Semite and Jew*, trans. George J. Becker (1948) (New York: Grove Press, 1962).

41. Harold Rosenberg was among those who objected to Sartre for, among other things, regarding Jews as an invention of anti-Semites. Rosenberg, *Discovering the Present*, 24–25, 270–287.

42. See my *Forms of Representation in Alois Riegl's Theory of Art* (University Park: The Pennsylvania State University Press, 1992).

43. Most impressive, along these lines, was Michael Fried's invocation of the concept of "grace" in his 1967 essay "Art and Objecthood," in *Minimal Art: A Critical Anthology*, ed. Gregory Battcock (New York: E. P. Dutton, 1968), 147.

44. On Ardon's Jewish themes, see Michele Vishny, *Mordecai Ardon* (New York: Harry N. Abrams, 1973). According to Ziva Amishai-Maisels, Ardon's landscapes of this period are responses to the Holocaust. *Depiction and Interpretation: The Influence of the Holocaust on the Visual Arts* (Oxford and New York: Pergamon, 1993), 256.

45. Benjamin Harshav has made a start on interpreting Chagall's art in the light of his Jewish heritage for an art historical audience in "The Role of Language in Modern Art: On Texts and Subtexts in Chagall's Paintings," *Modernism/Modernity* 1 (1994): 51–85.

46. Greenberg reprinted the essay in his *Art and Culture*, 171–174.

47. For a discussion of perceptual theories of art, see my *Forms of Representation in Alois Riegl's Theory of Art*, esp. 132–137.

48. Rudolf Arnheim, "The Gestalt Theory of Expression," *Psychological Review* 56 (1949): 156–171, esp. 158, n. 1 and 169. The author of the interesting study cited by Arnheim was born in Argentina to an Orthodox Yiddish-speaking family. His dissertation, under Franz Boas, was intended to refute the Nazi science of race by showing that gesture systems are environmental, not inherited. To compare the gestures with the "spirit" of the group with an eye to a physical explanation would have been hard to reconcile with this goal, although an attempt at an environmental explanation might well have been appropriate. David Efron, *Gesture and Environment* (New York: King's Crown, 1941); reprinted as *Gesture, Race, and Culture*, Approaches to Semiotics, no. 9, ed. Thomas A. Sebeok (The Hague and Paris: Mouton, 1972).

49. Bernard Berenson, *Aesthetics and History in the Visual Arts* (New York: Pantheon, 1948), 167. According to his preface, Berenson completed the manuscript in 1941, and the notes identify the passages cited as having been written in 1938.

50. Berenson is mentioned briefly in the major study of the phenomenon of Jewish self-hatred, Sander L. Gilman, *Jewish Self-Hatred: Anti-Semitism and the Hidden Language of the Jews* (Baltimore: Johns Hopkins University Press, 1986), 318–319.

51. Berenson, *Aesthetics and History in the Visual Arts*, 162–163.

52. Linda Nochlin noted the lack of relation between Pissarro's Jewish identity and his work in "Degas and the Dreyfus Affair: Portrait of the Artist as an Anti-Semite," in *The Dreyfus Affair: Art, Truth, and Justice*, ed. Norman L. Kleeblatt (Berkeley and Los Angeles: University of California Press, 1987), 96–116. Further remarks on the same subject appear in Richard I. Cohen, "The Visual Dreyfus Affair: A New Text?" in *Art and Its Uses*, 72–73.

53. Greenberg reviewed this book without great enthusiasm for Berenson's theoretical statements, but without mentioning the anti-Semitic remarks in it.

54. Ernst E. Herzfeld, *Archaeological History of Iran* (London: British Academy, 1935), 51–52. Berenson (*Aesthetics and History*, 159), quotes this passage with approval.

55. Postcolonial theory, for example, celebrates the "hybrid." For examples, see Bhabha, *The Location of Culture*. In the form of mixed media, complexity, and contradiction, notions like hybridity have also been a feature of postmodernist art theory.

56. In an important essay on Greenberg's political views, Robert Storr has analyzed Greenberg's use of the term "mainstream." "No Joy in Mudville: Greenberg's Modernism Then and Now," in *Modern Art and Popular Culture: Readings in High and Low*, ed. Kirk Varnedoe and Adam Gopnik (New York: Museum of Modern Art and Harry N. Abrams, 1990), 160–191.

57. Almost the same sentiments were expressed by Alois Riegl, for whom the "Kunstwollen," or artistic volition, of an age was analogous to its endeavors in other areas of cultural explanation. See especially Alois Riegl, *Spätrömische Kunstindustrie*, 400–405, and the essay "Stimmung in der moderne Kunst" (1899), in *Gesammelte Aufsätze*, ed. Karl M. Swoboda (Augsburg, Vienna: Benno Filser, 1929), 28–39. The strategy using scientific thought to explain the artistic concerns of a culture is still common. Svetlana Alpers, in *The Art of Describing: Dutch Art in the Seventeenth Century* (Chicago: University of Chicago Press, 1983), used the approach of relating science to art in order to discuss Dutch artists' fascination with optics.

58. The most important proponent of this view was Ernst Mach, *The Analysis of Sensations and the Relation of the Physical to the Psychical* (1885), trans. C. M. Williams, rev. Sydney Waterlow (1906) (New York: Dover, 1959). Explaining that Jackson Pollock's art is an attempt to cope with urban life, Greenberg wrote: "it dwells entirely in the lonely jungle of immediate sensations, impulses and notions, therefore is positivist, concrete" (2:166). Positivism also entered into his discussion of the "great change from three- to two-dimensionality which modern art has effected in pictorial space—a change that expresses our industrial society's abandonment of Cartesian rationality for empiricism and positivism" (2:203). See Donald B. Kuspit, *Clement Greenberg: Art Critic* (Madison: University of Wisconsin Press, 1979), 51–54.

59. Kuspit, *Clement Greenberg*, 30–56, has made an excellent case for the complexity Greenberg was willing to accept in art.

60. "Though virtually all American Jews were acutely aware that but for their parents' or grandparents' immigration they would have shared the fate of European Jews, this tended to deepen American loyalty and American identity, promoting an integrationist rather than a particularist consciousness." Peter Novick, "Holocaust Memory in America," in *The Art of Memory: Holocaust Memorials in History*, ed. James Young (Munich and New York: Prestel-Verlag and The Jewish Museum, 1994), 160.

61. See Edward Said, *Orientalism* (London: Routledge and Kegan Paul, 1978).

62. Rosenberg, "Jewish Identity in a Free Society," *Discovering the Present*, 259–269.

63. Sander Gilman has, in many works, but particularly in *Jewish Self-Hatred*, illuminated the role that knowledge of Jewish languages, Hebrew or Yiddish, plays in Jewish identity and anti-Semitism. Greenberg may well have been ignorant of Hebrew. His appreciative review of a Yiddish book of Jewish jokes actually points to this possibility. The book was printed in Roman letters. It suggests the existence of a potential audience, to which Greenberg may well have belonged, whose knowledge of Yiddish (a secular language normally written in Hebrew letters) is limited to speaking.

64. Storr also notes the relation between assimilation and Greenberg's formalism in "No Joy in Mudville: Greenberg's Modernism Then and Now," 160–191.

65. These statements of 1945 apply, respectively, to paintings by Hans Hofmann, who, however, perhaps "surrenders himself too unreservedly to the medium," and Arshile Gorky, with whose latest works Greenberg was considerably disappointed.

66. Kuspit, *Clement Greenberg*, 42.

67. Although it is often intimated that Greenberg's show of commitment was disingenuous. Storr, "No Joy in Mudville: Greenberg's Modernism Then and Now," 166.

68. As an example of the relation of formal aesthetics with political commitment, the work of Meyer Schapiro would contrast interestingly with that of Greenberg. See also "'It Is Not Going to Be Easy to Look into Their Eyes': Privilege of Perception in *Let Us Now Praise Famous Men*" (*Art History* 14 [March 1991]: 92–115) for a discussion of the difficulty of reconciling political effectiveness and art in another modernist context.

69. Susan Noyes Platt takes Greenberg's analysis of Judaism as authoritative. "Carefully dissected, the conservatism of his criticism—in the original sense of that term—becomes evident. It was the result of his Jewish heritage, described by Greenberg himself as emphasizing logic, abstraction, and the belief in an absolute." "Clement Greenberg in the 1930s: A New Perspective on His Criticism," *Art Criticism* 5 (1989): 59. In fact, it is Greenberg's description of that heritage that is relevant to his criticism, not the heritage itself, which can be described differently. For as nostalgic as he may have been for the spiritual life of the ghetto, Greenberg's heritage was not even that of a practicing Jew. Like his view of art, his traditional Judaism was his own invention.

SANDER L. GILMAN

THE JEW'S BODY
THOUGHTS ON JEWISH PHYSICAL DIFFERENCE

> Jews are inherently *visible* in the European Diaspora,
> for they look so different from everyone else; Jews are
> inherently *invisible,* for they look like everyone else.

"THE JEW'S BODY" IS AN ELABORATION OF THE AUTHOR'S EXTENSIVE RE-
SEARCH ON THE SCIENTIFIC AND HISTORIC THEORIES OF JEWISH "OTHER-
NESS." HERE HE ANALYZES HOW ATTEMPTS TO RECONSTITUTE THE JEWISH
BODY AND CHARACTER, WHICH CULMINATED IN THE HOLOCAUST, HAVE AF-
FECTED JEWISH CONSCIOUSNESS, LEADING TO COMPLEXITIES AND ANXIETIES
IN THE FORMATION OF MODERN JEWISH IDENTITY.

This is the contradiction that frames the anxiety about the body of the Jew in the
Diaspora—a body marked as different even in its sameness. Exploring the stereotype of the Jew's body means examining the cultural presupposition of Jewish difference. Even more so, for the artist, especially the Jewish artist, it means exploring
the anxiety about difference of character as well as body. Thus when the Lubavitcher
Manis Friedman, the dean of the Bais Chana Women's Institute in St. Paul,
preached that "Jews are different. Let's accept it and be thrilled," one can only agree
with the positive evocation of difference. But Friedman's sense of difference is cast
in a language that is itself contaminated with the sense of a negative Jewish difference, a difference of the Jewish body. He continues: "For 2,000 years we have denied our uniqueness. *We have tried to come to the world as if we were normal. Well,
guess what? The world hasn't bought it, and they never will.*"[1] According to Friedman,
Jews are not "normal." But what is the commonly understood antithesis of "normal"? It certainly is not "different" or "special" or "chosen." Rather, it is "abnormal,"
"diseased," "aberrant." What does it mean when those who celebrate a particular
Jewish difference speak of it only as being positioned on the far end of the normal-
abnormal scale?

Gilles Deleuze and Félix Guattari began to sketch the process of identity formation in their description of "becoming-Jewish" as the self-conscious separation
from the majority. They wrote in *A Thousand Plateaus*:

SANDER L. GILMAN *is Henry R. Luce Professor of Liberal Arts in Human Biology, The University of Chicago.*

SANDER L. GILMAN

Jews . . . may constitute minorities under certain conditions, but that in itself does not make them becomings. . . . Even Jews must become-Jewish (it certainly takes more than a state). But if this is the case, then becoming-Jewish necessarily affects the non-Jew as much as the Jew. Becoming-woman necessarily affects men as much as women. Conversely, if Jews themselves must becoming-Jewish . . . , it is because only a minority is capable of serving as the active medium of becoming, but under such conditions that it ceases to be a definable aggregate in relation to the majority. . . . Becoming-Jewish . . . therefore implies simultaneous movements, one by which a term (the subject) is withdrawn from the majority, and another by which a term (the medium or agent) rises up from the minority.[2]

This merging of the identity of the majority, which defines, with the minority, which is defined (and thus redefines the majority), is a process of constant construction and reconstruction of identity.

Such identity transformations have been understood as being internal, that is, purely psychological in their representation. "Becoming-Jewish," in the sense of Deleuze and Guattari, is understood as a process of identity formation. What I wish to illustrate in this essay is the complex, physical reconstitution of the Jewish body within the past century—its perception and internalization, as well as its actual physical alteration. What I hope to demonstrate is how this "becoming-Jewish" is a less fixed locus of difference than Deleuze and Guattari ever imagined because the common wisdom after the Shoah about the power of assimilation to annihilate Jewish identity is not only false, but also a simplistic attempt to deal with the complexity of identity formation both in the Diaspora and in contemporary Israel—for Israeli identity is in part a reflex of Diaspora Jewish identity. The assumption that the pressures of assimilation in the European and American Diasporas lead to perversions of the self and to a model of intense self-hatred is but one end of this spectrum. Identity is a complex thing and its deformations and reformations are varied in form and direction. Dealing with the idea of the difference of the Jewish body becomes part of the search for identity, especially for the visual artist of the late twentieth century.

Let us examine three sites in the creation of the Jewish body: the Jewish nose; the Jewish penis; and, finally, the debate about the mutability of the Jewish body in the Diaspora.

It is a visible body. The Jew's nose makes the Jewish face visible in the Western Diaspora. That nose is "seen" as an African nose, relating the image of the Jew to the image of the Black. It was not always because of any overt similarity in the stereotypical representation of the two idealized types of noses, but because each nose is considered a racial sign and as such reflects the internal life ascribed to Jew and African no less than it does physiognomy. The most widely read physiognomist of the eighteenth century, Johann Caspar Lavater, quoted the Storm and Stress poet

BAHNHOF FRIEDRICH-STR.   CENTRAL-HOTEL.

Bei'der grossen Wassersnot
Fand auch der kleine Cohn
den Tod!!!

Berlin unter Wasser

Fig. 1. A postcard from the fin de siècle showing the flooding in Berlin with the inscription: "In the great flood, little Kohn died!!!" Note the three qualities of the Jew's body: the prominent nose, the large feet, and the "diamond" ring. Here the physical and moral failings of the Jew are equated in the image of the dead Jew and his nose.

J.M.R. Lenz: "It is evident to me the Jews bear the sign of their fatherland, the orient, throughout the world. I mean their short, black, curly hair, their brown skin color. Their rapid speech, their brusque and precipitous actions also come from this source. I believe that the Jews have more gall than other people."[3] It is the character ascribed to the Jews which is written in the nose and on their skin. Jews bear the sign of the Black, "the African character of the Jew, his muzzle-shaped mouth and face removing him from certain other races," as Robert Knox noted at in the mid-nineteenth century.[4] The physiognomy of the Jew is like that of the Black: "the contour is convex; the eyes long and fine, the outer angles running towards the temples; the brow and nose apt to form a single convex line; the nose comparatively narrow at the base, the eyes consequently approaching each other; lips very full, mouth projecting, chin small, and the whole physiognomy, when swarthy, as it often is, has an African look."[5] This assumption that the Jewish prognathism was the result of the Jew's close racial relationship to, or intermixing with, Blacks becomes a commonplace of nineteenth-century ethnology. Both Aryan and Jewish fin-de-siècle anthropologists wrote of the "predominant mouth of some Jews being the result of the presence of Black blood" and the "brown skin, thick lips and prognathism" of the Jew as immutable facts.[6] It was, therefore, not only the color of the skin that enabled the scientist to see the Jew as Black, but also the associated anatomical signs, such as the shape of the nose. The Jews were quite literally seen as Black. Adam Gurowski, a Polish noble, "took every light-colored mulatto for a Jew" when he first arrived in the United States in the 1850s.[7]

The immutability of the Jew is tied to the Jew's physiognomy, which reflects the Jew's mentality. If the Germans (Aryans) are a "pure" race—and that is for turn-of-the-century science a positive quality—then the Jews cannot be a "pure" race. But what happens when the Jew attempted to stop being a Jew, to marry out of the "race"? Jewishness, in these cases, rather than being diminished, became heightened. The children were regarded as of mixed race—*Mischling*. The term *Mischling* in late nineteenth-century racial science referred to the offspring of a Jewish and a non-Jewish parent.[8] The Jewishness of the *Mischling* "undoubtedly signifies a degeneration: degeneration of the Jew, whose character is much too alien, firm, and strong to be quickened and ennobled by Teutonic blood, degeneration of the European who can naturally only lose by crossing with an 'inferior type.'"⁹ Such children can have "Jewish-Negroid" features.¹⁰ Language and, therefore, thought processes are a reflex of the racial origin of the "Black Jew." And "blackness" appears even more strikingly in mixed marriages, almost as nature's way of pointing up the difference and visibility of the Jew. This "taint" can appear among families "into which there has been an infusion of Jewish blood. . . . [It] tends to appear in a marked and intensely Jewish cast of features and expression."¹¹ As early as Edgar Allan Poe's "The Fall of the House of Usher" (1839), itself indebted to German literary models, the description of Roderick Usher, the last offspring of a highly inbred family (Poe hints at an incestuous relationship between him and his sister) is visualized as degenerate: "A cadaverousness of complex; an eye large, liquid, and luminous beyond comparison; lips somewhat thin and very pallid, but of a surpassingly beautiful curve; *a nose of a delicate Hebrew model*, but with a breadth of nostril in similar formations; a finely moulded chin, speaking, in its want of prominence, of a want of moral energy. . . ."¹² It is in the "mixed" breed, therefore, that negative qualities are most evident. As an anti-Semite said to the German-Jewish writer Jacob Wassermann during the 1920s, "whether, after conversion, they cease to be Jews in the deeper sense we do not know, and have no way of finding out. I believe that the ancient influences continue to operate. Jewishness is like a concentrated dye: a minute quantity suffices to give a specific character—or, at least, some traces of it—to an incomparably greater mass."¹³ Crossing the boundaries of race thus served to highlight the claimed inferiority of the Jews.

The image of the "Black Jew" is a powerful one in nineteenth-century Europe, especially for those Jews who desired to see themselves as "white," that is, Gentile. When, for example, Sigmund Freud, half a century after Knox's work, compared the unconscious with the preconscious, he evoked the image of the *Mischling* or "half-breed": "We may compare [these states] with individuals of mixed race who, taken all round, resemble white men, but who betray their colored descent by some striking feature or other, and on that account are excluded from society and enjoy none of the privileges of white people."¹⁴ The Jew remains visible, even when the Jew gives up all cultural signs of his or her Jewishness and marries out of the "race." It is the inability to "pass" that is central here, as well as the image of the mixed race. But what is the "striking feature" that marks the Jew as different, that marks the Jew as visible, even when the Jew desires invisibility?

It is a damaged male body, marked by the brand of circumcision. Jews only ritually circumcise their male infants. And indeed

Fig. 2. The visual stereotype of the Jew at the turn of the century was defined by the Jew's nose. The Butterfly *(May–October 1893).*

GHETTO STUDIES—NO. 7

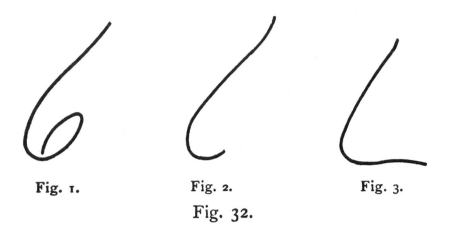

Fig. 1.   Fig. 2.   Fig. 3.

Fig. 32.

Fig. 3. Jewish scientists of the turn of the century accepted the existence of specific physiognomic qualities that defined the Jew. Here we have the creation of the idea of the "nostrility" of the Jew and its visual unmaking, at least in the form of a caricature. From Joseph Jacobs, Studies in Jewish Statistics *(London: D. Nutt, 1891).*

all the attacks on "female genital mutilation" heard in the past decade, for example in the recent work of Alice Walker, have likewise been leveled against the body and character of the male Jew.[15] The attacks on male circumcision by popular psychologists such as Alice Miller in the 1980s are but the most recent manifestation of the critiques of the Jewish body as representing the evil of the Jewish psyche. In her 1988 book *Banished Knowledge: Facing Childhood Injuries*, Miller argues that "*crimes against children represent the most frequent of all types of crime.*" "Child abuse" is not, however, only the physical and psychological maltreatment of children. It extends for her into the realm of the adult's treatment of the child's body, "the actual physical mutilation of small children," and thus into a devastating critique of "the cruel mutilation of children's sexual organs."[16] Miller argues that all circumcised males are inherently child abusers in that they insist on the circumcision of the next generation of males (an argument heard in the attacks on female circumcision).

Such arguments have a long history. One can turn to one of the most widely read sexologists of the beginning of the twentieth century, Paolo Mantegazza (1831–1901), for a "liberal" reading of the meaning of circumcision parallel to that given by Alice Walker and Alice Miller. The controversial centerpiece of Mantegazza's work is his trilogy on love and sex: *Physiology of Love* (1872), *Hygiene of Love* (1877), and *On Human Love* (1885).[17] Cited widely by sexologists from Cesare Lombroso, Richard Krafft-Ebing, Havelock Ellis, and Iwan Bloch to Magnus Hirschfeld, Mantegazza remained one of the accessible, "popular" sources for "scientific" knowledge (and misinformation) to the educated public at the turn of the century.[18] If we consult Mantegazza's chapter on the anthropology of sexual practices, which follows the one on "perversions," we find a detailed discussion of the "mutilation of the genitals" that recounts the history of these practices among "savage tribes," including the Jews.[19] Indeed, it is only in Mantegazza's discussion of the Jews that the text turns from a titillating account of "unnatural practices" into a polemic (echoing Spinoza's often cited comments on the centrality of circumcision for the definition of the Jew[20]) against the perverse practice of circumcision among Jews:

> Circumcision is a shame and an infamy; and I, who am not in the least anti-Semitic, who indeed have much esteem for the Israelites, I who demand of no living soul a profession of religious faith, insisting only upon the brotherhood of soap and water and of honesty, I shout and shall continue to shout at the Hebrews, until my last breath: Cease muti-

SANDER L. GILMAN

lating yourselves: cease imprinting upon your flesh an odious brand to distinguish you from other men; until you do this, you cannot pretend to be our equal. As it is, you, of your own accord, with the branding iron, from the first days of your lives, proceed to proclaim yourselves a race apart, one that cannot, and does not care to, mix with ours.[21]

Jews in German-speaking Europe found their own bodies used as the focus of debates about the meaning and source of health and disease. The primary means of avoiding these confrontations was to understate the meaning of circumcision. This attitude was also reflected in the debates about the need for circumcision among acculturated Jews in Vienna. The extraordinary, anonymous tale of "Herr Moriz Deutschösterreicher," written in the mid-1940s, begins with the argument between the father and the mother of this "Mr. Average German-Austrian Jew":

> Moriz Deutschösterreicher was born on June 2, 1891, in Vienna. His mother did not want him to be circumcised: 'It's crazy, Sandor, to purposely violate my child, think about when he goes into the army and they all have to bathe naked together, or what if he marries a Christian, how embarrassing. . . . If you are dumb enough and don't have him baptized, don't do this to him. Does one have to send such a poor worm with such a handicap into the world?' She cried day and night. But it didn't help a bit. Sandor agreed with his old mother—by himself he would have perhaps hesitatingly agreed, because he did not place much store in such things.[22]

Circumcision has no positive meaning in this context, except as a means of pleasing someone of an older generation.

The *topos* of circumcision as the sign of the problematic identity of Central European Jewry after the Shoah appears within other extra-German literary contexts. Simon Louvish, the brilliant Anglo-Israeli novelist, has presented the self-image of the "mad" Hungarian Jew, Yerachmiel Farkash-Fenschechter, whose life as "Friedrich Nietzsche" in a Jerusalem asylum is one focus of the first volume of

Fig. 4. At the fin de siècle, Jewish artists, such as Ephraim Moses Lilien, attempted to counter the image of the Eastern European Jew as ugly and deformed. Note the beneficent look of the eyes and the exotic, yet unexaggerated noses. From Maurice Fishberg, The Jews: A Study of Race and Environment *(New York: Walter Scott, 1911).*

Louvish's Avrom Blok trilogy, written in the late 1980s. (Here the "mad" Jew has so internalized the world which tried to destroy him in the Shoah that he became "Friedrich Nietzsche," the very philosopher claimed by his tormentors as their mentor.) In the novel, self-representation is associated with the act of circumcision and given a historical context: "by the time the Kecskemét mohel was cutting into the poor babe's ding dong the old order in Europe had crumbled." As an ironic sidebar, Louvish offers his microhistory of the meanings ascribed to circumcision as seen from an Israeli perspective:

> [Circumcision] was widespread in Pharaonic Egypt, they say. The Lord said to Abraham: 'And ye shall circumcise the flesh of your foreskin, and it shall be a token of the covenant between me and you.' 'Sure, sure, Boss,' said Abe, who had been promised a profusion of goodies. Siggy Freud, on the other hand, laid the blame on Moses, and blew the gaffe on the whole damn schmear: 'Circumcision,' said he, 'is the symbolic substitute for the castration which the primal father once inflicted upon his sons in the plenitude of his absolute power, and whoever accepted that symbol was showing by it that he was prepared to submit to the father's will, even if it imposed the most painful sacrifice on him.' But some anthropologists said it derived from the clipping of the vine, without which it would bear no fruit. A wag in Jerusalem's Ta'amon Café, though, had the last word on the issue, claiming Jewish boys were circumcised so that their foreskins should not get caught in their zips.[23]

This theological-historical discourse about circumcision, as mirrored in Louvish's microhistory, is of course ironic. His answer to circumcision is to dismiss it as trivial—circumcision is a practical social necessity given the "modern" replacement of buttons with zippers. For Louvish, neither Abraham nor Sigmund Freud has the answer to the centrality of Jewish male sexuality for the self-image of the male Jew. It is neither ritual nor repression. Louvish understands the importance of the act of circumcision for Central European Jewish males: it unwilling made them into Jews even as infants and marked that sign of difference onto their bodies. And that sign came to be a sign of sexual difference, for the Jew in Europe was traditionally seen as sexually deviant.

The theme of circumcision as a problem projected into Diaspora culture reappears in the Anglo–South African Jew Dan Jacobson's satire *The God-Fearer* (1992). Jacobson, following the lead of Clive Sinclair, postulates a lost world in which it was the Jews rather than the "Christers" who were in a majority and whose constant persecution leads to a "Christer" Holocaust. This inversion of history is set in the fabled land of Ashkenaz, the world of Central European Jewry, with its ghettos and clearly marked Other. But the Christers are marked by "the shaven faces of their menfolk" as well as by "the shamelessly uncut prepuces concealed within every pair of Christian breeches. One of the prizes of a successful pursuit of a Christer urchin was that you and your chums then had the opportunity to pull down his lower garment and to gaze your full, with fascination and disbelief, at the strange elongated, faceless, wormlike object thus revealed."[24] Here the sign of "how different they were from the majority" is hidden, and yet reflected in their shaven faces. Jacobson, like Louvish, sees circumcision as a mark of difference among Central European Jews, a mark that was read as a sign of their inferiority.

Jacobson's and Louvish's image reflects a Central European conceit that the inherent nature of Jewish sexuality was corrupt and corrupting. The definition of the Jew as a member of the covenant—one who is circumcised—places a focus on Jewish male sexuality in a unique manner. The Jewish male's psyche, like that of his body, is different. This is an ancient *topos* harking back to Tacitus's description of the Jews as the "projectissima ad libidinem gens"—the most sensual of peoples. The Jews' mental states, specifically the psychopathologies associated with the Jews, are closely linked to their intense sexuality from the very beginning.

In American culture of the late twentieth century, circumcision takes on a different meaning. Introduced into America as a hygienic practice (the rationale given by Jewish thinkers of the late nineteenth century), circumcision becomes not a sign of Jewish visibility but of Jewish invisibility. As more and more male children are medically rather than ritually circumcised, Jewish male physical identity comes to be one with the body of the "ideal" and healthy American. It is a sign of the mutable Jewish body, even if the fantasy of Jewish difference that arose when circumcision marked the Jewish male body as different seems to continue.[25]

It is a mutable body. Jews are physically different and yet they seem to be the same as everyone else. Werner Sombart, in his turn-of-the-century *The Jews and Modern Capitalism*, provides a clear image of the Jewish body as a sign of its adaptability:

> The driving power in Jewish adaptability is of course the idea of a purpose, or a goal, as the end of all things. Once the Jew has made up his mind what line he will follow, the rest is comparatively easy, and his mobility only makes his success more sure. How mobile the Jew can be is positively astounding. He is able to give himself the personal appearance he most desires. . . . The best illustrations may be drawn from the United States, where the Jew of the second or third generation is more difficult to distinguish from the non-Jew. You can tell the German after no matter how many generations; so with the Irish, the Swede, the Slav. But the Jew, in so far as his racial features allow it, has been successful in imitating the Yankee type, especially in regard to outward marks such as clothing, bearing, and the peculiar method of hairdressing.[26]

By the latter half of the nineteenth century, Western European Jews had become indistinguishable from other Western Europeans in matters of language,

Fig. 5. The physiognomy of the Jew matches the Jew's revealing voice and this at a time when British Jews were becoming more and more acculturated. There was no way to disguise the Jew, went such views, for he will always reveal himself. Punch, or the London Charivari *(October 27, 1883).*

dress, occupation, hair style, and places of residence. Indeed, if Rudolf Virchow's extensive study of over ten thousand German schoolchildren published in 1886 was accurate, Jews were also indistinguishable in terms of skin, hair, and eye color from most of those who lived in Germany.[27] Virchow's statistics sought to show that wherever a greater percentage of the overall population had lighter skin or bluer eyes or blonder hair, there a greater percentage of Jews also had lighter skin or bluer eyes or blonder hair. But although Virchow attempted to provide a rationale for the sense of Jewish acculturation, he still assumed that Jews were a separate and distinct racial category. George Mosse has commented, "the separateness of Jewish schoolchildren, approved by Virchow, says something about the course of Jewish emancipation in Germany. However rationalized, the survey must have made Jewish schoolchildren conscious of their minority status and their supposedly different origins."[28] Nonetheless, even though they were labeled as different, Jews came to parallel the physical types of people found elsewhere in European society.

The sense of the meaning of the Jewish body remains true among Jews even under the pressure of heightened anti-Semitism in the 1930s. Political awareness in no way mediated the notion that the permanence of the Jew's face marked the inherent difference between the Jew and the Aryan. In 1926, the eponymous heroine of Arthur Schnitzler's "Fräulein Else," a young girl about to be sold to an older man, an art dealer, to aid her bankrupt father, comments to herself: "You might as well be an old-clothes man as an art dealer—But, Else Else, what makes you say a thing like that?—O, I can permit myself a remark of this sort. Nobody notices it in me. I'm even blonde, a strawberry blonde, and Rudi [her brother] looks absolutely like an aristocrat. Of course, one can notice it easily in Mother, especially in her speech, but not at all in Father. Really they ought to notice it in me. More than that—let them notice it."[29] The "it," of course is the hidden taint, the visible invisibility of the Jewishness of her parents. In Schnitzler's world one can always tell who is a Jew, as the simple-mind Aryan Leutnant Gustl comments to himself at the theater: "They say the Mannheimers themselves are Jews, baptized, of course. . . . they don't look it—especially Mrs. Mannheimer . . . blond, beautiful

SANDER L. GILMAN

figure."[30] The German Jewish poet Georg Mannheimer, writing in exile in Prague in 1937, could evoke the "strange face" of the Jew:

> I know: you don't love us.
> We are not like the others.
> People who rest and people who wander
> Have a totally different face.
>
> I know: you don't love us.
> We have swum through too many streams.
> But, let us come to rest,
> Then we shall have the same face.[31]

Mannheimer's poem evokes the notion of the potential elimination of any "ugliness" associated with the "nomadic" nature ascribed to the Jew. Here it is not evolution, but rather acculturation that will alter the internalized sense of alienation marking the face of the Jew.

A parallel shift in the perception of the Jewish body can be found during the twentieth century in the United States. In 1910 the famed German Jewish anthropologist (and the founder of modern American anthropology) Franz Boas wrote a detailed report for Congress on the "Changes in Bodily Form of Descendants of Immigrants."[32] This report documented the change in body size, cephalic index, even hair color of the offspring of Jews, Sicilian, and Neapolitan immigrants born in the United States. Unlike their siblings born abroad, first-generation children were bigger, and had greater brain capacity and lighter hair color. Boas attempted to argue that racial qualities, even to the color of hair, change when the environment shifted and that racial markers were at least to some degree mutable. Needless to say, this view was contested in the science of his time. Some argued that the change could be explained by the shift from rural to urban life in America; others claimed that the "degenerate" types which had developed in Europe under capitalism were undergoing a kind of reversal in America, reemerging as the "pure" and healthier original European types. The idea that there could be a "new human race" evolving on American soil startled European scientists.

But these Eastern European Jewish immigrants were not only becoming physically more and more like other Americans, they were also growing into American culture.[33] As their body type altered, their culture changed. Not merely do second- and third-generation descendants of Eastern European Jewish immigrants not "look" like their grandparents, they "look" American. The writer and director Philip Dunne commented on the process of physical acculturation of Jews in southern California during the twentieth century:

> You could even see the physical change in the family in the second generation—not resembling the first generation at all. Of course, this is true all

across the country, but it is particularly noticeable in people who come out of very poor families. . . . One dear friend and colleague of mine was a product of a Lower East Side slum. He was desperately poor. And he grew up a rickety, tiny man who had obviously suffered as a child. At school, he told me, the goyim would scream at him. Growing up in California, his two sons were tall, tanned, and blond. Both excelled academically and in athletics. One became a military officer, the other a physicist. They were California kids. Not only American but Californian.[34]

But the more Jews in Germany and Austria at the fin de siècle looked like their non-Jewish contemporaries, the more they sensed themselves as different, and were so considered. As the Anglo-Jewish social scientist Joseph Jacobs noted in the late nineteenth century, "it is some quality which stamps their features as distinctly Jewish. This is confirmed by the interesting fact that Jews who mix much with the outer world seem to lose their Jewish quality. This was the case with Karl Marx."[35] And yet, as we know, it was precisely those Jews who were the most assimilated, who were "passing," who feared that their visibility as Jews would come to the fore. It was they who most feared being seen as bearing that disease, Jewishness, which the mid-nineteenth-century

Fig. 6. The physiognomy of race in the medical anthropology of the late nineteenth century. The Eastern Jew as the exemplary member of the "dark-skinned" races. Part of the frontispiece of Carl Ernst Bock, Das Buch vom gesunden und kranken Menschen *(Leipzig: Ernst Keil, 1893).*

German Jewish poet Heinrich Heine said the Jews brought from Egypt. For Heine, too, in his memorial to the German Jewish writer Ludwig Börne, it is the body that is the sign, specifically the "long nose that is a type of uniform, by which the King-God Jehovah recognizes his old retainers, even if they have deserted."[36]

Jews were assumed, for a thousand years, to look different, to have a different appearance, and this appearance came to have pathognomonic significance. Yet this very difference was also understood to be elusive—thus the introduction of the Jew's cap or the Jew's badge or, indeed, the ghetto in the Middle Ages, and the tattoo in Nazi concentration camps. While Jews were understood to be different, one form of that difference was their uncanny ability to look like everyone else (that is, to look like the idealization of those who wanted to see themselves as different from the Jew). For the Jewish scientist, such as Sigmund Freud, these "minor differences in people who are otherwise alike . . . form the basis of feelings of strangeness and hostility between them."[37] This is what Freud clinically labeled as the "narcissism of minor differences."

But are these differences "minor" from the perspective of either those labeling or those labeled? In reducing the basis of difference between "people who are otherwise alike," Freud was not only drawing on the Enlightenment claim of the universality of human rights, but also on the Christian underpinnings of these claims. For this "narcissism" fights "successfully against feelings of fellowship and overpower[s] the commandment that all men should love one another." It is the Christian claim to universal brotherly love that Freud was employing in arguing that the differences between himself, his body, and the body of the Aryan, are trivial. Freud comprehended the special place that the Jew played in the demonic universe of the Aryan psyche. But he marginalized this role to the Jew's function "as an agent of economic discharge . . . in the world of the Aryan ideal" rather than as one of the central aspects of the science of his time.[38] What Freud was masking was that Jews are not merely the fantasy capitalists of the paranoid delusions of the anti-Semites, but that they also mirror within their own sense of selves the image of their own difference.

Jewish internalization of images of Jews found in the larger society took the form of a heightened awareness of the "narcissism of minor differences." If Freud was right, such an internalization had to be either repressed or sublimated. The Jewish artist sublimated this sense of difference in creating works of art in which Jewish difference was encoded. In the world of American postmodern art (both here and in British exile), Jewish difference has come to be foregrounded. Jewish artists now incorporate the fantasies of Jewish difference in their art, just as African American artists, such as Carrie Mae Weems, bring the visual stereotypes of Blackness back into the world of high art. This is more than the evocation of difference; it is the realization that one lives in a world in which such images are present whether one wants them or not and that they must be dealt with. And whether they are images of Jewish difference or of difference associated with Jews on the basis of sexual orientation, color, or politics, these images must be dealt with not through repression but through confrontation.

Fig. 7. The standard caricature of the Jew in the West was that of the Eastern European Jew, usually in the form of a visual stereotype of the Wandering Jew. The Butterfly *(May–October 1893).*

NOTES

1. His comments are reported in Michael Specter, "The Oracle of Crown Heights," *The New York Times Magazine*, March 15, 1992, 34–76; quotation from 67.

2. Gilles Deleuze and Félix Guattari, *A Thousand Plateaus: Capitalism and Schizophrenia*, trans. Brian Massumi (Minneapolis: University of Minnesota Press, 1987), 291–292.

3. Johann Caspar Lavater, *Physiognomische Fragment zur Beförderung des Menschenkenntnis und Menschenliebe*, 4 vols. (Leipzig: Weidmann, 1775–1778), 3:98 and 4:272–274. This reference is cited (and rebutted) in Paolo Mantegazza, *Physiognomy and Expression* (New York: Walter Scott, 1904), 239.

4. Robert Knox, *The Races of Men: A Fragment* (Philadelphia: Lea and Blanchard, 1850), 134.

5. Ibid., 133.

6. A summary of this literature is offered in the chapter "Die negerische Rasse," in the standard racial anthropology of the Jew written during the first third of the twentieth century, Hans F. K. Günther, *Rassenkunde des jüdischen Volkes* (Munich: J. F. Lehmann, 1930), 143–149.

7. Adam G. de Gurowski, *America and Europe* (New York: D. Appleton, 1857), 177.

8. On the question of the definition and meaning of the *Mischling* see Paul Weindling, *Health, Race, and German Politics between National Unification and Nazism, 1870–1945* (Cambridge: Cambridge University Press, 1989), 531–532.

9. Houston Stewart Chamberlain, *Foundations of the Nineteenth Century*, trans. John Lees, 2 vols. (London: John Lane/The Bodley Head, 1913), 1:332.

10. W. W. Kopp, "Beobachtung an Halbjuden in Berliner Schulen," *Volk und Rasse* 10 (1935): 392.

11. Joseph Jacobs, *Studies in Jewish Statistics, Social, Vital and Anthropometric* (London: D. Nutt, 1891), xxiii.

12. Edgar Allan Poe, *Poetry and Tales* (New York: The Library of America, 1984), 321 (my emphasis).

13. Jacob Wassermann, *My Life as German and Jew* (London: George Allen & Unwin, 1933), 72.

14. All references are to Sigmund Freud, *The Complete Psychological Works of Sigmund Freud, Standard Edition*, ed. and trans. J. Strachey, A. Freud, A. Strachey, and A. Tyson, 24 vols. (London: The Hogarth Press, 1955–1974), 14:191. (Hereafter cited as *SE*.)

15. Alice Walker and Pratibha Parmar, *Warrior Marks: Female Genital Mutilation and the Sexual Blinding of Women* (New York: Harcourt Brace, 1993). See also Nahid Toubia, *Female Genital Mutilation: A Call for Global Action* (New York: Women, Ink., 1993) and Fran P. Hosken, *The Hosken Report: Genital/Sexual Mutilation of Females* (Lexington, Mass.: Women's International Network News, 1994).

16. Alice Miller, *Banished Knowledge: Facing Childhood Injuries*, trans. Leila Vennewitz (New York: Doubleday, 1990), 135–139; emphasis hers. See Lawrence Birken, "From Seduction Theory to Oedipus Complex: A Historical Analysis," *New German Critique* 43 (1988): 83–96.

17. The authorized German editions of Mantegazza are: *Die Physiologie der Liebe*, trans. Eduard Engel (Jena: Hermann Costenoble, 1877); *Die Hygiene der Liebe*, trans. R. Teutscher (Jena: Hermann Costenoble, [1877]); *Anthropologisch-kulturhistorische Studien über die Geschlechtsverhältnisse des Menschen* (Jena: Hermann Costenoble, [1891]).

18. On Mantegazza see Giovanni Landucci, *Darwinismo a Firenze: Tra scienza e ideologia (1860–1900)* (Florence: Leo S. Olschki, 1977), 107–128.

19. The relevant passages in the German edition, *Anthropologisch-kulturhistorische Studien über die Geschlechtsverhältnisse des Menschen,* are on 132–137. All of the quotations from Mantegazza are from the English translation: Paolo Mantegazza, *The Sexual Relations of Mankind*, trans. Samuel Putnam (New York: Eugenics Publishing Co., 1938).

20. Spinoza's text, often cited and often commented on in the nineteenth century, labels circumcision as the primary reason for the survival of the Jews as "they have incurred universal hatred by cutting themselves off completely from all other peoples." It also made them "effeminate" and, thus, unlikely to assume a political role in the future. Benedict Spinoza, *The Political Works*, trans. A. G. Wernham (Oxford: Oxford University Press, 1958), 63.

SANDER L. GILMAN

21. Mantegazza, *Sexual Relations*, 99.

22. *Herr Moriz Deutschösterreicher: Eine jüdische Erzählung zwischen Assimilation und Exil*, ed. Jürgen Egyptien (Vienna: Droschl, 1988), 5.

23. Simon Louvish, *The Therapy of Avram Blok: A Phantasm of Israel among the Nations* (London: Flamingo, 1990), 143. Unexpurgated version of the original novel, published in 1985.

24. Dan Jacobson, *The God-Fearer* (London: Bloomsbury, 1992), 60.

25. See my article "The Indelibility of Circumcision," *Koroth* (Jerusalem) 9 (1991): 806–817.

26. Werner Sombart, *The Jews and Modern Capitalism*, trans. M. Epstein (Glencoe, Ill.: The Free Press, 1951), 272.

27. Rudolf Virchow, "Gesamtbericht über die Farbe der Haut, der Haare und der Augen der Schulkinder in Deutschland," *Archiv für Anthropologie* 16 (1886): 275–475.

28. George L. Mosse, *Toward the Final Solution: A History of European Racism* (New York: Howard Fertig, 1975), 90–91.

29. Arthur Schnitzler, *Fräulein Else, a Novel*, trans. Robert A. Simon (New York: Simon and Schuster, 1925), 26–27.

30. Arthur Schnitzler, *Plays and Stories*, ed. Egon Schwarz (New York: Continuum, 1982), 256.

31. Georg Mannheimer, *Lieder eines Juden* (Prague: Neumann & Co., 1937), 31 (my translation).

32. This report was submitted to Congress on December 3, 1910, and issued on March 17, 1911. A full text was published by Columbia University Press in 1912. Boas summarized his findings (and chronicled the objections to this report) in his *Race, Language, and Culture* (New York: Macmillan, 1940), 60–75. An excellent reading of this problem is that of Carl N. Degler, *Culture versus Biology in the Thought of Franz Boas and Alfred L. Kroeber* (New York: Berg, 1989).

33. Boas, *Race, Language, and Culture*, 83.

34. Cited from an interview by Neal Gabler, *An Empire of Their Own: How the Jews Invented Hollywood* (New York: Crown, 1988), 242–243.

35. "Types," *The Jewish Encyclopedia*, 12 vols. (New York: Funk and Wagnalls, 1906), 12:295.

36. Heinrich Heine, *Werke*, ed. Klaus Briegleb, 12 vols. (Berlin: Ullstein, 1981), 7:31 (my translation).

37. *SE* 11:199; 18:101; 21:114.

38. *SE* 21:120.

RIV-ELLEN PRELL

WHY JEWISH PRINCESSES DON'T SWEAT
DESIRE AND CONSUMPTION
IN POSTWAR AMERICAN JEWISH CULTURE

ANTHROPOLOGIST RIV-ELLEN PRELL PROPOSES THAT A STUDY OF JEWISH
CULTURE MUST INCLUDE SERIOUS CONSIDERATION OF ISSUES OF GENDER,
THE BODY, AND SEXUALITY. HERE SHE FOCUSES ON REPRESENTATIONS OF
THE JEWISH "WOMAN," "WIFE," AND "MOTHER," USING SOURCE MATERIAL AS
VARIED AS SONG LYRICS, PHILIP ROTH, AND STANDUP COMEDY, IN AN EFFORT
TO DISMANTLE THE INTERNAL AND EXTERNAL STEREOTYPES OF BOTH EROTI-
CIZED AND DE-EROTICIZED JEWISH WOMEN, AND DOMINANT AND POWERLESS
JEWISH MEN.

In 1928, a young New York Jewish woman, H.B., wrote to the Yiddish newspaper *The Day*, decrying the fact that Jewish professional men constantly attacked Jewish women for their extravagance. "As a man creates his own God," she wrote, "so does he create a woman in his own image."[1]

As they became more Americanized, Jewish men did not stop constructing images of Jewish women. The grandsons and great-grandsons of immigrants, safely located in the privileged middle class, continue to create Jewish women in their own image, and that image has become even harsher than the one H.B. disputed in 1928. Innumerable contemporary images of women in film and television, literature, and humor created by Jewish men portray women not only as mercenary, but as lacking any sexual appeal.

If Jewish women are the reflected image, then the original may be discovered in images of Jewish manhood. Indeed, for every unerotic woman there is a Jewish man who is powerless, dominated, and unable to find sexual satisfaction with his Jewish wife or girlfriend.

De-eroticized Jewish women and powerless Jewish men are not mere literary tropes. They are accusations men and women hurl at one another as they negotiate their passage toward adulthood and, for some, into marriage. They are stereotypes masquerading as men and women whose hyperreality, the result of their sheer redundancy in the culture, makes them important to investigate.

RIV-ELLEN PRELL, *an anthropologist, is associate professor of American Studies at the University of Minnesota.*

American Jewish experience is gendered in the representations of Jewish women that developed shortly after World War II. These portraits are consistent and ubiquitous, and they are created by Jewish comics, novelists, and film makers. They circulate throughout American Jewish life not only in the media, but in ordinary conversations as well.

The Jewish woman is represented through her body, which is at once exceptionally passive and highly adorned. She simultaneously lacks sexual desire and lavishes attention on beautifying herself. She attends to the needs of no one else, expending great energy on herself instead. This popularly constructed Jewish woman performs no domestic labor and gives no sexual pleasure. Rather, her body is a surface to decorate, its adornment financed by the sweat of others.

This representation of the Jewish woman emerged specifically within the postwar period. It is preceded in time by representations of the "Jewish mother" and the "Jewish wife." Wives were a dominant subject of Jewish humor for both Europeans and immigrant Americans. Mothers appeared later in American Jewish humor, dominating it until the 1970s.[2] All these types of Jewish women can be found in Jewish humor today. Each representation emerged in a different period, however, and remained dominant until it was replaced by the next. Jewish princesses do not necessarily grow into Jewish mothers, and Jewish mothers in no sense began their lives as princesses.

Immigrant American Jewish literature and music initially celebrated an idealized mother capable not only of perfect love, but also of superhuman, slavish labor. As the immigrant's yearning for "home" in Europe, epitomized by the mother, diminished with time, the image changed. Jewish mothers came to symbolize the excesses of nurturance and the pressures of guilt.

In both cases, saintly or smothering, the Jewish mother, in contrast to the post–World War II Jewish American princess, is imagined as having an exceptionally active body. For example, in the song "My Yiddishe Momme," which was introduced by Sophie Tucker in 1925 and went on to international success, the lyrics describe the momme in the following way: "I see her at her daily task in the morning's early light. / Her willing hands forever toiling far into the night." Toil is not mentioned in the Yiddish version, but that version emphasizes sacrifice—"She would have leaped into fire and water for her children."[3] The English-language version portrays an extraordinarily physically active person who never rests. Elizabeth Stern's memoir, *My Mother and I* (1917), paints a similar portrait. She writes: "I can never remember my mother in my childhood in any other than one of two positions: standing in the corner, her foot rocking the cradle, and her hands stitching, stitching. Mother eked out the family income by making aprons—by hand."[4] Her labor and activity are central to her representation in the work of songwriters, film makers, and novelists of the period.

The sentimentalized Yiddishe momme is transformed in the 1940s, and for decades thereafter, into a symbiotic martyr. Her activity is increasingly portrayed in terms of her capacity to induce her children's guilt or repress her husband. Nevertheless, her early cultural portrait of physical exertion is directly inverted in the subsequent representation of the "princess's" passive body.

After World War II, the Jewish woman is represented as demanding, withholding, and passive. According to postwar humor, the Jewish wife and daughter are infamous for their indifference to domestic care-taking and nurture of their husbands and fathers. For example, a recently circulating joke asks, "What is a JAP pornography film? Debbie Does Dishes." A variant of the joke asks, "Did you hear about the new JAP horror movie? It's called Debbie Does Dishes."[5] The joke plays on the title of a pornographic film of the 1980s, *Debbie Does Dallas*, substituting for the male fantasy of a woman's sexual availability to a city of men a Jewish woman's purported disgust at the thought of laboring over dishes.

This and a host of jokes about a Jewish woman's refusal to clean or cook— "What does a Jewish American Princess make for dinner? Reservations"—cast her as an unwilling participant in any form of domestic labor. Another joke asks, "What does a JAP like most about being married? Having a maid."[6] Domesticity in all forms is repulsive. An unusually long joke on the subject underlines this aversion:

> To her family's delight, the JAP landed a prize husband, the son of an English duke. After the honeymoon, the couple came to the United States to live. The JAP began to instruct her husband, who had grown up on a huge country estate, on more informal ways of life in the USA.
>
> On the second day back she took her husband to a supermarket. Darling," she said, "I'll push this cart. You walk along and put all your favorites into the cart." He trotted off ahead of her, then returned with an armful of packages.
>
> She inspected them, pointing. "Drop this in the cart. And this. And this." Suddenly, she spied a large steak. Her face formed an expression of deep disgust and she said, "No. You must never buy anything like that."
>
> "But why?" her husband asked.
>
> "It needs to be cooked."[7]

Such Jewish women do not transform the raw into the cooked, or nature into culture. If the domestic realm belongs to women, then this Jewish woman defies her gender because she cannot be domesticated. Whether the jokes concern cooking or cleaning, the humor rests on the JAP's rejection of any work.

Another related series of jokes represents women refusing another activity parallel to domestic labor. They do not participate actively in sex. Jewish women are portrayed as either indifferent to sex or passive when they participate.

"How do you get a JAP to stop having sex? Marry her."

"What's the definition of a Jewish nymphomaniac? A woman who makes love once a year."

"What is the difference between a JAP and Jello (or spaghetti)? Jello moves when you touch (eat) it."

The Jewish woman does not have an active, sexual body. A number of jokes, in fact, cast her as dead or comatose, so extreme is the construction of her body as inactive. The point is illustrated by a longer joke.

> A prince enters a castle, and finds a beautiful woman lying on a bed. He tiptoes into her room and ravishes her. As he leaves, he is approached by the lord of the castle.
> Lord of the Castle: "Have you seen my poor daughter? She's been in a coma since her horse threw her last week."
> Prince: "In a coma! I thought she was Jewish."[8]

Less elaborate versions of the story also play on the woman as a corpse and the man as the corpse's partner. A popular story attributed to Woody Allen includes the following dialogue: "A man sees his ex-wife and asks if they can't make love again. She responds, 'Over my dead body.' He rejoins, 'Isn't that how we always used to do it?'"

Another joke recently found its way into the recording of a rap group called Two Live Jews, a send-up of the rappers Two Live Crew, who were accused of obscenity. One song on the album is called "Jokes." A rapper tells the following joke: "Mildred and I had doggy sex last night. I sat up and begged and she rolled over and played dead."[9]

The alternative to the Jewish woman's deathlike passivity is her active refusal to participate in sexual relations. "What is Jewish foreplay? Twenty minutes of begging."[10] Refusing to have sex or being a passive partner is an image central to the cultural representation of the Jewish woman. She is inactive in all areas of the domestic realm—whether the kitchen or the bedroom.

Domestic and sexual "labor" are parallel because each ties women to reciprocal relationships with men. If men support women, then women provide men with a range of domestic services. Women withhold their part of the contract in postwar American middle-class life. In humorous anecdotes or jokes, men are reduced to necrophilia or humiliation in order to experience sexual pleasure.

The Jewish woman's refusal to participate in a relationship is made even clearer in her lack of activity in another form of labor—childbirth. Joan Rivers, an American Jewish comedienne, describes a Jewish labor as follows: "I had a Jewish delivery. They knock you out with the first pain and wake you up when the hairdresser shows."[11] The Jewish woman will thus not even participate in the one form of labor unique to her sex, and essential for the production of life itself.

According to these caricatures and stereotypes, the Jewish woman labors neither to produce nor reproduce, a characterization based on the concept of an inactive body fundamentally defined as nonproductive or non-reproductive.

Jewish women, then, do not sweat. Their inactivity results in a central transformation of their bodies. *Mad* magazine's description of campus "types" lists "the princess" (discreetly dropping the Jewish descriptor) "wish(ing) scientists would hurry up to find a cure for perspiration."[12] The sweatless Jewish woman possesses a body that is less than human, is incapable of exertion, and withholds pleasure.

These representations are not peculiar to jokes alone. A similar portrait of a Jewish woman appeared in the 1974 film *The Heartbreak Kid*, based on the Bruce Jay Friedman short story "A Change of Plans."[13] In the film, although not in the original short story, it is the classically passive Jewish woman's body that brings disaster upon her. The film concerns the brief marriage of Lila Kolodny and Lenny Cantrow, and his subsequent pursuit of another woman, whom he meets on his honeymoon. Neither Lenny nor Lila is affluent, nor is their Judaism portrayed through elaborate Jewish rituals or symbols. They are physically typed as Jews (dark hair); they live in New York; their wedding includes the words "Mazel Tov" when a glass is broken at the conclusion of the ceremony. These minimal clues seem sufficient to alert the viewer to the film's backdrop of middle-class Jewish life.

The new groom grows increasingly unhappy and even repulsed by his wife during their first few days together. She talks during sex. She eats sloppily. But it is her inactivity that allows his distaste to blossom into passionate pursuit of another woman. Lila cannot swim, and she is so badly sunburned the first day that she must spend the rest of the honeymoon lying immobile in their hotel room. It is on the very beach where Lila's pale and inactive body was burned that Lenny, now free of ailing Lila, meets Kelly Cochran, the embodiment of a beautiful WASP woman. Kelly swims, runs, and moves gracefully. Her class and culture in every way oppose Lila's. Kelly's athletic body is especially desirable to Lenny.[14] By the third day of the honeymoon, Lenny has abandoned Lila to begin his pursuit of Kelly, which will take him to the WASP heartland of Minnesota, leaving behind his ethnicity, religion, and class. The message is that the Jewish woman's passive body is inadequate, leaving her cut off from relationships with men.

The inactive, deathlike body, however, is only one aspect of the image of Jewish women. This body, passive and sweatless, exists to be adorned, a surface for self-display of wealth and style. The Jewish woman will not serve or please men but depends upon them to adorn herself. Her own lack of productivity requires others to sweat for her. Her excessive adornment, moreover, is not designed to attract men, but only to indulge herself.

The connection between the Jewish woman's passive body and her adorned body is complex. The Jewish woman's body can be constructed as the site of adornment only if it is passive. Her sexual feelings are both created and canceled by adornment. The Jewish woman is represented more frequently through her adorned body than through her passive one. Wealth, bargains, self-indulgence, designer clothes, and many forms of consumer excess are all associated with the Jewish woman.

A series of jokes emphasizes that the Jewish woman is capable of erotic feelings, but that they are inseparable from shopping and consumption. "How do you give a JAP an orgasm? Scream 'Charge it to Daddy.'" Or from a Joan Rivers album: "Jews get orgasmic in department stores. They scream 'Charge it, charge it,' and they start to shake."[15] An interesting variant places the source of the orgasm on adornment itself. "How do you know when a JAP is having an orgasm? She drops her nail file." In this joke, adornment is simultaneous with sexuality. Sexuality, however, is also opposed to adornment. A companion joke presents the following dialogue: "The scene is in bed: He: 'Can I do anything?' She: 'Sure, as long as you don't touch my hair.'"[16] The Jewish woman's erotic desire is inseparable from her desire to be adorned.

A sexualized image of consumption in the person of a young Jewish woman was also offered in the early days of the *Saturday Night Live* television program in the 1970s. Gilda Radner, one of the original members of the company, frequently portrayed a newly married, suburban Jewish woman. She also performed a mock commercial for a product called "Jewess Jeans," a send-up of designer jeans. She is dressed for the commercial in tight jeans with the Star of David embroidered on the hip pocket. She wears many gold chains, a gold Star of David, dark glasses, and chews gum. She sings, backed up by a multiracial chorus of women wearing identical tight jeans, through glossy red lips that appear on the screen before her entire body is revealed.

> Jewess Jeans.
> They're skintight, they're out of sight.
> Jewess Jeans.
> She's got a life style uniquely hers,
> Europe, Nassau, wholesale furs.
> She shops the sales for designer clothes,
> She's got designer nails and a designer nose.
> She's an American princess and a disco queen.
> She's the Jewess in Jewess Jeans.

If the viewer has any doubts about the meaning of the commercial, the narrator's voice announces, "You don't have to be Jewish to wear Jewess Jeans," and Gilda responds, "But it doesn't hurt."[17] The inseparability of her clothes, nails, and cosmetically produced nose focuses our attention quite clearly on the body of the "Jewess," representing both her gender and Jewish affluence.

In humor above all, but also in film and fiction, the Jewish woman maintains an immovable and impermeable appearance. Whether she fakes an orgasm by pretending she is shopping or achieves it by a similar fantasy, this woman's polysemous body is the site of elaborate adornment. She is not a producer but a consumer. When the Jewish woman of popular culture might be expected to be productive—in the domestic sphere for example—her body performs no labor. She passively resists the desires of others. When her body is presented as a site for adornment, her desire is voracious. She must have it all. The passive body is one of consuming desire with no object of desire other than the self.

WOMEN'S BODIES

Why are Jewish women's bodies a site of symbolic elaboration? What forms of differentiation and what ideas about American Jewish experience are constructed upon this body, which is at once passive and elaborately decorated? If, after all, American Jews more frequently encounter themselves in film, jokes, and family gatherings than in synagogues or sacred study, then these representations provide consistent clues to American Jewish life.

Why is the woman's passive body such a powerful feature of American Jewish humor and popular culture? The passive female body is a surprising representation in Western culture, where portrayals of women's unbridled sexuality and their intimate link to the natural world are far more common. Western culture's deeply Christian roots are evident in the dual representations of women as virgins and whores. Women are frequently portrayed as either without desire and sexuality or as nothing but their sexuality. A passive body that is still an object of sexual desire is unusual. The Jewish woman's passive body may be most closely connected to the idealized Victorian woman who, though married, found activity in general, and sexuality in particular, distasteful. Queen Victoria is rumored to have given her daughter the same advice she received the evening before her marriage: "Lie still and think of England." The Victorian woman, no less than her monarch, understood the importance of duty and virtue, even in the service of sexuality. The Jewish woman appears to have no sense of duty, but is nevertheless still and passive. The image, then, is unique, but lays claim to middle-class respectability embodied in Victorian visions of womanhood and the family. The representation of the Jewish woman both inverts and borrows from Victorian domesticity.

That legacy creates a representation full of contradictions, not within womanhood itself, but within a single woman. The Jewish woman is passive but voracious, (sometimes) sexual but unavailable, dependent upon men but inaccessible to them, and capable of great pleasure, but incapable of it in the "natural" world of mutual sexuality.[18] Cultural critic John Fiske argues that "the struggle over the meaning of the body and the validation of its pleasure is a power struggle in which class, gender, and race form complexly intersected axes."[19] Any study of the body, therefore, depends on developing its social contexts. For Jews, gender, race, and class are each symbolized by and experienced through the Jewish woman's body, which specifies a Jewish ethnicity situated in middle-class affluence and dependent on the male as a producer. This contradictory body, with its demand for and denial of pleasure, suggests powerful conflicts that complicate Jewish gender relations embedded within the middle class.

Fiske's view is widely supported by a growing literature that recognizes the body's cultural representation as an important and largely neglected site for understanding how human experience is regulated and represented, as well as how humans resist domination. Fiske suggests that the middle class and the dominant culture have long felt threatened by the exercise of pleasure, by men's and women's refusal to regulate their sexuality according to narrow and Church-controlled norms. "'Unruliness' was characterized by the middle class as immoral, disorderly, and economically improvident"; it is also potentially subversive, a venue for participation in cultural forms outlawed by those in power.[20]

Pleasure, however, in the case of Jewish women, is a complex matter, because they are portrayed neither as lusty, nor as dominated by sexual desire. The image of Jewish women is conceived in more purely aesthetic terms—they seek beauty, the point of their consumption. Beauty, however, is typically associated with subordination to a class-designed and class-regulated aesthetic. The image of the perfectly coiffed woman wearing very expensive, stylish clothing is both a critique of excess and praise for beauty, success, and aesthetics. Ironically, these representations of Jewish women do not symbolize subordination or control, but precisely their opposite: the passive bodies of Jewish women cannot be regulated. Jewish women resist by their passivity because they lack the capacity for productivity. This image denies the women represented a sense of embodied power while casting them as passively voracious and capable of inducing others to produce. The link between body and pleasure in particular is what appears convoluted and dissociated in this representation.

The sociologist Bryan Turner writes in *The Body and Society* that "every mode of production has a mode of desire."[21] Every society must reproduce itself and its members, and these processes are linked to desire, which is socially controlled. The representation of Jewish women as passive, in all its ramifications, began with the entry of American Jews—particularly descendants of Eastern Europeans—into the consumer culture at the time this culture came to dominate the American economy. The representation, as I suggested, took on particular force after World War II. The distorted mode of desire embodied by the Jewish woman's representation is linked, then, to the consumer society that depends on insatiable desires for its continuance.

The centrality of consumption to the American economy began before 1935, that is, before American Jewish humor and literature began portraying wives as voracious leeches. The seeds of such economic relations developed much earlier in the century and Jews played important entrepreneurial roles in fostering their growth.[22] Scholars have recently begun to debate precisely how acculturating consumerism was for American ethnics from 1890 to 1930.[23] Some argue that consumerism emphasized ethnic ties until 1930, and others that it hastened acculturation as early as 1890. The consumer economy alone, however, cannot be the foundation for this view of the Jewish woman's body. Rather, the distorted pleasures so central to this image are best understood in the social relationships surrounding consumption—family, work, and ethnic ties—that developed after World War II.

The representation of the Jewish woman as young, demanding, and withholding appears to be particularly associated with the period of unprecedented affluence for white Americans, including their mass migration to the suburbs. Jews shared in these middle-class developments, participating in both the economic opportunities and the move into single-family homes beyond the city and urban ethnic communities. Suburban parents produced children whose life experiences differed dramatically from their own. A psychiatrist writing at the time, Joseph Adelsen, carefully spelled out the causes of and dreams for suburban life.

> We had as a nation emerged from a great war, itself following upon a long and protracted Depression. We thought, all of us, men and women alike, to replenish ourselves in goods and spirit, to undo, by exercise of collective will, the psychic disruptions of the immediate past. We would achieve the serenity that had eluded the lives of our parents. The men would be secure in stable careers, the women in comfortable homes, and together they would raise perfect children. It was the zeitgeist, the spirit of the times.[24]

The vast majority of Jews realized this very dream. What they probably did not anticipate was how dramatically their own children's lives would differ from theirs. Both the experience of this suburban dream and the way children differentiated themselves from their parents created the social relationships that generated the popular culture upon which stereotypes of the Jewish woman's body are dependent.

Through the 1950s, for example, Jewish males were far more likely to be in business than in the professions.[25] Their children, whose young lives were shaped in the immediate postwar period, were more educated and more often directed toward professions than business. Like the mainstream society, they had a vast array of consumer items available to them as well, and experienced neither the Depression nor the Second World War. This younger group continued to work in only a small number of occupations, as Jews have since their arrival in the United States. They were, however, different occupations, which required more education. The daughters of these families came of age during the second wave of feminism in the United States and anticipated staying in the workforce even when they had children, a pattern that differed dramatically from their mothers' experience.

This demographic information, drawn from a major Northeastern city, but typical of American Jewish experience, suggests that the uniqueness of the humor and other forms of popular culture in the 1970s arose directly from the experiences of the generation creating the culture. Both men and women were more likely to be employed. Wage earners probably had less autonomy than did their fathers or parents, and they were more firmly entrenched as white-collar professionals whose success depended on education and formal training. At the same time these American Jewish children were the products of unprecedented suburban affluence. Their childhoods must have been somewhat paradoxical: they were simultaneously expected to enjoy life and their parents' indulgences, yet to be self-disciplined, hard-working, and capable of the deferred gratification that produces middle-class success.

In short, these children fell prey to a common problem in the life of the American middle class, a problem exacerbated by an economy that began to weaken in the 1970s. Barbara Ehrenreich argues in *Fear of Falling* that the middle class keeps its children in the same class position not by passing on land and capital, but primarily by instilling self-denial and self-discipline in them.[26] Its capital, in contrast to the upper class's real capital, is skill and knowledge earned at a high price that demands forswearing the rewards of a consumer society.[27] The American Jewish middle class, then, entered the affluent society with a vengeance, enjoying the fruits of postwar affluence and working to keep its children firmly entrenched in that society by investing in their education and encouraging success and consumption. But these children were given a narrow path to travel. Their achievements were predicated on denial, yet their indulgence was proof of their parents' success. They were urged to do both, and to reward their parents by creating a duplicate middle-class life predicated on endogamous Jewish marriage, affluence, and children to be further indulged by grandparents.

There is no question that these children followed this path, but not as clones of their parents. With the hindsight of the 1990s we now know that the economic success that awaited them required two incomes to their parents' one and a diminished sense of independence and autonomy that came from entering the corporate world and corporate models of medicine, law, and accounting, rather than self-employment. Even consumption items became impossible to control, and the clear sense of what was appropriate to own in the 1950s and 1960s was supplanted by an infinite variety of possibilities. By the 1980s, both men and women began new consumer roles; for example, women buying cars and men buying clothes. After 1960 Jews began to intermarry until, by the late 1980s, the percentage of intermarriage reached about 30 percent of all Jews. The suburban family hardly exists any longer, given the widespread employment of women and the advent not only of American feminism, but also of a specific Jewish feminism that began in the 1970s, which criticized the "ideal" family and "normal" sex roles.[28] From the 1970s on, this young adult generation began to enter different professions, different marriages, and different forms of consumption from those of their parents. With these differences came the new, very antagonistic and deadly representations of Jewish women's bodies, and the somewhat more persistent Jewish men's self-portraits as weak and dominated.

The period's representation of the Jewish woman as inactive and unproductive, as an impermeable consumer, bears an uncanny likeness to the role of the entire middle class in the consumer economy. Jews' close association with the middle class, not surprisingly, is central to this representation. The middle class increasingly found itself anxious, passive, and preyed upon as postwar affluence began to decline in the 1970s. Unlike the producers or "self-made men" of earlier days, the middle class is now professional and technocratic. Its members must work to produce affluence, but the nature of the work, dependent on denial and abstraction, is difficult to measure other than by what can be bought by the income it produces. Encoded in the Jewish woman's passive and adorned body is the very paradox of middle-class work. The highly decorated surface rests upon an unproductive foundation. Indeed, the woman's body absorbs labor and investment without, in the parodied image, production or reproduction.[29]

The suburbs promised happiness, ease, companionate marriage, and loving families.[30] According to Ehrenreich, it produced men so burdened by supporting their families that multiple subversions developed—the Playboy philosophy, the Beat generation, and humanistic psychology—all dedicated to rationalizing men's lack of responsibilities to women and children.[31] The children of that era, the boys in particular, assumed a nurturing environment that placed their needs first, as males and children. Not only did the nature of middle-class life change with the 1970s, but its promises of pleasure did not include women singlemindedly devoted to the needs of husbands who supported them.

If, as Turner suggests, modes of production and desire/sexuality are linked, then Jews' active participation in *both* the consumer culture and its professional/managerial class is reflected in the representation of the woman's body that does not sweat. Jews have negotiated their passage into the mainstream of American culture through the middle class. Gender, embodied by the woman, symbolizes Jewish American experience. The woman's body, freed from labor, but requiring others to work, reveals the anxiety that is the patrimony of the middle class. The passive body, and the bitterness that creates its representation, incorporate this anxiety. Jewish humor casts men as victimized by women and their insatiable wants. "Embodied" in that passive female body is a consumption-driven economic system in which men are rendered unproductive as surely as women are. Work is abstract, its products difficult to identify. Consumption is almost infinitely variegated and, as such, inevitably disappointing. Sweat evaporates. Woman's sexuality is, in humor, subsumed by her consumerism because she embodies the economic system that depends on manipulation rather than manufacture, consumption rather than production. In the popular culture, the Jewish male is portrayed as shackled to a ferocious taskmaster who drives him to finance what he cannot enjoy as he continually works to satisfy her. Work cannot seem to satisfy or succeed as it once did, and it results in a sense of loss.

The Jewish American princess, beautifully adorned, is the realization of aspirations for success. But Jewish men, like so many men of the middle class, not only resent and reject their place in the economy, but also see themselves as failing to reap the rewards of sexual satisfaction. They construct marriage and marriage partners as the dark side of the social world. Jewish women "energize" nothing. Instead, they absorb energy, leading men to experience their disappointment and their success as the same thing. Marriage and work cannot establish manhood, yet manhood is impossible without them.

Therefore, it is their relationship to women and their role within the family that best came to symbolize for fathers, and particularly sons, the disappointment with middle-class suburban life. The life that promised pleasure, leisure, security, and satisfaction is inverted in a popular culture of withholding women. Elisa New, reviewing a recent book about the murder of a suburban Arizona Jewish woman by her husband, whose successful defense was that his wife behaved like a Jewish princess, writes:

> Indeed, what Veblen did not anticipate—though Henry James did when he noted the "growing" divorce between the American woman (with her comparative leisure, culture, grace) and the male American immersed in the ferocity of business—was that, in a country without a landed class, it would fall to women to exercise the tastes their husbands labored to support; that the leisure class in America could only be a female class whose lifestyle was preserved through intrafamilial class warfare. It is this warfare that we see explode in the comedy of the fifties, where the American man as Provider is a disgruntled or bemused prole, shackled to supporting his wife's conspicuous spending. And it is this warfare that is not incidentally so standard in the repertoire of those Borscht Belt comics who are our mainstream American comics. When Rodney Dangerfield, Shecky Green, and Alan King pillory their wives, it is not to reveal that the wrangling over the Visa card is unique to the Jewish marriage. It is rather to point with rueful humor to the Americanization of that marriage.[32]

Americanization was virtually indistinguishable from suburban affluence. As Jews successfully entered the mainstream, abandoning much of their unique ethnic culture by the 1930s, their spending habits and consumption patterns as well as their types of employment all hastened their Americanization. The tension between men and women symbolized through their family division of labor is further proof, as New contends, of this complete Americanization and, with it, the benefits and disappointments of middle-class life embodied in affluent women, a sign of poisoned success. Work, family relations, and rampant Americanization are each expressed in the Jewish woman's passive and adorned body. The humor of the 1950s comics was to escalate, with American Jewish affluence, into the 1970s humor of the Jewish American princess.

I have described a popular culture that envisions women as symbols of men's economic and cultural desires. As such, women appear largely as a representation of male experience. Women are, nevertheless, actors in this drama of middle-class life. As noted, a central part of the transformation of suburban life was both women's employment and their dissatisfaction with the suburban family. In particular, Jewish women created a Jewish feminism that addressed quite specifically their rejection of the narrow range of roles idealized by their community. Jewish mothers came in for considerable discussion in the 1970s.[33] The Jewish American princess humor developed in precisely this period. Many Jewish women rejected male dominance of every aspect of Jewish life—ritual, advanced religious education, secular boards, the rabbinate, the cantorate, as well as an unabashed cultural preference for male children. As Jewish women, supported by the larger feminist movement, abandoned their roles as "Jewish mothers," fundamentally defined as self-sacrificing, they were portrayed more frequently as "princesses." Jewish women's widespread entry into the paid labor force, at a much younger age than their mothers, continued to be translated as the denial of men's desires.

What form a Jewish American popular culture of young Jewish comediennes, film makers, novelists, and writers will take remains to be seen because this work is only now being produced. Film maker and humorist Elaine May and comedienne Joan Rivers, who gained attention and popularity in the 1960s and 1970s, have echoed many of the views of Jewish women and of their male peers. There is little question that different voices and images will soon emerge that will address the issues which remain central to middle-class American Jewish life.

The consumer culture, the middle-class path to Americanization, the economic and cultural upheavals that developed in the 1970s, and second-wave American feminism can all be traced to the sweatless body of the Jewish woman. The convoluted desire that locates pleasure in consumption but not mutual sexuality is the product of postwar American pains and disappointments anesthetized by the devouring pleasures of the consumer society.

SWEATING PRINCESSES

I have suggested that the passive body cannot sweat for lack of exertion and that passivity is tied to a new form of labor and economy in which Jewish males found themselves at the onset, and then more fully at the end, of World War II. It would be misleading, however, if I did not acknowledge the existence of a prominent Jewish princess who did sweat, one who may have defined the very contours of the representation itself. It is the very nature of her sweat that may best demonstrate my point because her sweat is a metaphor for leisure and consumption.

Brenda Patimkin is the central character of Philip Roth's novella *Goodbye, Columbus*. First published in 1959, this story and Herman Wouk's *Marjorie Morningstar* (1955)[34] are the sources of the two first postwar Jewish princesses. *Goodbye, Columbus* is a far richer text for analysis with more complex emotions than one finds in jokes and much of the popular culture I have described here, and yet there

Goodbye, Columbus.

are uncanny similarities between Roth's work and Wouk's. Roth's novella—it appears in retrospect—used the Jewish woman's body symbolically in a way that anticipated its power to represent economic, social, and cultural transformation.

When Neil Klugman, son of the lower middle class in Newark, New Jersey, first sees Brenda, it is at an upper-class suburban country club where his cousins are members. Drawn to Brenda's beauty, he calls her for a date. When he inquires if he can meet her after tennis: "'I'll be sweaty after,' Brenda said. It was not to warn me to clothespin my nose and run in the opposite direction; it was a fact, it apparently didn't bother Brenda, but she wanted it recorded."[35] And when Neil slyly inquires "'How will I know you?' Brenda responds, 'I'll be sweating'" (18).

Thus begins a passionate romance between a Jewish lower-middle-class male, out of college, working in a library and "not a planner," with the daughter of a family that epitomizes American Jewish success. Brenda's father is a transitional figure between prewar and postwar American Jewish life. His manufacturing business, Patimkin Kitchen and Bathroom Sinks, transformed the Patimkins into the nouveau riche when the War Department installed his sinks in all military barracks. To Neil Brenda says, "Money! My father's up to here with it" (26).

In this suburban world of the 1950s, upper-class success is associated with all sorts of physical exertion. Brenda's brother is a large, successful athlete, a "crewcut proteus" who appears to Neil to be a giant as capable of drinking the country club pool dry as of swimming in it. Brenda is good at every sport. Even her mother was a New Jersey tennis champion as a girl. However, none of this sweat is productive. The only producer, Brenda's father, is portrayed as "sweet," "not too smart," and crude. His business is located in the "Negro section" of Newark, once home of Jewish immigrants, including Neil's grandparents. His work and its location attach Ben Patimkin to an older order. The Patimkin children and wife sweat the sweat of leisure, locating them in the suburban world of postwar affluence.

Neil, always the outsider to this Short Hills suburban rambler, notes the artificiality of their environment. The air he says is "by Westinghouse" (22) in contrast to his aunt and uncle's apartment in Newark, where they escape the heat by sitting in the alley. Looking out the Patimkin picture window, he describes their oaks: "I saw oaks, though fancifully, one might call them sporting goods trees. Beneath their branches, like fruit dropped from their limbs, were two irons, a golf bag, a tennis can, a baseball bat, basketball, a first baseman's glove, and what was apparently a riding crop" (21–22).

When Neil discovers their basement refrigerator—brought from Newark—completely full of fruit, he wonders that the trees produce sporting equipment and the machines yield fruit. Through the eyes of a Jewish man who remains exceptionally ambivalent about the climb up the social ladder, everything in the Patimkin world is artificial. The sweat, the fruit, and the sporting equipment are all produced through leisure and artificiality. Even Brenda's nose, a topic of discussion at their first meeting, was artificially created by plastic surgery.

Unlike latter-day Jewish princesses, Brenda is erotic and physically and sexually active. But in the end, she fails Neil by her loyalty to her parents, and, one must assume, to her social class. In their final fight, precipitated by her mother's discovery of the diaphragm Neil insisted Brenda buy, she says, "Neil, you don't understand. They're still my parents. They did send me to the best schools, didn't they? They have given me everything I've wanted, haven't they?" (134).

Through the novelist's eye, we see the contours of both the "mode of production" and the "mode of desire" that will come to dominate postwar America, and American Jews in particular. The producers' work ethic, epitomized by Mr. Patimkin—"A man works hard he's got something. You don't get anywhere sitting on your behind, you know. . . ." (93)—rings hollow in this world of consumption and leisure. And what lies beneath the initially sweet passions of Neil and Brenda's affair is a fundamental differentiation by social class in their attitude toward how firmly love is embedded in consumerism, adornment, and the decorated body. Their passion is an illusion, incapable of cementing real ties. As it wanes, so sexuality will soon disappear from the representations of Jewish women, and all that remains will communicate the world of leisure and consumption. People who produced without words will be replaced by those whose living depends on words and abstractions. Their success will be rewarded by wealth, which they will use to purchase prestigious consumer items.

What ultimately perplexes Neil is the source of his attraction to Brenda. He finds in her suburban world two types of pleasure and desire—sex and affluence. Brenda is only one of many to tell Neil that when he loves her he will never have to worry again. As he waits to meet Brenda after her appointment to be fitted for a diaphragm, he contemplates this relationship. He is sitting in St. Patrick's Cathedral to escape the heat. He finds himself making a silent speech that might pass for a prayer directed to an audience he calls God. He asks: " 'What is it I love lord? Why have I chosen? If we meet You at all, God, it's that we're carnal and acquisitive, and thereby partake of You. I am carnal and I know You approve, I just know it. But how carnal can I get? I am acquisitive. Where do I turn now in my acquisitiveness? Which prize is You?' " (100).

Neil Klugman continues: "'Which prizes do you think, schmuck? Gold dinnerware, sporting goods trees, nectarines, garbage disposals, bumpless noses, Patimkin sinks, Bonwit Teller. . . .' "(100).

Neil finds it difficult to separate his various desires and does not know which to trust. His desire for Brenda depends on her uniqueness, but he finds it difficult to assure himself that she is different from the women and world he believes were created by new Jewish affluence.

Matters are resolved when Brenda finally cannot join her sexual relationship with Neil and her loyalty to her family and its affluence. Neil is about to propose marriage just as he learns that Brenda's parents have discovered their sexual liaison. She remains loyal to her parents and all that they have given her. Her mother's final words to Brenda in the letter revealing her discovery of Brenda's sexual relationship—"this is some thank you for all we gave you" (129)—seem definitive. Brenda will reject Neil, her right to sexuality, and her independence in order to stay in the orbit of affluence and leisure. Roth has constructed a Jewish princess against whom Neil can rebel, rejecting his rightful inheritance as the next male generation. Neil asserts his independence and perhaps "manhood" against the Jewish woman, who is made to embody the modes of production and desire.

Goodbye, Columbus provided the outline of a set of relations that would generate the American Jewish humor of the 1970s. The manufacturers' wealth of the war years created the children whose enlarged vistas revealed affluence and professionalization. Their (almost always male) success was marked by their ability to maintain the affluence of their fathers and fathers-in-law. The consumer culture generated an unceasing and insatiable set of demands. American Jewish men, inheritors of a long tradition of "overdemanding wife" jokes, translated the frustrations of their class and epoch into the Jewish woman, whose body became a surface reflecting affluence, purchased at a high price. Even Brenda's sexual and physical exertions cannot allow her to transcend her overdetermined role as the "glittering prize" of male success. Her sweat of leisure will soon evaporate, leaving Jewish women with passive bodies. Neil, who rejected this world, forswears not just a social class but an American Judaism that he ineluctably linked to the synagogue, organizations, and empty ritual observances of the Patimkins' suburban life. Neither Neil nor Philip Roth, for that matter, cease to be Jews. But their sense of American Jewish life as inseparable from middle-class consumerism defines their rite of passage to adulthood and with it the rejection of American Jewish women who will rarely again appear as a source of erotic desire in Roth's work.[36]

AMERICAN JEWISH GENDER SYSTEMS

I have argued that gender systems persist in American Jewish culture, particularly as we recognize that American Jewish life is fully embedded in the economy and culture of middle-class American life. And yet Jewish ethnicity persists, and one of its most potent forms is the popular culture and literature that American Jews produce. Jewish women are represented in these media in terms of a passive and repressed body, but one often beyond the control of men. This representation focuses very powerfully on the body because the woman's body is made to symbolize forces of both production and reproduction, consumption and deferred gratification, repression and the fulfillment of desire. In short, whether the Jewish woman is portrayed as sweating in sports, or not sweating at all, exerting herself, or refusing to move, desire for her and her desire are always frustrated by the lack of the active body or physical productivity. Understanding these images and how desire is linked to economy tells us a great deal about the elusive American Jewish culture.

NOTES

This essay is a revised and abridged version of one previously published in *The People of the Body: Jews and Judaism from an Embodied Perspective,* ed. Howard Eilberg-Schwartz (Albany: SUNY Press, 1992). Versions of this essay were presented in 1989 at the Conference on Social Scientific Approaches to Judaism, Toronto, and The American Studies Association meeting, New Orleans. I benefited from discussions of the essay at these conferences. I would like to acknowledge the very thoughtful comments of the following colleagues on an earlier draft of this article: Harry Boyte, Howard Eilberg-Schwartz, Sara Evans, Steven Foldes, Amy Kaminsky, Rebecca Mark, Elaine May, Lary May, Cheri Register, and Naomi Scheman. I was assisted by Nicole Pineda's thorough library research and wish to acknowledge her help. This essay was written in the months of mourning immediately after the death of my mother, Mary Prell. Though it would cause her chagrin, with the deepest love I dedicate this essay to her memory for reasons so numerous that they are impossible to detail.

1. *The Day,* January 15, 1928.
2. G. Rothbell, "The Jewish Mother: Social Construction of a Popular Image," in *The Jewish Family: Myths and Realities,* ed. Steven M. Cohen and Paula Hyman (New York and London: Holmes and Meier, 1986), 114.
3. M. Slobin, *Tenement Songs: The Popular Music of the Jewish Immigrants* (Urbana: University of Illinois Press, 1982), 198, 204.

RIV-ELLEN PRELL

4. E. G. Stern, *My Mother and I* (New York: Macmillan, 1917), 212.

5. J. Allen, *500 Great Jewish Jokes* (New York: Signet, 1990), 21.

6. Ibid., 15.

7. Ibid., 131.

8. S. W. Schneider, "'In a Coma! I Thought She Was Jewish': Some Truths and Some Speculations about Jewish Women and Sex," *Lilith: The Jewish Women's Magazine* 5 (Spring–Summer 1977).

9. This rap, a string of Jewish jokes in song, is framed by responses between the two rappers. On some occasions one laughs and on others there are attempts to silence the jokes. As Irving tells this joke, Moishe continually says, "Don't say it; it's not funny." The rap also ends with a string of obscene words in Yiddish, with parenthetical comments about "talking dirty" and "getting arrested," references to the censorship of Two Live Crew's music. Two Live Jews both represent Jewish women in stereotyped fashion and resist the interpretation throughout the album.

10. Folklorist Alan Dundes suggests that such jokes are part of a larger ethnic slur tradition that criticizes insensitive males who are oblivious to female sexual needs. He includes in the genre jokes such as "What is Irish foreplay? Brace yourself Bridget." "What is Italian foreplay? Hey you awake?" or "Slamming the front door and announcing, 'Hey Honey I'm home'" ("The J.A.P. and the J.A.M. in American Jokelore," *Journal of American Folklore* 98 [1985]: 456–475).

11. Joan Rivers, *What Becomes a Semi Legend Most?* (Geffen Records, n.d.).

12. *Mad* magazine (January 1987): 22–23.

13. Bruce J. Friedman, "A Change of Plans," in *Black Angels: Stories by Bruce J. Friedman* (orig. 1962; New York: Simon and Schuster, 1966), 80–90.

14. The *shiksa* is a representation of the non-Jewish woman closely linked to the Jewish woman. They affect one another through contrasts and depend upon one another to create either stereotype. See Riv-Ellen Prell, "Rage and Representation: Jewish Gender Stereotypes in America," in *Uncertain Terms: Negotiating Gender in American Culture*, ed. Faye Ginsburg and Anna Lowenhaupt Tsing (Boston: Beacon Press, 1990), 248–268. On the *shiksa* in literature, see R. C. Jaher, "The Quest for the Ultimate Shiksa," *American Quarterly* 35 (Winter 1983): 518–541.

15. Rivers, *What Becomes a Semi Legend Most?*

16. This joke was printed in Leslie Tonner's book, *Nothing But the Best: The Luck of the Jewish Princess* (New York: Coward, McCann and Geoghegan, 1975) and reprinted in her article for *Cosmopolitan* "The Truth about Being a Jewish Princess" (September 1976): 226. The joke is described as a warning to Jewish princesses who want to marry and may be overly interested in their appearance to the detriment of their ability to "catch" a husband by being sexually available.

17. In the Jewish Video Archives, The Jewish Museum, New York. Levy's rye bread produced a series of popular advertisements in the 1970s that showed a variety of ethnic groups eating rye bread sandwiches. The caption announced "You don't have to be Jewish to love Levy's real Jewish rye." Radner's line punctures the artificial pluralism of the Levy's commercial.

18. Bartky argues that women's pleasure and agency are part of her embodiment. Women also play roles in the styles they wear. They are not simply victims of patriarchal culture. Nevertheless, she argues that though women tend to respond to men's desire, style may allow for certain forms of resistance against patriarchy. She wants to explore the "dialectic of the image" at work in women's pleasure in self-display. S. Bartky, "Women, Bodies and Power: A Research Agenda for Philosophy," *Newsletter on Feminism and Philosophy* (American Philosophical Association) 89 (1989): 79–80.

19. John Fiske, *Understanding Popular Culture* (Boston: Unwin Hyman, 1989), 50.

20. Ibid., 75, 97.

21. Bryan Turner, *The Body and Society: Explorations in Social Theory* (Oxford: Basil Blackwell, 1984), 249.

22. Lary May, *Screening Out the Past: The Birth of Mass Culture and the Motion Picture Industry* (Chicago: University of Chicago Press, 1983); A. Heinze, *Adapting to Abundance: Jewish Immigrants, Mass Consumption, and the Search for American Identity* (New York: Columbia University Press, 1990).

23. Heinze, *Adapting to Abundance*; L. Cohen, "Encountering Mass Culture at the Grassroots: The Experience of Chicago Writers in the 1920s," *American Quarterly* 41 (March 1989): 6–33.

24. Cited in E. May, *Homeward Bound: American Families in the Cold War* (New York: Basic Books, 1988), 58.

25. S. Cohen, *American Modernity and Jewish Identity* (New York: Tavistock, 1983), 87; M. Sklare and J. Greenblum, *Jewish Identity and the Suburban Frontier: A Study of Group Survival in the Open Society*, 2d ed. (Chicago: University of Chicago Press, 1979), 25–27.

26. Barbara Ehrenreich, *Fear of Falling: The Inner Life of the Middle Class* (New York: Pantheon Books, 1989).

27. Ibid., 15, 84.

28. S. W. Schneider, *Jewish and Female: Choices and Changes in Our Lives Today* (New York: Simon and Schuster, 1984).; C. Baum, P. Hyman, and S. Michel, *The Jewish Woman in America* (New York: Dial Press, 1975).

29. George Lipsitz links early television to the transformation to a consumption economy. *The Goldbergs*, the popular program that made the switch from radio to television, abounds with examples of growing affluence directed toward transforming these immigrant Jews into people of civility and self-conscious consumers. "The Meaning of Memory: Family, Class, and Ethnicity in Early Television," in *Time Passages: Collective Memory and American Popular Culture* (Minneapolis: University of Minnesota Press, 1990), 39–76.

30. May, *Homeward Bound*.

31. Barbara Ehrenreich, *The Hearts of Men: American Dreams and the Flight from Commitment* (New York: Anchor Books, 1983).

32. Elisa New, "Killing the Princess: The Offense of a Bad Defense," *Tikkun* 4 (March–April 1988): 17–18.

33. See Prell, "Rage and Representation: Jewish Gender Stereotypes in America," for a discussion of this stereotype.

34. Herman Wouk, *Marjorie Morningstar* (New York: Doubleday and Company, 1955).

35. Philip Roth, *Goodbye, Columbus and Other Short Stories*. (1959; rpt. Boston: Houghton Mifflin, 1989), 8. All future page references in the text are to this edition.

    In Roth's preface to the thirtieth anniversary edition of "Goodbye, Columbus," he singles out *Commentary* magazine for providing models and inspiration for critiques of American Jewish life. He found in *Commentary* of the forties and fifties an attitude of "ineluctably Jewish self-scrutiny" in fiction that examined everyday lives of Jews—their passions, customs, and family relations. Roth's depiction of Short Hills Jewish life intended to do more than draw on local color. He clearly understood himself to be offering a critique of American Jewish life that he accomplished through his depictions of men and women in the Patimkin family (xii).

    Critical attempts to understand "Goodbye, Columbus" may be found in Michael Aaron Rockland, "The Jewish Side of Philip Roth," *Studies in American Jewish Literature* 1 (Spring 1975): 29–37; and D. Walden, "Goodbye, Columbus, Hello, Portnoy—and Beyond: The Ordeal of Philip Roth," *Studies in American Jewish Literature* 3 (Winter 1977–1978). A feminist critique of Roth may be Found in S. B. Cohen, "Philip Roth's Would-be Patriarchs and Their Shikses and Shrews," *Studies in American Jewish Literature* 1 (Spring 1975): 16–29.

36. Baum, Hyman, and Michel, *The Jewish Woman in America*, also consider Roth and Wouk in their study. My interpretation is in basic agreement with theirs, but they use the texts for different purposes.

MAURICE BERGER

THE MOUSE THAT NEVER ROARS
JEWISH MASCULINITY ON AMERICAN TELEVISION

THIS ESSAY DISCUSSES THE PARADOXICAL REALITY THAT THE ANTI-SEMITIC
STEREOTYPES OF JEWISH MASCULINITY SHOWN ON AMERICAN TELEVISION
SINCE THE 1950S WERE OFTEN CREATED BY JEWS THEMSELVES. THE AU-
THOR ANALYZES THESE VARIOUS NEGATIVE CONSTRUCTIONS OF JEWISH MEN
ON PRIME-TIME TV AND INVESTIGATES THE COMPLEX SET OF CIRCUMSTANCES
THAT LED TO THESE UNFLATTERING CHARACTERIZATIONS.

In an essay on the need for definitions of masculinity to be less rigid, the cultural
critic Homi Bhabha recalls a question that his barrister father repeatedly asked
him as a child in India: "Are you a man or a mouse?" Bhabha remembers thinking that he really didn't want to choose, caught as he was between "two different
creeds and two different outlooks on life."[1] His father was confronting him with
a question that almost every young man must face in one form or another: How
do you want to express your power as a man? There is a particular sense of irony
for Bhabha, however, for while men might expand and enrich their masculinity
by refusing to make this choice—the very point of Bhabha's narrative—the answer to the father's inquiry did not entirely lie with the son. For the dark-skinned
child was, in some sense, defined by the social order of colonialism, a hierarchy
that most often denied men of color the status of full manhood.

Since Jewishness is not as visually immediate as skin color, the drama enacted
by Bhabha and his father metaphorically parallels, in a far more subtle way, the
dilemma of the Jewish male in postwar American popular culture, a telegenic
universe where the sensibilities of Jewish masculinity have been assigned, through
stereotypes, rather than chosen. In the forty-five years since the advent of prime-
time TV, Jewish men have seen their identities disguised, their mannerisms
mocked, and their masculinity voiced as the quiet peeps of a mouse.

Unlike the conditions of de jure or de facto segregation, colonialism, or even,

---

MAURICE BERGER *is a Senior Fellow at The Vera List Center for Art and Politics, New School for Social
Research, New York.*

to a certain extent, postcolonialism, where men of color are defined and catego-rized by their white oppressors, such anti-Semitic stereotypes were more often than not produced by Jewish men themselves. Nevertheless, Jewish men on prime-time television have assumed a plethora of negative or subordinated roles: passive fathers married to domineering, often vulgar Jewish women; nebbishy husbands and boyfriends involved with beautiful Gentile women; neurotic Jew-ish American princes; self-deprecating nerds; loyal sidekicks; and cross-dressing or effeminate men. This behavioral or professional pigeonholing has in turn spawned consistent and durable stereotypes.

Such stereotyping is, of course, endemic to American popular culture: African American men and women, for example, have long been associated with insipid character types designed to help lessen white fears about people their soci-ety has enslaved and oppressed. In order to better understand the function and effects of these representations in culture, the African American literary critic Sterling A. Brown divided the range of these tropes in American literature into seven categories: the contented slave, the wretched freeman, the comic Negro, the brute Negro, the tragic mulatto, the local color Negro, and the exotic primi-tive.[2] In the years following Brown's assessment in 1933, such types have been con-tinually updated in the formulaic narratives of American television, from Amos 'n' Andy in the 1950s to junk dealer Fred Sanford and erstwhile "household man-ager" Benson in the 1970s and '80s.

It is also important to understand that despite television's formulaic struc-ture, the content of programs often attempts to capture contradictory positions in order to reach as broad an audience as possible. As such, even the most rigid stereotypes are usually ameliorated by some positive features: Fred Sanford, for example, is savvy and generous; Benson is the most canny member of the house-hold. As Douglas Kellner has written on this issue: "The forms of TV narratives and codes tend to be conservative. American television is divided into well-defined genres with their dominant conventions and formulas. . . . But like all ideology in advanced capitalism, television is full of contradictions. The regions of television ideology contain conflicting conceptions of such things as the family and sexuality, and power and authority; these conflicts express ideological and social changes in advanced capitalism."[3]

Some of the stereotypes that marked Jewish masculinity in nineteenth- and early twentieth-century culture and science were also appropriated for TV, and they too fit into distinct categories—the exotic or vulgar ethnic, the subordinated or passive *schlemiel*, the validated Jew, the neurotic, the inferred Jew, and the fem-inized Jew—cynically designed to undermine or ameliorate Jewish manhood.

Jewish women have fared even less well. While Jewish female characters are rare on American television, they usually appear as overbearing mothers, self-hating *schleps*, or spoiled princesses. Although Molly Goldberg (Gertrude Berg) on *The Goldbergs* (1949–1955) or Sophie Berger (Marion Ross) on *Brooklyn Bridge* (1991–1993) are portrayed as powerful and considerate women, most Jewish tele-

vision mothers come off as controlling and hypercritical monsters: Rhoda Morgenstern's compulsive mother (Nancy Walker) on the situation comedy *The Mary Tyler Moore Show* (1970–1977), for example, reveals her intimate marital problems to Rhoda's thoughtful best friend Mary Richards and then cruelly admonishes the young woman for listening; Paul Buchman's mother on the sitcom *Mad About You* (1992–) barges in on her son and daughter-in-law's bedroom lovemaking, sneering, "Can't you skip an evening?"; and the repressive, comedic matriarch (Renee Taylor) on *Daddy Dearest* (1993) emotionally demolishes several students at her grandson's grade school.

These wicked depictions, like those of Jewish men, serve to undermine the authority of the Jewish subject. The Jewish mother's dysfunctionalism—her inability to respect emotional boundaries, her disregard of her children's privacy or feelings, and her over-controlling nature—renders her undesirable as a parent. The self-deprecating neurotic, exemplified by Rhoda Morgenstern on *The Mary Tyler Moore Show* or Brenda Morgenstern (Julie Kavner), Rhoda's bank-teller sister on the sitcom spin-off *Rhoda* (1974–1978), especially in contrast with her elegant WASP counterparts, continually undermines herself through whining entreaties that further denigrate her feminine voice. The Jewish American

Fig. 1 (left). The Goldbergs.

Fig. 2 (right). Brooklyn Bridge.

Fig. 3. Rhoda.

princess's refusal to engage in domestic chores, her ambivalence toward and competitiveness with other women, and her reluctance to participate in sex or "to be an animated partner who experiences or gives pleasure" render her inactive in the domestic, political, and sexual realm; rather than powerful in her femininity, she is emotionally and intellectually sterile.[4]

Most media constructions of male-female relationships pit heterosexuals against each other in a simplistic battle for power and control, but gender representations of Jews are charged in addition with issues of race and class. Depictions of subordinated or passive Jewish men, for example, are often motivated less by conflicts between the sexes and more by network executives who fear the wrath of disaffected non-Jewish men, a significant sector of the viewing audience, who often perceive Jews as "rich and powerful" competitors. Thus, the cultural construction of Jewish masculinity must be understood as part of a "partial gender system, embedded within the larger culture's, but uniquely differentiated from it."[5]

The wider significance of this partial system is exemplified by one of television's most insidious masculine stereotypes: the feminized Jew. Given the rarity of the reverse construction, that of the hypermasculine or macho Jew, it is almost inconceivable that Jewish actors such as the stars of *Bonanza* (1959–1973), Lorne Green and Michael Landon, could have actually played their roles as robust Jewish cowboys—a role afforded to only one character on American television, Nathan Shotness on *Have Gun Will Travel* (1957–1963). Depictions of Jewish men in drag, who in turn usually portray vulgar Jewish mothers or princesses, rarely suggest the kind of positive blurring of gender boundaries associated with more affirmative acts of cross-dressing. On the contrary, Jewish drag—exemplified by such characters as Mother Marcus (Harvey Corman), the big-boned, Yiddish-accented Jewish matriarch of the ersatz soap-opera *As the Stomach Turns*, a regular skit on *The Carol Burnett Show* (1967–1978); or Linda Richmond (Mike Myers), the *verklemt* yenta-host of the weekly cable gab-fest *Coffee Talk*, a regular skit in recent years on *Saturday Night Live* (1975–)—usually embraces misogynist stereotypes while simultaneously fueling anti-Semitic suspicions about Jewish men as weak, disempowered, and unmasculine.

These characters do little to advance the kind of powerful "drag" sensibility that can undermine society's rigid definitions of who we are. Since sexuality, gay, straight, or bisexual, is always a *presentation* communicated by surface expressions such as dress, gesture, and voice, it is possible to construct oneself in ways that question society's normative standards of gender and sexuality. To reenact openly the complexities of one's sexuality through forms of drag, argues social theorist Judith Butler, is to acknowledge the extent to which sexual identity is always a mask, always contingent on the personal choice of how to reveal and present it.[6] Any questioning of normative standards is rare on American television, although the

Fig. 4. Milton Berle: Mr. Television.

Toronto-based half-hour comedy series *The Kids in the Hall* (1992–1995) has distinguished itself with its weekly share of men dressed as strong or combative women who radically challenge various repressive social and cultural norms. But with the possible exception of Milton Berle's burlesque transvestism on *The Milton Berle Show* (1948–1959), where gender roles were creatively parodied and confused, most Jewish drag on TV neither questions masculine power nor liberates the boundaries of gender.

The feminization of the Jewish male body ultimately perpetuates longstanding stereotypes about Jewish masculinity. It was precisely this desexualized, ambivalent body that underlay the understanding of the

Jew in the arts and sciences of the late nineteenth and early twentieth centuries. Indeed, in almost all "legitimate" medical and biological discussions of pathology from 1880 to 1930, Jews represented the absolute negation of Aryan health and purity: their sexual practices were seen as depraved, their bodies as diseased, their anatomy as abnormal, their minds as predisposed to insanity and hysteria. Even Sigmund Freud's own understanding of the constructions of gender to some extent appropriated these paradigms of the feminized Jewish male body.[7] In Freud's unconscious mind, the Jewish male—understood as weak and castrated (i.e., circumcised) by biological science—would be defensively compared to other social "inferiors," most specifically women. The scientific charges leveled at the Jewish male inevitably influenced Freud's theories of gender difference, trauma, and castration anxiety; through his assumption of the role of neutral male scientist, a role that, at least temporarily, set him apart from his more suspect Jewish brothers, Freud's "fabrication" of the image of the fragile, hysterical female allowed him to assuage "his own anxiety (which he expressed in private) about the limitations ascribed to the mind and character of the Jewish male."[8]

Freud's increasingly liberal view of homosexuality may similarly be related to his self-protective need to override theories that placed gayness in the same orbit of pathology as Jewishness. Freud initially hypothesized that paranoia was the result of

Fig. 5. The Odd Couple.

MAURICE BERGER

unresolved homosexual conflict, but he ultimately concluded that homosexuals could be completely "healthy" in their sexuality. In a letter written in 1935, for example, Freud argued that homosexuality had "no advantage, but is nothing to be ashamed of, no vice, no degradation, it cannot be classified as an illness; we consider it a variation of sexual function."[9] Thus Freud's understanding of the homosexual as "different but not ill," may have been driven by his need to undermine the scientific imperative to parallel Jews and gays in order to prove their mutual predisposition to remain fixated at an earlier, and hence atavistic, stage of sexual development.

Fig. 6. The Jack Benny Program.

Not surprisingly, stereotypes of the unmanly, powerless Jew—sexist and anti-Semitic constructions designed to allay fears of Jewish intelligence, wealth, or political power—are also exemplified by Jewish male characters on television who hint at effeminacy or homosexuality. Felix Unger (Tony Randall) on *The Odd Couple* (1970–1975), for example, the fey, fastidious photographer who tends to the needs of his slovenly roommate, sportswriter Oscar Madison (Jack Klugman), reads as both effeminate and closeted. The comedian Jack Benny, as well, with his limp-wristed mannerisms, lisp, and aristocratic bearing reenacts certain gay stereotypes of the 1950s and '6os. These men share another brotherhood as well: that of the closeted Jew who celebrates Christmas, assimilates into his nondescript urban surroundings, and almost never alludes to his ethnic background. As such, Unger and Benny suggest an unconscious relationship between sexuality that is nascent and unspoken and Judaism that is unarticulated; both bespeak a kind of internalized self-doubt that strives to deny personal identities and any sense of pride. Like their counterparts in drag, these men neither challenge gender roles nor radically blur the boundaries of sexuality; instead, their affectations and sensibilities serve to trivialize the Jewish presence.

Fears of this presence have been mollified, as well, by the ubiquitous stereotype of the passive or subordinated *schlemiel*. The weak father—Martin Morgenstern (Harold Gould) on *The Mary Tyler Moore Show*, or Jules Berger (Louis Zorich) on *Brooklyn Bridge*, to name two—represents the most obvious example of this cultural construction. Continually henpecked by the Jewish female, the Jewish father is shy, quiet, and usually unopinionated; he is often berated or ignored by his wife and children, who overrule him and undermine his authority.

This balance of power is also evident in the role of the loyal, homely, jester-like Jewish sidekick of the handsome, powerful Gentile—a role exemplified by Rob Petrie's wisecracking underling Buddy Sorrel (Morey Amsterdam) on *The Dick Van Dyke Show* (1961–1966). The stereotype of the neurotic Jewish American prince also serves to perpetuate the subordinated Jew theme. Characters such as Miles Silverberg (Grant Shaud) on the situation comedy *Murphy Brown* (1988–) or Dr. Joel Fleischman (Rob Morrow) on the drama *Northern Exposure* (1990–1995) endlessly *kvetch* about their circumstances, power, social standing, and appearance despite their relative good looks and professional success. They are, in effect, nerds with talent and power (Silverberg is the producer of a hit TV news magazine; Fleischman a physician paying off his student loans by practicing in a remote village in Alaska) who are in some ways as asexual and socially inept as their princess counterparts.

These stereotypes of social obedience—in which minority men must make themselves less threatening in order assuage the fears of the dominant culture—have plagued African American and other men of color for decades. As bell hooks writes:

> Representations of black males that portray them as successful yet happily subordinated to more powerful white males break with the old stereotypes of the lazy darky. The neocolonial black male is reenvisioned to produce a different stereotype: he works hard to be rewarded by the great white father within the existing system. . . . Black males who do not conform to [these] roles . . . are deemed dangerous, bad, out of control—and most importantly, white hating. The message that black males receive is that, to succeed, one must be self-effacing and consumed by a politics of envy and longing for white male power.[10]

It is, of course, ironic that some Jewish men, both fearful and desirous of WASP power, have represented themselves on television as "happily subordinated" despite considerable power in Hollywood; unlike the African American male, who is usually at the mercy of white institutions to generate or control how and when he is depicted, the Jewish male is most often subordinate only in *front* of the television camera.

The reasons for this self-denigration, as the social critic Todd Gitlin has observed, are both complex and troubling. For one, ethnic characters of any kind on television, appealing as they do to the identity interests of particular minority groups, may limit a program's potential audience. Brandon Tartikoff, the former president of NBC Entertainment, maintains that an explicitly Jewish show like *The Goldbergs*—a half-hour situation comedy about an extended immigrant Jewish family in the Bronx—would fail today because the demographics of the prime-time viewing audience have broadened.[11] When television was in its infancy, and television sets were expensive, access to TV belonged mostly to middle-class people living in major cities, an audience that was, in effect, disproportionately Jewish. If suppliers are self-censoring, they also realize "that a large part of the audience prefers its Jews Gentile,"[12] that to a certain extent anti-Semitism and apprehensions about the unknown have informed middle-class attitudes toward Jewishness in American popular culture. As Tartikoff himself admits, it is not at all farfetched to imagine a network executive concluding that "we don't want this because it's Jewish."[13]

Moreover, the imperative to maintain good ratings and, by extension, sponsors, by neither disturbing nor offending viewers all but ensures ethnic neutrality. Carl Reiner's original scripts for what became *The Dick Van Dyke Show*, for example, were originally written with the Jewish comedian himself as the lead. In the end, network executives "de-Jewishized" and "Midwesternized" the show, casting instead the WASPish Van Dyke.[14] In the early days of television, when big sponsors had the power to control the content of programming, racist and anti-Semitic strategies were an even more pervasive part of network practices. A former casting executive at CBS recalls the virulence of these biases:

> I remember some guy from [a top advertising agency] telling me he wanted his shows to look like the covers of the *Saturday Evening Post*, and I said, "You mean you don't want any Negroes or Jews." . . . And he said, "Well, no, I mean, but I, you know, I want it to look like the cover of the *Saturday Evening Post*. . . ." You saw very few Jewish actors who looked like Jewish actors. I'd cast Jack Carson and they'd say, "He seems ethnic." There were all these wonderful euphemisms. He certainly didn't look like the cover of the *Saturday Evening Post*.[15]

The networks' fear of Jewish ethnicity, as Gitlin has argued, led many Jewish writers in the 1950s and '60s to create stories about non-Jewish ethnic situations—such as Paddy Chayevsky's *The Catered Affair* (1955), about an Irish family—in order to discreetly communicate Jewishness while avoiding the charge of being "too Jewish."[16]

Internalized anti-Semitism and fears about the public's perception of Jewishness may also have played an important role in the formation of these concerns. Until very recently, network executives, many of them Jewish, rarely produced shows with Jewish characters or content. Moreover, these characters, unlike the working-class, Yiddish-accented denizens of *The Goldbergs*, were most often represented as assimilated or inferred Jews, a practice that continues to the present day. The world of Jack Benny or George Burns, for example, submerged the comedians' "Jewishness . . . within the context of their eccentric and essentially Gentile ensembles."[17] These "crypto Jews" never self-identify as Jews even though their ethnicity is apparent:[18] Benny goes Christmas shopping on an episode of *The Jack Benny Program* (1950–1965); Jerry Seinfeld lives in a kind of ethnic limbo on the situation comedy *Seinfeld* (1990–); and even Barney Miller (Hal Linden) on the situation comedy of the same name (1975–1982), a New York City police precinct captain, maintains an ethnically vague profile. "We never said Barney was Jewish and we never said he wasn't," explains the show's creator Danny Arnold. "We deliberately called him Miller because it was an ethnic nonethnic name."[19] In a certain sense, this ambivalence parallels the real-life tendency of network media moguls self-protectively to underplay their own Jewishness in order to defuse "any real or conceivable anti-Semitic charge that Jews are too powerful in the media."[20] Thus, driven by this desire as well as his possible embarrassment at the specter of working-class, unassimilated Jewish ethnicity, CBS founder William S. Paley reportedly refused to invest in the hit Broadway musical *Fiddler on the Roof* because it was "too Jewish."[21]

The fear of being "too Jewish" has resulted in what may be the most persistent Jewish male character type on American television: the nebbish who is, in effect, validated by his Gentile girlfriend or wife. Essentially an updated video version of the long-running Broadway hit *Abie's Irish Rose*, about a rich Irish girl who marries a poor Jewish boy, the validated Jew represents the vast majority of Jewish male character types on TV. Indeed, in recent years, when TV executives have apparently been more comfortable with Jewish characters, the validated Jew—a conceit that de-minoritizes its subject while simultaneously underscoring his marginal status—has appeared in many forms: on the situation comedy *Chicken Soup* (1989), the ultra-ethnic Jackie Fischer (Jackie Mason) chases after an Irish Catholic divorcee (Lynn Redgrave); on the drama *L.A. Law* (1986–1992), tax lawyer Stuart Markowitz (Michael Tucker) marries his colleague Ann Kelsey (Jill Eikenberry); on the situation comedy *Love and War* (1992–1995), Jack Stein (Jay Thomas) and his WASP girlfriend Wally Porter (Susan Dey) celebrate Christmas and Hanukkah together, each secretly hoping the other will convert; on *Mad About You,* Paul Buchman (Paul Reiser) and his blond, WASP wife Jamie (Helen Hunt) build a life together in Greenwich Village; and on the comedy *Flying Blind* (1992–1993), Jewish corporate drone Neil Barash (Corey Parker) is continually shot down by his exotic Gentile girlfriend (Tea Leoni).

These character relationships exploit two stereotypes simultaneously: the undesirability of Jewish women and the need for wimpy *schlemiels* to be validated and enhanced by *shiksas*. The validated Jewish male is usually shy, self-deprecating, and generally attractive and sweet—the quintessential nice Jewish boy. His love interest is most often cool and critical; she demands respect and often makes

Fig. 7. Bridget Loves Bernie.

her partner beg for her affection. Joel Fleischman on *Northern Exposure*, for example, is attracted to the gamine bush pilot, Maggie O'Connell; she is at once flirtatious, withholding, and taunting. While Joel endlessly agonizes about his own Jewishness (and his commitment to his mostly unseen difficult princess girlfriend back home in New York), the alluring, carefree Maggie holds out the possibility of liberation from the world of the "too Jewish." On what may well be television's most anti-Semitic program, the situation comedy *Bridget Loves Bernie* (1972–1973), Bernie Steinberg (David Birney), an aspiring writer and part-time cabbie, is married to the wealthy Bridget Theresa Mary Colleen Fitzgerald. As their in-laws spew bigoted venom—"You Jews aren't as clannish as they say," suggests Bridget's patrician, Republican father to Bernie's frumpy, immigrant parents—the couple argues incessantly. Bernie invariably yields to his wife's wishes, always the lowly Jew groveling for the approval and attention of his angelic wife.

If there is one character in the recent history of American television who would seem to exemplify a more complex and positive Jewish masculinity it is Michael Steadman (Ken Olin), the protagonist of the drama *thirtysomething* (1987–1992). Defying traditional media paradigms of Jewish masculinity, he is rugged, handsome, and virile. He is surrounded, as well, by the usual signifiers of successful American men on TV: the beautiful WASP wife (named, appropriately enough, Hope, and played by Mel Harris), the adorable and healthy children, the closely knit group of ethnically neutral white friends, and the large, comfortable house in an upscale suburban neighborhood. Despite his good standing, Michael quakes with anxieties about his social position, gender, and religion: the existential angst of the baby boomer who must work twice as hard to match the economic status of his parents; the frustrations of the yuppie who senses that his

Fig. 8. thirtysomething.

lifestyle is culturally and intellectually bankrupt; the tensions of the businessman who wants to remain ethical and caring in the face of cutthroat, competitive masculinity; and the apprehensions of the Jew who must define his identity through the lens of intermarriage and the generational indifference to Jewish ritual and history.

The issue of Michael's ambivalent relationship to his Jewish identity forms the basis of one of the series' most powerful, albeit problematic, episodes. Faced with the question of whether his first son should be circumcised, Michael is forced to consider his own commitment to Judaism. Hope, the couple's friends, and Michael's mother and her new compan-

ion, Dr. Ben Teitelman (played by Alan King)—a pushy and unabashedly ethnic Jew who continually embarrasses the elegant and sensitive protagonist—also struggle with their own issues of religious identity and community. Michael eventually arrives at an apotheosis: he not only sanctions and plans the *bris,* in effect symbolically embracing his own Jewish maleness, but also honors Teitelman with the role of *sandek.*[22]

Despite the surprisingly frank discussion of issues that haunt and embarrass Jews (and often mystify non-Jews), the show's tidy conclusion is disturbing. Although Michael's inner turmoil would seem to be resolved, the viewer learns little of the deeper meaning of his place in society as a white, heterosexual, Jewish man. The show's writers fail to broach the tenuous status of Jewish masculinity itself, an identity shaped by the historical vicissitudes of fear, jealousy, assimilation, and anti-Semitism. As such, circumcision serves as a simplistic signifier of a mythical Judaism rather than as a complex metaphor of the way Jewish men initially signify their masculinity, through a phallus that is cut, exposed, and, paralleling Michael's own feelings about his Jewishness, made vulnerable. Yet, Michael's vulnerability, centered as it is on the fear of appearing "too Jewish" rather than on the real dangers and complexities of being both a Jew and a man, seems narcissistic and overwrought.[23]

This is not to say that, with regard to the issues of Jewish stereotypes, Michael is neither a complex nor a sympathetic character. Michele Wallace, in a brilliant analysis of the seemingly racist stereotypes in the silent-film work of African American director Oscar Micheaux, has argued that one must be careful not to misunderstand or underestimate the director's subtle, underlying attempts to actually countermand certain racist stereotypes by attenuating them. It is precisely the cultural and social ambivalence toward blacks that Micheaux locates in his films—an ambivalence that, more often than not, exposes the underlying racism of these stereotypes. Micheaux's attempt to focus on race in seemingly brutal ways in his film *Within Our Gates* (1919), Wallace concludes, was really a remarkable attempt to question and expose the grotesque racism of D. W. Griffith's *Birth of a Nation,* released a few years earlier.[24] There is no doubt, as well, that Michael Steadman represents a subtle, and even powerful response to decades of anti-Semitic renderings of Jewish men on American television. Yet, in some ironic way, he still personifies and re-creates the very conflicts and anxieties that have driven decades of American Jewish writers, directors, and producers to deny their ethnicity and neutralize their presence in the medium.

Ultimately, Michael Steadman's compromised representation of Jewish masculinity skirts the outermost threshold of television's tolerance. Even the most reasoned and complex Jewish characters in recent network programs are "kept within carefully defined limits," writes John J. O'Connor. "Like all other groups, Jews will rarely get beyond the bounds of familiar and generally comforting stereotypes."[25] But television has, on occasion, sanctioned complex and even provocative views of non-Jewish masculinity, from Archie Bunker (Carroll O'Connor) on *All in the Family* (1971–1983) to cartoon patriarch Homer Simpson (Dan Castellaneta) on *The Simpsons* (1990–). Yet, from the earliest days of prime-time television it has been clear that Jewish characters, indeed any overtly ethnic roles, would have a difficult time surviving. One need only look at TV's first positive exemplar of Jewish manhood—the tailor Jake Goldberg, Molly's thoughtful and hardworking husband—to realize the profound truth of this assertion. In a tragic omen for the future of Jewish men on television, the actor who played Jake, Phillip Loeb, was unceremoniously forced off the air in 1952—a victim of Hollywood's notorious blacklist. With Loeb's tragic suicide several years later, Americans were sent the subliminal, but no less powerful, message that difference was undesirable and that only fathers with the bluest eyes could really know best.

NOTES

1. For more on this story, see Homi K. Bhabha, "Are You a Man or a Mouse?" in *Constructing Masculinity*, ed. Maurice Berger, Brian Wallis, and Simon Watson (New York and London: Routledge, 1995), 57. Bhabha is quoting Sigmund Freud, "Notes upon a Case of Obsessional Neurosis" (1909), in vol. 7 of *The Complete Psychological Works of Sigmund Freud, Standard Edition*, ed. James Strachey (London: Hogarth Press, 1954), 128.
2. For more on Brown's analysis, which first appeared in the essay "Negro Character Types as Seen by White Authors" (1933), see Henry Louis Gates, Jr., "The Face and Voice of Blackness," in *Facing History: The Black Image in American Art*, ed. Guy McElroy (San Francisco: Bedford Arts Publishers, 1990); reprinted in *Modern Art and Society: An Anthology of Social and Multicultural Readings*, ed. Maurice Berger (New York: Harper-Collins, 1994), 51–52.
3. See Douglas Kellner, "TV, Ideology, and Emancipatory Popular Culture," in *Television: The Critical View*, ed. Horace Newcomb (New York and Oxford: Oxford University Press, 1982), 400.
4. See Riv-Ellen Prell, "Why Jewish Princesses Don't Sweat: Desire and Consumption in Postwar American Jewish Culture," in *People of the Body: Jews and Judaism from an Embodied Perspective,* ed. Howard Eilberg-Schwartz (Albany: SUNY Press, 1992), 334.
5. Ibid., 331.
6. For an important discussion of this issue, see Judith Butler, "Imitation and Gender Insubordination," in *Inside/Out: Lesbian Theories, Gay Theories*, ed. Diana Fuss (New York and London: Routledge, 1991), 15–29.
7. The following paragraphs on Freud and Judaism are indebted to Sander L. Gilman, *Freud, Race, and Gender* (Princeton: Princeton University Press, 1993).
8. Ibid., 37. Nowhere was this transposition more dramatic than in Freud's negative internalization of the prevailing scientific fear of the circumcised phallus into theories on gender difference, trauma, and castration anxiety. While circumcision was seen as a form of "savage" castration by the anti-Semitic minds of the period, Sander Gilman has persuasively argued that this view of the cut penis as the signifier of a more feminine, and hence, more Jewish male body may have unconsciously motivated Freud's displacement of the perceived weaknesses of the Jewish male onto women. For more on this issue, see ibid., 49–92.
9. Sigmund Freud, *Briefe, 1873–1939,* ed. Ernst and Lucie Freud (Frankfurt: Fischer, 1960); as as quoted in ibid., 136.
10. bell hooks, "Doing It for Daddy," in *Constructing Masculinity*, ed. Berger et al., 104.

11. For more on the issue of Jews in television, see Todd Gitlin, *Inside Prime Time* (New York: Pantheon, 1985), 184.

12. Ibid.

13. Tartikoff as quoted in ibid.

14. For more on this issue, see ibid., 185–186.

15. Ethel Winant as quoted in ibid., 184.

16. Ibid., 185.

17. Albert Auster, " 'Funny You Don't Look Jewish . . .': The Image of Jews on Contemporary American Television," *Television Quarterly* 26 (Summer 1993): 66.

18. Jeffrey Shandler, as quoted in Frank Lovece, "Deck the Halls with Boughs of Challah," *FanFare*, December 12, 1992, 24. For more on the issue of the "crypto Jew," see Shandler, "The Bris Comes to Prime Time Television," *The Forward*, November 30, 1990, 23.

19. Danny Arnold, as quoted in John J. O'Connor, "They're Funny, Lovable, Heroic—and Jewish," *The New York Times*, July 15, 1990, 30.

20. Gitlin, *Inside Prime Time*, 184.

21. Auster, "Funny You Don't Look Jewish," 65.

22. The *sandek* or *sandak* holds the child on his knees during the circumcision; equivalent to a godfather. For discussions of this groundbreaking episode, see Michael Lerner, " 'Thirtysomething' and Judaism," in *Tikkun* 5 (October 1990): 6–8; Jay Rosen, "Thirtysomething," *Tikkun* 4 (July–August 1989): 29–33; and Shandler, "The Bris Comes to Prime Time Television," 23, 28.

23. The show, however, was not without its insightful moments. The disillusionment of Michael and his business partner, Elliot Weston (Timothy Busfield), for example, painfully unfolds in a series of episodes that chart the economic failure of their company, a narrative that subtly drains away the American Dream from the hazy world of TV suburbia. But if Michael represents the end of capitalism's free ride, he also suggests a counter idealization: that of the reformed hippie poised to save himself (and the world around him) from the irresponsible, overly permissive, and failed liberalism of the 1960s. Yet, to those who remain committed to the ideals and the values of the period, his compromises might seem at best hollow and cynical. In the world of *thirtysomething*, these stalwart believers—represented by such characters as Gary (Peter Horton), an idealistic, long-haired college professor, and Michael's cousin Melissa (Melanie Mayron), a photographer living a lonely, bohemian life—come off as foolish, naive, or self-destructive. "Television for the past two decades has been convincing [these people] that they really don't exist," writes Michael Lerner. ". . . That they'd be smarter to be like Michael Steadman and put most of their energy into having and holding a good job and raising their children."

   As an updated exemplar of the responsible postwar, upper-middle-class American male—a kind of angst-ridden, circumcised *Father Knows Best*—Michael turns his back on the rich history of idealistic men and women who have dominated Jewish politics and culture for most of this century. After years of rejecting the evils of a selfish and greedy status quo, often through the fighting of racism, anti-Semitism, greed, and injustice, many formerly liberal middle-class Jews replaced humanitarianism, altruism, and religious belief with anti-intellectual or conservative thinking bent on maintaining economic stability and nostalgically reinstating the values of an earlier and seemingly more prosperous time. It is this shift that Michael most dramatically exemplifies. So entrenched is his pragmatism, for example, that he ignores the spiritual foundation of Hope's discomfort with capital punishment—a position predicated on her conviction that murder of any kind is wrong. "Oh, come on," Michael replies, "the state takes a convict and puts him in a hole for sixty years where he's made into an animal, raped . . . I mean, who are we kidding? That's taking a life just as surely as flipping the switch on the electric chair." Michael's position essentially empties out the principled moral complexity of Hope's argument and replaces it with what Jay Rosen has called a "superior grasp of reality, before which all principles shrink into irrelevance." For a more critical reading of the show, see Lerner, "'Thirtysomething' and Judaism," 6–8 and Rosen, "Thirtysomething," 29–33.

24. See Michele Wallace, "Oscar Micheaux's *Within Our Gates* and the Evolution of Black Stereotypes in American Cinema," in *Oscar Micheaux and His Circle: The Silent Years*, ed. Charles Musser, Jane Gaines, and Pearl Bowser (Washington, D.C.: Smithsonian Institution Press, 1996).

25. O'Connor, "They're Funny, Lovable, Heroic—and Jewish," 30.

RHONDA LIEBERMAN

JEWISH BARBIE

THIS PIECE FIRST APPEARED IN THE AUTHOR'S MONTHLY COLUMNS FOR *ART-FORUM*. THIS SERIES, "GLAMOUR WOUNDS," LAUNCHED HER INSISTENTLY JEWISH AND FEMINIST PERSPECTIVE ONTO THE PAGES OF A MAJOR CONTEMPORARY ART PERIODICAL. "JEWISH BARBIE" IS A CRITICAL BUT AMUSING DELIBERATION ON A YOUNG JEWISH WOMAN'S STRUGGLE FOR SELF-ESTEEM IN THE FACE OF IMPOSSIBLE STEREOTYPED IDEALS.

In the century of Calvin Klein, Ralph Lauren, and Dinah Shore, need we ask who but a Jew is best at packaging unwhiny blonde fantasy figures? I don't know about you, darlings, but ever since I found out that Kathie Lee Gifford was née Epstein, I don't assume *anything*. Why be surprised, then, that Barbie, the ultimate *shiksa* goddess, was invented by a nice Jewish lady, Ruth Handler (with her husband, Elliot, co-founder of Mattel)? Indeed, the famous snub-nosed plastic ideal with the slim hips of a drag queen is in fact named after a real Jewish princess from L.A., Handler's daughter, Barbara (who must have been hell to know in junior high school!). Her brother is named Ken. What would it be like, I imagined, if Barbie's Jewish roots were to show? A Barbie High Holidays kit would be nice, a welcome addition to the multicultural rainbow that is the contemporary doll scene, where the shelves of our community toy outlets are integrated with dolls of color. How about Hanukkah Barbie (with a little bush)? Nose-Bob Barb (with pre-op detachable beak)? Bat Mitzvah Barbie—stunning! Barbie Looking for a Bargain . . . Not!

Conspiracy Theory still believes in the "Big Other," like a shadow government organizing everything according to some kind of coherent agenda, the psychotic notion that "we are all connected"—when, in fact, we're all just slacking along in contingency. Nevertheless, when Barbie was born, in 1959, in a parallel universe an *Other* Barbie emerged, with all the qualities *repressed* from the Barbie

RHONDA LIEBERMAN *is a writer living in New York. "Jewish Barbie" appeared as two articles: copyright © Artforum (March 1995) "Je m' appelle Barbie" and (April 1995) "Goys and Dolls."*

we have come to know in our one reality system; for example: Barbie—blonde, Jewish Barbie—brunette or frosted; Barbie—no thighs, Jewish Barbie—thighs; Barbie—mute, Jewish Barbie—whines incessantly about perceived injustices. Jewish Barbie is not evil, merely *repressed*; the conscious system we call "reality" can't recall where it has stored her information. UnErase™, a software program developed by computer tycoon Peter Norton, is a special retrieval system for deleted computer data. Norton discovered that this material is not destroyed by the computer, but simply "forgotten." The computer simply "forgets" where it filed it, much as the conscious mind "represses" material it would rather not recognize (due to unconscious conflict or whatever). Thanks to Norton's software device we are now able to retrieve the Jewish Barbie files from the disarray of the one-reality system as we consciously know it. It is strictly a coincidence, by the way, that "repression" was discovered by Freud—a Jew.

Here then are some highlights, retrieved by UnErase™, of the life led in a parallel universe by Jewish Barbie, who exists, but is *repressed*, by the defensive layer of the ego, by society, and most cruelly of all, by Barbie herself.

Early trauma: in 1969, at the age of ten, Jewish Barbie goes to see Ali MacGraw playing a "young, beautiful, and very spoiled Jewish princess" in *Goodbye, Columbus*. She admires pert nose-bobbed heroine Brenda Patimkin and is shattered to learn later that MacGraw is a *shiksa,* her nose, *real!* A foreshadowing of many betrayals.

During her teen years, Jewish Barbie stars in the teen division of Shaynah Punim Models, run with a velvet oven mitt by Mrs. Gottlieb, who launches her onto the cover of *Jewesse Today* with a dazzling promotional technique: "Jewish Barbie, I can't get a *latke* into that girl. She's too thin—you'll love her." Jewish Barbie blazes in the limelight. In the early 1970s it's Jewish Barbie in *Hebrew Vogue*, Jewish Barbie in *The Punim* (a trendy British mag), Jewish Barbie in *Modern Shaynah* dazzling the public as This Year's JewGirl, partying down with David Cassidy. Stunning.

Yet underneath her glamorous and always well-made-up exterior stir the longings of a complex creative soul, craving intimations of immortality available only through the less popular arts. As a young diva, Jewish Barbie looks to Barbra as a beaconness of Jewish glamour in a world hostile to multitalented strong women who should be worshipped. Inspired by the body art of '70s women artists, she expresses her esthetic urges—between modeling gigs—by fashioning exquisite chopped liver sculptures of Barbra in her various movie roles and album jacket looks, from *Je m'appelle Barbra*—bohemienne ingenue in black turtleneck and armful of ethnic bangles cleverly rendered with zesty pepper rings—to *Season's Greetings from Barbra*, in front of festive holiday tree, chopped-liver Barbra wholesome in pert reddish pageboy done in carrot slivers, white collar and cuffs in mashed potato. Also stunning.

Not surprisingly, as both talented sculptress and Young Hadassah Beauty

1973, Jewish Barbie alienates her peers, mostly with modeling stories (which she loves to tell, in detail). "She was like *JewGirl* cover-shoot this, *Yeshiva* Covergirl 1974 that," remembers an ex-friend from Young Judea, Jill Schwartz, still seething somewhere in New Jersey. Longing to trade war stories from the top of the glamour heap, Jewish Barbie repeatedly tries to reach her estranged twin, Barbie. But Barbie never returns her calls. Jewish Barbie wwwwhines and wwwwhines: "Why is the b-i-t-c-h snubbing me? She must think I'm fat. . . . I wrote her when I made my summer-camp drama debut starring in *Katz*, about Jewish cats who work in the garment district. I thought she'd be so cute as a cameo mod *shiksa* cat from London, but did I get even a postcard? Nothing." A couple of years later, *Cats*, the Anglicized version, becomes a huge hit on Broadway.

At age nineteen, soon to be runway geezer material, savvy Jewish Barbie plans for her modeling golden years—her twenties—as the face for a fragrance. Her people at Shaynah Punim approach Calvin Klein and Ralph Lauren but they aren't havin' it. According to Calvin (strictly off the record): "We can't have Jewish Barbie selling Eternity. No way." Ralph Lauren, same. "Jewish Barbie on Safari? Forget it. I can't work with her—she always calls me Ralph Lipschitz."

As another slap in the face, during the enlightened marketing heyday of Barbies of color a friend brings her back a chocolate bar from Israel—with Barbie on the wrapper! Barbie, she discovers, is working the Israeli market—as a blonde, obvious *shiksa*. "They have Barbies of color like Sun Lovin' Malibu Christie," complains Jewish Barbie. "They have 'Fiesta' Hispanic Barbie—and they totally ignore me! Talk about chutzpah!" As repressed material in a parallel universe, it is nothing but *tzouris* whenever Jewish Barbie tries to surface in our mainstream reality system. Exasperated, she blows her bangs out of her eyes and looks her destiny in the face. She thinks, "I totally need a haircut," and bemoans the hell that is her life as repressed material.

Her parents nudge her: "Enough with the modeling already. When are you going to marry Jewish Ken, a doctor? Daddy and I are going to Aruba. We made out our will. When are we going to see our grandBarbies?" Now in college, studying art history at Boston University, Jewish Barbie flouts her family through an excessive interest in the Virgin Mary. She rebels against her plastic background, cramming her apartment with Central American textiles and effigies of the Virgin. "Up until now," she writes in her diary, "I've been a puppet for Shaynah Punim and my parents. . . . Barbie hates me. *Everyone* thinks I'm annoying." She glances around her Beacon Hill apartment strewn with shopping bags and that morning's rejected outfit choices. "I will console myself," she resolves, "by studying the decay of communities under capitalism."

Spiritually adrift on a college campus in New England, Jewish Barbie had become a bit of a mess. Betrayed by Shaynah Punim Models and her parents, who deployed her as a tool in their own narcissistic agendas, she felt really unsupported. Repressed from our one reality system, by destiny deprived of the groundwork for mental health, Jewish Barbie bravely strove to be validated on

RHONDA LIEBERMAN

her own terms. Reading and obsessively underlining *The Anxiety of Influence* by Harold Bloom, she worked through murderous revenge fantasies against Barbie, who categorically refused to recognize her existence, despite many prank phone calls and unwanted pizza deliveries from Jewish Barbie's high-spirited college pals. Now she had *real* friends, by the way, from the college eating disorders clinic. A popular peer counselor, Jewish Barbie conducted a passionate seminar entitled: "I'm O.K., You're Barbie," healing many other young women—and some young men—by coping with her own pain.

It was during this period that her excessive interest in alternative Central American spiritual practices as subverting the centralized Catholic Church blossomed into full-blown Frida Kahlo worship and concomitant fetishism of Guatemalan shrines. She accepted a grant (Manischewitz Studies in Post Colonialism) to study indigenous domestic shrines, combining as it did her authority issues with the aesthetics of the classic Bev Hills Catholic-wannabe. She intuitively grasped the importance of keeping a tidy altar, and the significance of shrines, like shopping, as ways for people to express their spirituality through stuff. These were dark years, with no dry cleaners.

Years later, still with a soft spot for Central America, Jewish Barbie moves to a loft in SoHo big enough for a basketball game, is semi-embarrassed about it, but not enough to move. The combination of her plastic roots and her underdog identification continues to be a spiritual challenge. It is only after she returns to NYC that she learns that "real" Ken—the son of Barbie's inventors—was down in Central America too, with a highly developed social conscience, doing research on "low self-esteem among people of color." They were like two Barbie figures with issues, passing in the night, circling around the same symptomatic spots. As for Barbie, she has never recognized the existence of Jewish Barbie and never will; Jewish Barbie has accepted this, and goes on with her life, in SoHo. Still working through her plastic roots, she has an overdeveloped interest in "the body" and in work combining photos and text. She can occasionally be spotted purchasing perfect produce at Dean & Deluca or at openings at the Drawing Center.

(*Enter Rod Serling.*) Jewish Barbie does not exist in our reality. Split off from Barbie at the moment of her creation, Jewish Barbie fractioned off, became her own reality, and just went on from there forever, like the unconscious. Yet back in our reality, glimpses of this alternative Barbie universe can be sighted, like obscene sprouts of enjoyment coming to the surface, symptomatic pimples typically aggravated by a complex of Jew/goy issues. For example, a 1986 made-for-TV movie starring Farrah Fawcett as a Nazi-hunter, *The Beate Klarsfeld Story*, depicts the trial of Nazi Klaus Barbie in Lyons. In front of an embassy we see people with signs saying "Barbie = S.S.! Barbie = S.S.!" Privy to top-of-the-line therapy, Jewish Barbie does not take this personally, reading the whole made-for-TV movie in terms of psychoanalytic projection. While it is creepy to associate Barbie with the Nazi Klaus Barbie, Barbie is creepy, too, Jewish Barbie reasons. As a phantasmatic social body ego, Barbie sews herself up around the incarnation of her own impossibility—represented, of course, by Jewish Barbie. As the support for the Barbie fantasy, Jewish Barbie becomes an unwanted semiotic leftover coded obscene, satanic. Recurrent failure to recognize this empirical leftover's prior, founding function—well, that's the way Barbie gets off! Jewish Barbie is the libidinized scapegoat covering the gap through which Barbie's own impossibility comes to consciousness! For Barbie to emerge into representation, Jewish Barbie keeps on telling herself, "*She must misread me. For her to exist, I must be repressed! I'm not evil!*" she continues to tell herself. . . .

In another symptomatic event, in 1990, militant Barbies abetted by guerrilla artists in California rebelled against their makers, switching voice boxes between Barbies and G.I. Joes as a political statement about oppressive gender construction through toys. G.I. Joes surprised their owners by suggesting "Let's Go Shopping!"; rogue Barbies announced "Vengeance Is Mine!" Organized under the acronym BLO (Barbie Liberation Organization), rogue Barbies flouting Mattel uncannily echoed PLO resistance to the state of Israel. Just this week, doing research at Toys-'R'-Us, I saw Native American Barbie and Dutch Girl Barbie; Jewish Barbie remained conspicuously absent.

Barbie historian and reader M. J. Lord has observed, "The daughter of Polish Jewish immigrants, Ruth Handler (Barbie's creator) coded with her fashion dolls the same sort of phantasmatic 'America' that Louis B. Mayer had coded in his movies." As we have seen, *Goodbye, Columbus* deploys Ali MacGraw, a WASP, as a Hollywood Jewish princess only *acting* like she'd had a nose job. ("I was pretty," she explains, "Now I'm prettier.") The Tori Spelling Effect performs a recent twist: in the TV series *Beverly Hills 90210* we see the Tori Spelling Effect at work through the technique of Displace the Jew. The daughter of producer Aaron Spelling, overlord of international cheesy sitcom empire, the real Jewish princess of the show, Tori Spelling, plays a conspicuously Catholicized virgin. The Displace the Jew effect is clinched by the Andrea Zuckerman character, coded "Jew" by her not-to-the-manor-born anxiety, her academic overachievement, and her eyeglasses (signifying nonbabehood). This character—played by Gabrielle Carteris, who is Greek—is in fact a decoy, set up as a scholarly Semitic foil to the blonde, bob-nosed Tori, who emerges, by contrast, ethnically cleansed.

Since I couldn't interview Tori Spelling, I recently had a chat about "passing" with emerging glamorous Jewess Rebecca Odes, from New Jersey via Vassar, who has just gone blonde (but who was also fetching as a brunette): "It's like this reverence. It's like you're walking down the street and you grace the world with your blonde presence." Having recently appeared in *Spin*, Rebecca was wearing an ultra-snappy outfit: butter yellow ribbed turtleneck, beige fake-fur chubby jacket, frosted lipstick, hip-hugger jeans, long legs with heels. Long blonde hair represents the final frontier of Rebecca's thoughtful journey into total self-construction as babe: "It's almost like you don't have to dress up anymore. . . . I feel like I go into a store and it's like Hey, Miss America. I think that blondeness is so cultur-

RHONDA LIEBERMAN

ally revered. . . . It's like a reverse scale, like blondes are assumed to be attractive until proven otherwise. *Long* blonde hair, that is. When you see someone with long blonde hair from far away, you think, like, babe. When you look close up and they have like half a face . . . ," her voice trails off. Whatever.

Trying to think of other Jewish babes in the media without much success, we kept circling back to Barbra in *The Owl and the Pussycat*, where she wears the mod bra with the hands on it. The up-and-coming-supermodel Shalom might be a breakthrough, we thought, only to learn that she is neither from Israel nor Jewish: "My parents were hippies," she disclosed in a blurb on the occasion of her first *Cosmo* cover, revealing herself as another faux Jew. "The weird thing," continued my recently blonde interlocutor, "is how blondeness totally changes your arbitrary self-identification issues. Like I was watching *Charlie's Angels* and now I identify with the blonde, Farrah—I'm no longer Sabrina! It's so liberating." With blonde radar up, you begin to see "there's hardly a natural blonde in the media. You know Pamela Anderson in *Baywatch*—I saw a picture of her from high school—dyed blonde!" Ohmigod. Now we were outing the dyed blondes. We imagined a world of dyed blondes, a glamour nation like Denmark in World War II, when the king foiled the Nazis by having the whole country wear yellow armbands, contaminating the ID code, ingeniously marking *everyone* a potential faux.

In his essay "Nomad Thought," Gilles Deleuze refers to Nietzsche's task: transmitting "something that does not allow itself to be codified—to transmit it to a new body—to invent a body, that can receive it and spill it forth." [Cutaway: Jewish Barbie stops in her tracks, on her way uptown to Barney's.] This new body could seem monstrous according to recognizable codes [Jewish Barbie frowns] but it's a philosophically healthy contamination [then she smiles, sort of]. Nietzsche was calling out to the philosophers of the future, the new philosophical flesh, like something out of *Videodrome*, addressing and thereby creating an audience of nomad rogue readers who would practice "legitimate misreading," making monsters out of what we read through the distorting lens of desire, spawning new and strange conjunctions, the metabolic products of reading as contamination, rather than reproducing codes faded by familiarity and thus sterilized into prepackaged "identities" and stuff we've already known and labeled.

Although no one should find their "identity" ready-made in a text, strong misreading can create strange new life, or at least potential. Deleuze describes a career "misreading" Western thinkers from Spinoza, Leibnitz, and Kant to Nietzsche and Bergson: "I imagined myself approaching an author from behind and giving him a child that would indeed be his but would nonetheless be monstrous." Finding in these philosophical big guys the genealogy of his own nomad agenda, Deleuze had his way with them, legitimately misreading them to articulate his concept of "deterritorialized" thought, transmitting "intensity" rather than "identity." It's true that finding the Jewish Barbie files is an act of monstrosity—the monstrosity of reading. This is a good, not a scary, thing, as Jewish Barbie would learn in a seminar entitled "I'm O.K., I'm Nietzsche," available to philosophically discriminating shoppers in a parallel universe near you.

Photo still from performance of The Third
Seder, *at The Jewish Museum, New York,
1995. Conceived and produced by Neil
Goldberg, Joan Hocky, and Alicia Svigals,
featuring choreography and performance by
David Dorfman, performance pieces by
Joan Hocky and Tony Kushner, stage design
by Neil Goldberg, music by The Klezmatics,
play by Sarah Schulman.*

"NOTES ON AKIBA" WAS ORIGINALLY WRITTEN AND PERFORMED AS PART OF
THE THIRD SEDER AT THE JEWISH MUSEUM, NEW YORK, ON THE NIGHT BE-
FORE THE FIRST SEDER, 1995. WITH POIGNANT HUMOR AND PAINFUL HON-
ESTY, THE PLAY DRAMATIZES A CONTEMPORARY EXEGESIS ON THE STORIES
OF JEWISH EXODUS AND EXILE AND INFUSES THEM WITH PRESENT-DAY POLIT-
ICAL AND SOCIAL CONCERNS.

TONY

This is Michael Mayer.

MICHAEL

This is Tony Kushner. These are notes on Akiba. This is exegesis, or, elaboration.

TONY

OK OK let me begin by apologizing, OK, so I wrote this in a hurry so I wrote
this in haste so I wrote this on the fly on a fucking *AIRPLANE* I wrote this so
it's not funny so it makes no sense so it doesn't work so don't laugh so don't
come so sue me it's not like anyone's *paying* me to do this, not like anyone's *paying* me to do this and *HIM*, he never saw the script before an hour ago, so forget memorizing it he is totally confused but the haste is appropriate, the
airline is appropriate, I travel too goddam much, my father was a goddam wandering Aramean, alright, so sue me, WHAT ARE YOU DOING HERE
ANYWAY don't you have company coming tomorrow night shouldn't you be
at home now on your hands and knees scouring for *hametz* DID YOU GET
EVERY CRUMB *ARE YOU SURE?* HE is not responsible for this The Klezmatics are not responsible for this the clarinetist is so hot he reminds me of my

TONY KUSHNER *is a playwright living in New York City. A volume of his recent writing, entitled* Thinking about the Longstanding Problems of Virtue and Happiness: Essays, a Play, Two Poems, and a
Prayer, *has just been published by Theatre Communications Group.*

father shouldn't you be at home cooking for your father don't you have company have a family have friends have a father coming over what are you an animal or something I worry about you don't get hurt don't get shot drive safely wear a condom I alone am responsible I alone bear responsibility I cannot bear the responsibility it is insupportable it is impossible it is imponderable.

This, by way of prologue.

(Pause.)

MICHAEL
In some Sephardi Seders the celebrants lash each other with leeks.

(They lash each other with leeks.)

TONY
Ow.

MICHAEL
They do this because in the desert the people complained to Moses, missing the fish and onions they enjoyed eating in Egypt. The leek-lashing is to remind them that there is a high price to pay for tasty things sometimes. The price for fish and leeks in Egypt was the lash. The Passover practice, in coastal villages of the Mediterranean, of lashing each other with fish, died out by the fourth century C.E.; Hellenizing influences are credited with the eventual replacement of fish-whips with the more manageable leek.

The more one elaborates . . .

TONY
Elaborates. E-LAB-OR-ATES. *Elaborates.*

MICHAEL
. . . on the departure from Egypt the more praiseworthy one is.

TONY
But my father skipped it.

MICHAEL
Everyone does.

TONY
So I said to him, you skip it!

TONY KUSHNER

MICHAEL

Everyone does.

TONY

Every year. Right after the Four Questions. Do the Four Questions and then start the story and then you get to that bit and then, SKIP.

MICHAEL

The *Fier Kashe*.

(Pause.)

TONY

Right.

MICHAEL

I like saying the Hebrew. *Fier Kashe*. The delicious nasalities, the slides, the wide-open vowel sounds, the abrupt syncopation.

TONY

They skip it because it's like, oh, it's like one of those medieval Jewish numerological things, one of those . . . (gestures). *Fier Kashe* by the way is Yiddish, not Hebrew.

MICHAEL

Every letter has a value.

TONY

So he said of course he said I don't skip it.

MICHAEL

Oh bullshit.

TONY

But he does. Who doesn't? Everyone does.

MICHAEL

"*Echad,*" the Hebrew word for "one," has letters the numerological value of which adds up to thirteen: hence the thirteen verses in the game that begins "Who knows one," hence "Who knows thirteen I know thirteen thirteen are God's attributes etc."

TONY

These attributes, by the way, what are they?

MICHAEL

They are immensely potent emanatory demi-divine entities suffused through-out the world of prayerful visionary journeying as mystical lights as described in kabbalah, Jewish magic.

TONY

A nervy thing to invoke at the tail end of what is let's face it a children's counting game.

MICHAEL

We read in the Zohar that . . .

TONY

But what really makes my gorge rise is that he can't *admit* he skips the whole, you know, that part that bit that Tarfon that whatsitsname.

MICHAEL

Akiba.

TONY

Right, Akiba, *that* bit which everyone skips because it's like who knows what it's about so like what is the big fucking deal about skipping it, I've only been going to his fucking goddam Seder for forty years practically and I like think I would know if he skips it or not and believe me *he skips it* but what's *sick* is that he can't admit he skips it because you know why? Because his *FATHER* never skipped anything not one part not one bit not one word of Hebrew every word, every detour and digression, with his father they would sit for hours and hours the Seder would take hours, and he of course cannot is like *molecularly* incapable of conceiving that he maybe does *less* than his *FATHER* did because it's like Jewish men, it's this sick thing, isn't it, it's this sick thing, this sick sick sick sick sick thing they have with their fathers, all Jewish men have it or is it all men period or is it just me? It's sick. I told him that.

MICHAEL

What?

TONY

That it's sick, sick, a crazy competitive . . . and . . .

MICHAEL

What did he say?

TONY

He said, "It's . . . That's a sick thing to say to your father." But. I mean really, like, *out of the house of bondage*, right?

MICHAEL

Totally.

TONY

I mean *please*.

(Pause.)

MICHAEL

A favorite Passover treat of Jewish American kids of the '30s, '40s, and '50s was to break up matzah crackers, remember when we used to call them matzah crackers, my family did anyway I grew up in Maryland, was to break up matzah crackers into a bowl and cover the broken pieces with condensed milk and Fox's U Bett syrup and then with a fork you mash the pieces and the condensed milk and syrup into a sticky lavender-gray gluten, a paste. This paste represents the bricking mortar Jews in *mizrayim* made *with* straw *before* Pharaoh took the straw away, punitively, and then mortar had to be made *without* straw, which is *haroset*. The matzah represents the pious deflation of the pridefulness of man and woman as they approach God during this Holy Week of Remembrance, not puffed up with the yeast of their pretensions and their vainglories. Flat. Broken up in pieces in a bowl, the matzah means basically the same thing as it does whole, in a box. The condensed milk is known as the Milk of Affliction. It represents canned food, the food of haste, of fallout shelters, especially in the '50s and early '60s. The meaning of Fox's U Bett Syrup is obscure. It is not a traditional component of *Shulhan Arukh*, the Prepared Table.

TONY

Do you think what I said is like self-hating, the sick thing part, is that . . . ?

MICHAEL

No. I mean it's not necessarily true, but it . . .

TONY

Oh, it's *true*. It is *true*. It's just maybe also it's self-hating, I worry about that because, I love Passover I really do but it's my family. You skip you don't elaborate you don't quibble you don't haggle you don't explicate or enumerate or niggle or nit-pick you hasten through the hard parts, you go right from the questions and then skip over these tired old men, who cares about tired old men let's get to the kids, the young people, the wise one and the wicked and the *gornisht* slow one and the one who knows not what to ask. For whom, specifically, copious elaboration is salutary. But who gets short shrift while everyone is guiltily aware that wedged into this crack between the Questions and The Story and The Kids, between the easy, folksy bits, the stuff about kids that's basically only in there to keep the kids from sliding under the table or keep them awake or not kicking up fusses because they don't really care about the Exodus, "for you and not for me," right, that's kids, what do kids care about but *kids,* right, so over the centuries you learn to stick in all this stuff about kids so they stay awake and don't fidget and you can *schlep naches . . .*

MICHAEL
Schep.

TONY
What?

MICHAEL
You *schep naches,* you *schlep . . .* other things.

(Pause.)

TONY
. . . and, and look how good my kid is he . . . *performs,* he really *performs,* he *memorizes,* he is *prepared,* a *performer,* he's four years old he can barely read *Green Eggs and Ham* and look he has memorized lengthy strings of what are to him nonsense syllables which he will now produce flawlessly on command because he knows like *the whole year to follow and his life along with it will be cursed, the crops will fail and Elijah won't come because YOU FORGOT WHAT COMES AFTER MAH NISHTANAH ETCETERA* and like that's not affliction?

(Pause.)

MICHAEL
There are fifteen verses to "Dayenu." One verse each for each of the steps that led up to the door of the First Temple. Hence the song's ladderlike structure. Passover songs appeal to children primarily through games of simple mastery, building, accumulating, accelerating, challenges to reading proficiency and lung capacity.

TONY

So now we are going to read and do exegesis on the part everybody skips.

"A tale is told of Rabbi Eliezer, . . .

MICHAEL

Eliezer ben Hyrcanus, first and second centuries, a Mishnaic sage, a *tanna,* teacher of Akiba.

TONY

. . . Rabbi Joshua, . . .

MICHAEL

A creator of post-Temple Judaism. They all were, actually, the ones who survived.

TONY

. . . Rabbi Eleazar ben Azariah, . . .

MICHAEL

Named head of the Sanhedrin when he was eighteen.

TONY

. . . Rabbi Akiba, . . .

MICHAEL

Didn't survive. The greatest Mishnaic *tanna* of them all. When Moses was receiving the Commandments from God on Sinai he asked God why there were all the little curlicues on Hebrew letters, the points and the thorns and God said turn around and Moses did and lo, he was looking, two thousand years in the future, looking through a window into Rabbi Akiba's yeshiva in Bene-Berak, and Akiba was doing exegesis on the five books of Moses which Moses of course had yet to write, and Moses turned back around again and God said, "That man Akiba is so smart he will be able to interpret even the curlicues on the letters of the words of the books you will someday write."

TONY

. . . Rabbi Tarfon. "

MICHAEL

Also didn't survive. His two most famous sayings are: "The day is short the task is great the workers are lazy the reward is much the Master is insistent."

TONY

And he also said: "The task cannot be completed by you, but neither are you free to desist from the task."

MICHAEL

This is from the Haggadah:

"A tale is told of Rabbi Eliezer and Rabbi Joshua and Rabbi Eleazar ben Azariah and Rabbi Akiba and Rabbi Tarfon who reclined together at Bene-Berak. And they recounted the departure from Egypt all night until their students came to them and said 'Masters, the time has come to recite the morning *Shema.*'

"Said Rabbi Eleazar ben Azariah, 'I am like unto a man seventy years old'"— this is because his hair had turned white prematurely when, at the age of eighteen, he was made head of the Sanhedrin, and so he was "like" a seventy-year-old but actually much younger.

TONY

He is the wise son. I am the wicked son.

MICHAEL

"I am like unto a seventy-year-old, yet I never found biblical proof as to why the Exodus from Egypt should be recited in the evening service until ben Zoma . . ."

TONY

Elaborate, be praiseworthy.

MICHAEL

—Ben Zoma a Jewish mystic who went to Heaven and lost his mind as a result—

TONY

The thirteen attributes, no doubt.

MICHAEL

Possibly.

TONY

Go on.

MICHAEL

". . . explained the verse, 'so that you may remember the day of your departure from the land of Egypt all the days of your life (Deuteronomy chapter 16 verse 3).'

"'The days of your life'" implies the daytime, while 'all the days of your life' implies the nights. And the sages amplify this by saying, 'The days of your life' refers to this world; 'all the days of your life' to Messianic times as well."

And now we will perform an exegesis on the traditional lack of exegesis concerning this passage.

TONY

The reason people skip over this hardly lengthy section has something to do, I think, at least on the surface, with the tension set up in the form of the Seder between the forward-moving motional urgency of appetite, on the one hand, and the profound reluctance on the other hand of true critical thought to move ahead. Wait, wait, there is more to glean, there is always more. Also, everyone has stored up in her or his actual memory or probably after three or four thousand years of Seders probably stored in your genetic memory are nightmare Seders of days gone by when fathers and sons competed for the honor of being most praise-worthy, elaborating and prolonging as these rabbis did till dawn.

MICHAEL

The rabbis who nobody wants to hear from anymore return in the Haggadah a second time in the Plague section.

TONY

Counting the fingers and the fingerbones of God.

MICHAEL

Multiplying plagues. Two hundred and sixty plagues. Four hundred plagues. In this way exalting the Miracle of Liberation.

TONY

This bit is also skipped over.

MICHAEL

Because it is lengthy, confusing, too close to dinner to be endured, and exceedingly blood-curdling.

TONY

It contains a Ten Plagues mnemonic, *D'TZaKH ADaSH B'AHaB.* The letters of which contain the first letters of the ten plagues. *D'TZaKH ADaSH B'A-HaB* translates literally, "A scorpion bit my uncle."

MICHAEL

This ancient mnemonic apparently inspired Jewish communities in North Africa and in Tijuana, Mexico, to compose a Pesach counting song, "A Scorpion Bit My Uncle," but the traditional song has been largely abandoned in this century, due to the arrival of modern insecticides and a concomitant lessening of the anxieties provoked by the mnemonic. In countries to which the scorpion is not indigenous, the song never caught on.

TONY

This fear of skipping, of cheating, of eliding, effacing, passing over with many a secret sigh of relief the imponderably weighty inheritance of millennia of Jewish intellectual, theological, political, historical, mystical *effort*. The imponderability creating as symptom the desire to skip.

MICHAEL

The propensity to skip.

TONY

Yes.

MICHAEL

Gracefully, but guiltily.

TONY

Yes.

MICHAEL

I know what you mean. The elegant uneasy skip of the dilettante. The "I don't need to know that" as opposed to the injunction "Know everything, know it all. Even the curlicues: Know them." Be praiseworthy.

TONY

Which symptom producing the ache of insufficiency. The tribal genetically-encoded Darwinian anxiety of inexorable decline down through the generations, the entropic cooling down unto Death.

MICHAEL

And hence of course how perfect that what we skip is this brief odd strobic glimpse of these particular five men, these protean daddies, their massive hairy forearms, wound tightly, perhaps even a little cruelly, with the leather phylactery straps, their bulky foreheads bound and bearing boxes enshrining tiny curled-up parchment leaves representing leaves of flame upon which are inscribed letters of flame representing words and sounds which are the dark crackle of midnight devouring Holy Fire. Tented with *tallises,* fringey with *tzitzis.* Reclining. On pillows. Talking and singing through the night.

TONY

That is too elaborate. Perhaps.

MICHAEL

Talking about the Exodus. What has passed. How the future is to receive it. How to carry the imponderable burden of it.

TONY

Judaism has as a distinguishing feature its unreasonable difficulty. It is unappeasably hard. You must remember. You must remember everything. You must write down what you remember. You must read what you have written every year. Not once a year but for a whole week. And even worse you must *understand.* And even worse you must *elaborate* on that understanding.

MICHAEL

The freeing of the slave only commences the wandering of the now-homeless. The freed slave is still unfree. Only after his arrival in some safe shelter is the freed slave free. The Exodus is also an affliction.

TONY

A woman in the town I grew up in searched her house the night before Pesach with a candle searching out the *hametz* as is traditional, and she made a big pile of crumbs but forgot to burn them and left the unburned *hametz* in the dustpan in the utility closet and maybe it's a coincidence but from her chicken soup, which she thought the room was cold enough to let stand outside the refrigerator overnight because the refrigerator was full of *kugel* and whatnot and so everyone at the Seder table the next night got botulism and had to go to the emergency room.

MICHAEL

Why is this night different from all other nights? On all other nights gay Jewish men are channeling their mothers. On this night gay Jewish men are channeling their great-great-grandmothers from the Russian Pale.

(Pause.)

MICHAEL

The rabbis reclining at Bene-Berak that we skip over in the Haggadah are plotting rebellion against the Roman Empire. Perhaps instead of recounting the Exodus as they are supposed to have been doing they are working out strategies of resistance. This garrison is weak, that one is vulnerably positioned, we might roll big stones off the tops of those cliffs and bash in the skull of that centurion, this captain, that governor. Is Death a part of the miracle that brings liberation?

TONY

For instance God Forgive me God Forgive me, but how is Senator D'Amato doing with those chest pains?

MICHAEL

Perhaps the young students rushing in in the story to warn the rabbis that day has arrived are speaking in code: Perhaps "Hear O Israel" in this instance means "Put away the maps, the Romans are nearby." This is conjecture and so inappropriate as elaboration. Akiba declared Bar Kochba Messiah and commenced the rebellion.

TONY

Bar Kochba is slain.

MICHAEL

And Akiba is tortured and slain.

TONY

And the Temple is destroyed and the Diaspora begins. A condition of permanent Exodus.

MICHAEL

A liberation and also an affliction. In some Haggadahs the Akiba section ends with a quadruple benediction: The Place, God, The Torah, God. "Ha-Makom," Hebrew for "The Place," is one of God's many names.

TONY

Toward which perhaps we are wandering.

(Pause.)

TONY

I apologize for my earlier fit of pique. It's the stress, the stress, I'm under a lot of stress.

MICHAEL

Who isn't?

TONY

    We all are.

MICHAEL

    We are.

TONY

    Blessed is The Place. Blessed is God, giver of the Torah. Blessed is the Torah.
    Blessed is God.

MICHAEL

    H'ag Sameach.

END

NOTE

Copyright © 1995 by Tony Kushner. "Notes on Akiba" was originally written for and performed at *The Third Seder*, The Jewish Museum, New York, April 13, 1995. The historical information contained in this piece comes from a variety of sources: my usual rabbinate—Bloom, Scholem, Yerushalmi, Steinsaltz—and an important new guest at the table, Ira Steingroot. Everything factual in the piece, indeed everything you could ever want to know about Passover, can be found in Steingroot's remarkable, indispensable, delightful, and erudite *Keeping Passover*, published by HarperCollins.

Ken Aptekar
"Albert. Used to be Abraham," 1995
Oil on wood with sandblasted glass and bolts
30" x 30"
Courtesy of Jack Shainman Gallery,
New York

Ken Aptekar
"Goldfinch. Used to be Goldfarb," 1995
Oil on wood with sandblasted glass and bolts
30" x 30"
Collection of Wil Foster, New York
Courtesy of Jack Shainman Gallery,
New York

Helene Aylon
The Liberation of G-d, 1990–1996
Mixed media installation
Variable dimensions
Courtesy of the artist

Neil Goldberg
Shecky, 1992
Matzahs, photographs, and mixed media
Approximately 18" x 30" overall
Courtesy of the artist

Neil Goldberg
Untitled (hinged matzahs), 1992
Matzahs and mixed media
6½" x 6½" x variable angles
Courtesy of the artist

Neil Goldberg
Workout Tallis, 1994
Cloth prayer shawl, wrist grips
30" x 2" x 48"
Courtesy of the artist

Photo still from performance of *The Third
Seder,* at LaMama E.T.C., New York, 1993
Conceived and produced by Neil Goldberg
and Alicia Svigals, featuring choreography
and performance by David Dorfman,
performance piece by Richard Elovich, stage
design by Neil Goldberg, music by The
Klezmatics, and play by Sarah Schulman
Photo by Beth Phillips Studio
Courtesy of Neil Goldberg

Photo still from performance of *The Third
Seder,* at The Jewish Museum, New York,
1995. Conceived and produced by Neil
Goldberg, Joan Hocky, and Alicia Svigals,
featuring choreography and performance by
David Dorfman, performance pieces by Joan
Hocky and Tony Kushner, stage design by
Neil Goldberg, music by The Klezmatics,
play by Sarah Schulman.
Photo by Oren Slor.
Courtesy of Neil Goldberg.

Kenneth Goldsmith
Bob Dylan, 1995
Mixed media on paper
62" x 45"
Courtesy of Bravin Post Lee, New York

Dennis Kardon
Jewish Noses, 1993–1995
Oil on Sculpey
49, each approximately 5" x 3" x 2½"
Courtesy of the artist and
Richard Anderson Fine Arts

Dennis Kardon
Lover's Quarrel, 1994
Oil on linen
30" x 36"
The Jewish Museum, New York, Museum
purchase with funds provided by Livia and
Marc Straus, 1995–101

Deborah Kass
Four Barbras (the Jewish Jackie Series), 1992
Silkscreen on acrylic on canvas
9, each 20" x 24"
Collection of Arthur G. Rosen

Deborah Kass
Sandy Koufax, 1994
Silkscreen ink on canvas
72" x 64"
Courtesy of the artist

Deborah Kass
Triple Silver Yentl (My Elvis), 1992
Silkscreen on acrylic on canvas
72" x 96"
Collection of William Ehrlich and Ruth
Lloyds

Cary Leibowitz
I'm A Jew how 'bout U?!!, 1995
Acrylic on wood
77" x 40"
Courtesy of Michael Klein Gallery, New
York

Cary Leibowitz
Jew, Jew Lover, Jew Wannabee, Honorary Jew,
1993
Rubber stamps
4, each approximately 2" x 1½"
Courtesy of the artist

Cary Leibowitz
Untitled (jewelled yarmulkes), 1992
4, each approximately 8" in diameter
Mixed media
The Jewish Museum, New York,
Gift of the Artist, 1994–83–86

Cary Leibowitz
*Kosher Hot Dog Yarmulke (Please Don't
Forget Eleanor Roosevelt)*, 1995
*German Yarmulke (Thanks for
Remembering)*, 1995
*Swedish Yarmulke (Please Don't Forget Raoul
Wallenberg)*, 1994
*Stonewall Yarmulke (Shalom Independence
July 4th 1776/June 27th 1969)*, 1994
4, each approximately 8" in diameter
Mixed media
The Jewish Museum, New York,
Gift of the Artist, 1995–97–100

Cary Leibowitz and Rhonda Lieberman
Chanel Hanukkah, 1991
Mixed media
Variable dimensions
Collection of Patricia A. Bell, Madison,
N.J., collection of Anne Pasternak and
Michael Starn, and courtesy of the artists

Rhonda Lieberman
Barbra Bush, Hanukkah/Christmas 1994
Mixed media
36" x 25" x 25"
Courtesy of the artist

Rhonda Lieberman
Chanel (Matzah) Meal, 1991
Matzah meal and paper
Approximately 7½" x 4½" x 2"
Courtesy of the artist

Rhonda Lieberman
Pushy/Cushy/Tushy (Sandra Bernhard triptych
from the series "Purse Pictures"), 1994
Mixed media
3, each 12" x 11"
Courtesy of the artist

Beverly Naidus
What Kinda Name Is That?, 1995
Laser prints on paper and mixed media
Variable dimensions
Courtesy of the artist

Nurit Newman
Complex Princess, 1995
Matzah meal and mixed media installation
Variable dimensions
Courtesy of the artist

Rona Pondick
Swinger, 1992
Mixed media
28" x 20" x 10"
Collection of Clyde and Karen Beswick,
Los Angeles

Rona Pondick
Untitled (series of "legs"), 1992–1993
Mixed media installation
Variable dimensions
Courtesy of Sidney Janis Gallery

Rona Pondick
Little Bathers, 1990–1991
Mixed media
Variable dimensions
Collection of Livia and Marc Straus

Archie Rand
The Chapter Paintings, 1989
Mixed media on canvas
54, each 36" x 24"
Collection of the artist

Elaine Reichek
A Postcolonial Kinderhood, 1994
Mixed media installation
Variable dimensions
Courtesy of Michael Klein Gallery,
New York

Adam Rolston
Untitled (from the series "Nose Job"), 1991
Ink on glassine
3, each 17" x 14"
Courtesy of the artist and Fawbush Gallery

Adam Rolston
Untitled (Horowitz Margareten Matzohs), 1993
Synthetic polymer on canvas
72" x 72"
The Jewish Museum, New York, Museum
purchase with funds provided by Barbara S.
Horowitz, 1994–698

Adam Rolston
Untitled (Manischewitz American Matzos),
1993
Synthetic polymer on canvas
72" x 72"
Collection of Livia and Marc Straus

Ilene Segalove
Jewish Boys, 1987
Silver print
47½" x 36"
The Jewish Museum, New York, Museum
purchase with funds provided by Aimee and
Monroe Price, the Morris Fox Bequest, and
the Mrs. Chauncey Newlin Fund, 1993–31

Art Spiegelman
Maus: A Survivor's Tale, Vol. 2, Chapter 1,
pages 11–25, 1983–1986
Pen and ink, paper collage, and white
gouache on paper
15 plates, each 8⅓" x 11"
Courtesy of Art Spiegelman

Art Spiegelman
19 Preliminary sketches and one photograph
for *Maus: A Survivor's Tale,* Vol. 2,
c. 1983–1986
Pencil, colored crayon, and markers on
tracing paper and woven paper
Variable dimensions
Courtesy of Art Spiegelman

Allan Wexler
Indoor Sukkah, 1991
Mixed media installation
38" x 108" x 42" overall
Courtesy of Ronald Feldman Fine Arts Inc.,
New York

Allan Wexler
Sukkah model series:
1. *Study Model for Sukkah, Earth Wall
Raised*, 1988
Plaster, balsa wood, sand
15½" x 13⅛" x 8½"
The Jewish Museum, New York, Museum
purchase: The Jewish Museum New
Generation Council, 1992–164

2. *Study Model for Sukkah, Dining Building
with Furniture Touching Earth and Sky*, 1988
Balsa wood
7¼" x 7⅙" x 7⅙"
Courtesy of Ronald Feldman Fine Arts Inc.,
New York

3. *Study Model for Sukkah, Dining Room
with Walls as Projections*, 1988
Balsa wood
12" x 15" x 17"
Courtesy of Ronald Feldman Fine Arts Inc.,
New York

Hannah Wilke
Venus Pareve, 1982–1984
Painted plaster of paris self-portraits
18 of 20, each 10" x 5" x 2"
Collection of Frayda and Ronald Feldman
and courtesy of Ronald Feldman Fine Arts
Inc., New York

Hannah Wilke
Venus Pareve, 1982–1984
Chocolate cast self-portraits
One at 10" x 5" x 2" and various fragments
Courtesy of Ronald Feldman Fine Arts Inc.,
New York

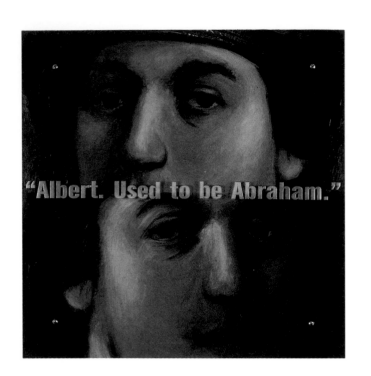

1. KEN APTEKAR
"Albert. Used to be Abraham." 1995

2. KEN APTEKAR
"Goldfinch. Used to be Goldfarb." 1995

134

4. NEIL GOLDBERG
Shecky, 1992

5. Kenneth Goldsmith
Bob Dylan, 1995

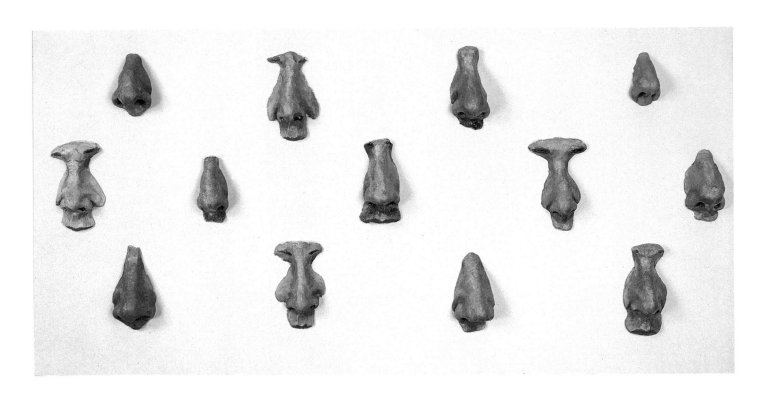

6. DENNIS KARDON
Detail, *Jewish Noses,* 1993–1995

LEFT TO RIGHT:
TOP ROW: *Meyer Vaisman, Helene Winer, Jay Gorney, Deb Kass;*
MIDDLE ROW: *Janet Kardon, Josh Decter, Adam Bellow, Laurie Simmons, Andrea Bellag;*
BOTTOM ROW: *Haim Steinbach, Nan Goldin, David Deutsch, Rona Pondick*

7. DENNIS KARDON
Detail, *Jewish Noses,* 1993–1995
Adam Bellow

138

8. DEBORAH KASS
Four Barbras (the Jewish Jackie Series), 1992

9. DEBORAH KASS
Detail, *Four Barbras* (the Jewish Jackie Series),
1992

10. CARY LEIBOWITZ
I'm A Jew how 'bout U?!!, 1995

11. CARY LEIBOWITZ AND RHONDA LIEBERMAN
Chanel Hanukkah, 1991

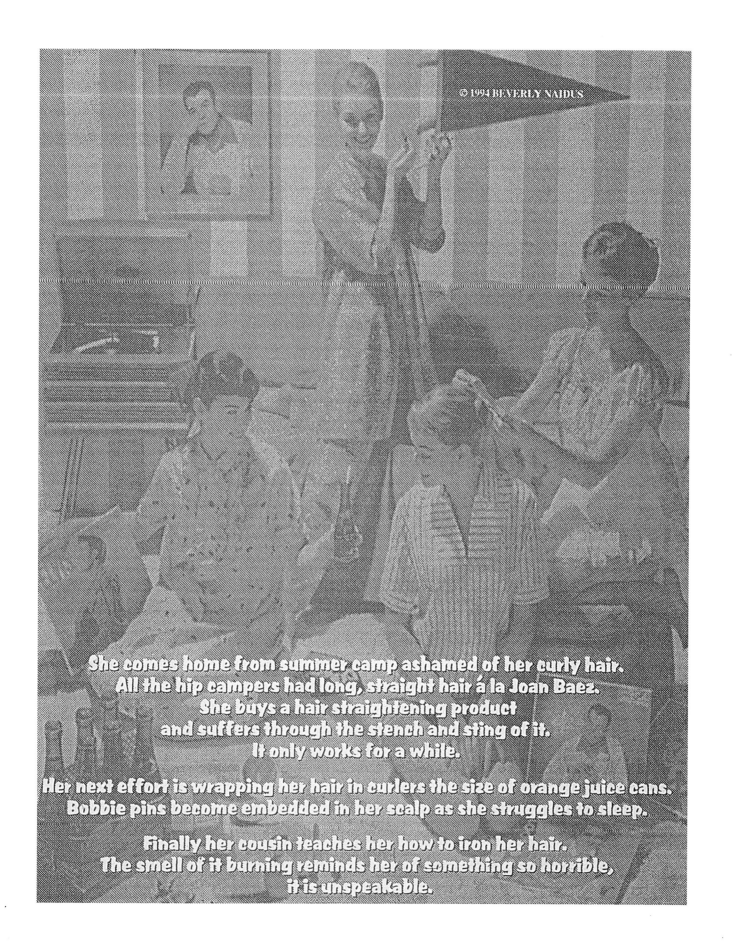

She comes home from summer camp ashamed of her curly hair.
All the hip campers had long, straight hair á la Joan Baez.
She buys a hair straightening product
and suffers through the stench and sting of it.
It only works for a while.

Her next effort is wrapping her hair in curlers the size of orange juice cans.
Bobbie pins become embedded in her scalp as she struggles to sleep.

Finally her cousin teaches her how to iron her hair.
The smell of it burning reminds her of something so horrible,
it is unspeakable.

143

14. NURIT NEWMAN
Complex Princess, 1995

15. NURIT NEWMAN
Detail, *Complex Princess,* 1995

16. RONA PONDICK
Swinger, 1992

145

17–30. ARCHIE RAND
Details from *The Chapter Paintings*, 1989

LEFT TO RIGHT:
TOP ROW: (5) *Chayye Sarah*, (7) *Vayyetsey*, (11) *Vayyigash*, (20) *Tetsaveh*, (24) *Vayyikra*, (29) *Acharay Moth*,
MIDDLE ROW: (35) *Naso*, (39) *Hukkath*, (40) *Balak*, (46) *Ekev*, (51) *Nitzavim*,
BOTTOM ROW: (53) *Haazinu*, (1) *Bereshith*, (27) *Tazria*

31. ELAINE REICHEK
Untitled (Jesse Reichek) from *A Postcolonial Kinderhood,* 1994

32. Adam Rolston
Untitled (Manischewitz American Matzos), 1993

Jewish Boys

It was the first day of Jewish summer camp.
The director gave a lecture.

**"No pairing off! Pairing off causes trouble.
You are here to set an example, not a fire."**

We giggled. Everyone had pairing off on their minds.

That afternoon we went swimming.
I wore a new blue bikini with little white polka dots.
As I dove in the water I heard

"Come see me right now young lady!"

over the loudspeaker.
I went dripping into the director's office.

"Your bathing suit is too small."

He was upset: "But Schlomo," I pleaded,
"This bathing suit is special."
I showed him the label across the inside of the top.
"MADE IN ISRAEL." My bathing suit was small
but it was Jewish.

"Hmmm. All right. But it's going to be trouble."

An hour later all the counselors in training
wanted to walk me to my bunk. Schlomo was right.
The swimsuit was trouble.

33. ILENE SEGALOVE
Jewish Boys, 1987

34. Art Spiegelman
Preliminary sketch for *Maus: A Survivor's Tale, c.* 1983

35. Alan Wexler
Indoor Sukkah, 1991

KEN APTEKAR

Born in Detroit, Michigan, 1950

EDUCATION

M.F.A. Pratt Institute, 1975
B.F.A. University of Michigan, 1973

SELECTED ONE-PERSON EXHIBITIONS

1995 Palmer Museum of Art, Pennsylvania
State University, University Park
*Rembrandt Redux: The Paintings of
Ken Aptekar*
1994 Jack Shainman Gallery, New York
Rembrandt's Problem
1990 Margulies Taplin Gallery, Coral Gables
1989 Bess Cutler Gallery, New York
1984 Sid Deutsch Gallery, New York
1983 The New Museum of Contemporary Art,
New York
On View
1980 Art Galaxy, New York
1979 Art Latitude, New York

SELECTED GROUP EXHIBITIONS

1996 California Center for the Arts Museum,
Escondido
Narcissism: Artists Represent Themselves
(catalogue)
John Michael Kohler Arts Center,
Sheboygan, Wis.
Beyond the Male Pale (catalogue)
1995 Centenaire de la Municipalité de La
Rouche, Québec
Art sans Frontières
Corcoran Gallery of Art, Washington, D.C.
Recent Acquisitions
The New Museum of Contemporary Art,
New York
Human/Nature
Walters Art Gallery and The Contempo-
rary, Baltimore
Going for Baroque
1994 Center for the Arts at Yerba Buena Gar-
dens, San Francisco
New Old Masters
UCLA Wight Art Gallery, Los Angeles,

in conjunction with The New Mu-
seum of Contemporary Art,
New York
Bad Girls West (catalogue)
1993 Corcoran Gallery of Art, Washington, D.C.
*43rd Biennial Exhibition of Contempo-
rary American Painting* (catalogue)
Flint Institute of Arts, Flint, Mich.
The Purloined Image (catalogue)
1992 School 33 Art Center, Baltimore
Decoding Gender
1991 Carnegie Mellon Art Gallery, Pittsburgh
New Generation, New York (catalogue)
Snug Harbor Cultural Center, Newhouse
Center for Contemporary Art,
Staten Island
Drawing Time
1990 Artists Space, New York
Post-Boys & Girls: Nine Painters
(catalogue)
Pfizer, Inc., New York (loan exhibition or-
ganized by the Museum of Modern
Art, New York)
In Bloom
1989 University Art Museum, State University
of New York at Binghamton
Gender Fictions (catalogue)
1987 The New Museum of Contemporary Art,
New York
*The Other Man: Alternative Representa-
tions of Masculinity* (catalogue)
1986 Art in General, New York
Group Painting Exhibition
1982 Just Above Midtown/Downtown,
New York
What I Do For Art (catalogue)
1978 Franklin Furnace Archive, Inc., New York
Two-person exhibition of bookworks

SELECTED BIBLIOGRAPHY

1995 Hagen, Aernout. "Ken Aptekar kiest uit
Rembrandts hoedencollectie." *Kroniek
van Het Rembrandthuis* (Chronicle of
the Rembrandt House), no. 1.
1994 Grimes, Nancy. "Ken Aptekar at Jack
Shainman." *Art in America* 82
(November).
Edelman, Robert G. "The Figure Returns:

* Performance was videotaped.

43rd Corcoran Biennial." *Art in America* 82 (March–April).

Risatti, Howard. "43rd Corcoran Biennial." *Artforum* 32 (March).

Roth, Charlene. "Bad Girls." *Artweek*, March 10.

Drohojowska-Philp, Hunter. "And Then They Were Bad . . ." *Los Angeles Times*, January 16.

1993 Baker, Kenneth. "Contemporary Painting Celebrated in D.C." *San Francisco Chronicle*, November 7.

Gibson, Eric. "Who Are the New Stars of Painting?" *The Washington Times*, November 2.

1991 Raynor, Vivien. "Bedrooms and Drawings." *The New York Times*, February 17.

1990 Hess, Elizabeth. "Yesterday's Children." *The Village Voice*, December 4.

Henry, Gerrit. "Ken Aptekar at Bess Cutler." *Art in America* 78 (June).

Saslow, James. "Rethinking Masculinity: Ken Aptekar." *The Advocate*, May 22.

1989 Atkins, Robert. "New This Week: Ken Aptekar." *Seven Days*, December 5.

1984 Zimmer, William. "Kenneth Aptekar at Sid Deutsch." *Arts Magazine* 59 (May).

1982 Glueck, Grace. "Critics' Choices." *The New York Times*, June 20.

HELENE AYLON

Born in Brooklyn, New York, 1931

EDUCATION

M.A. Antioch College West, 1980

M.F.A. (Equivalency) State University of San Francisco, 1974

B.F.A. Brooklyn College, 1960

SELECTED ONE-PERSON EXHIBITIONS AND COLLABORATIONS

1995 SONY Jumbotron at Times Square, New York
    two sacs en route (video meditation played hourly)

University Art Museum (facade), University of California at Berkeley
    Bridge of Knots: The 50th Anniversary Commemoration of Hiroshima/Nagasaki

1992 Creative Time, New York, and tour
    The Earth Ambulance 1982–1992 (and performance)

1989 Cleveland Center for Contemporary Art
    Stretchers (and performance*)

1979 Betty Parsons Gallery, New York
    Formations

White Columns, New York
    Formations Breaking (and performance*)

1976 List Visual Arts Center, Massachusetts Institute of Technology, Cambridge
    Transformations: Paintings That Change in Time (catalogue)

1975 Betty Parsons Gallery and Susan Caldwell Gallery, New York
    Paintings That Change in Time (brochure)

1972 Max Hutchinson Gallery, New York
    Shadowlands I and II (brochure)

1970 Max Hutchinson Gallery, New York

SELECTED PERFORMANCES

1992 Ma'alot and Mitzpe Ramon, Israel
    Stone Carrying II*

1991 Hofstra University, Long Island, N.Y.
    The Liberation of G-D

1989 Cleveland Center for Contemporary Art
    Mirror Covering

Institute for Contemporary Art, P.S. 1 Museum, Long Island City, N.Y., and Fort Mason, San Francisco
    Inquiry: The Trial of the Sands of Time*

University of Iowa Multi-Media Workshop
    Earth. Desert. Salt . . . Sands, Faultline, Shoreline*

1988 The Jewish Museum, New York
    Four Questions (with Mierle Laderman Ukeles)*

1987 Women's Building, Los Angeles
    Mirror Covering

1985 Japan
    Current. two sacs en route: two sacs float on Japan rivers*

1983 Dag Hammerskjold Plaza at the United Nations, New York
    Senecca Delivery*

1982 Cross-country, Strategic Air Command (SAC) bases and Bunche Park and Dag Hammerskjold Plaza at the United Nations, New York
    Terrestri: "Rescued" Earth*

U.S.S.R.
    Somniloquy: Pillowcase Exchange

1981 *Geder hatova* (The Good Fence), Israel-Lebanon border
    Border Earth Dust*

Haifa Museum and Vadi Salib, Israel
    Stone Carrying/Stone Sacs*

1980 San Andreas Fault, Death Valley, Pacific Ocean, and Women's Building, San Francisco
    Sand Carrying/Sand sacs (with Anna Halpprin and Pauline Oliveros)*

SELECTED GROUP EXHIBITIONS

1994 Aldrich Museum of Contemporary Art, Ridgefield, Conn.
    Paintings in Transition

Artists Space, New York
    Stones in Transition 1991: Stone Carrying, Arab and Jewish Women 1981

1993 Museum of Modern Art, New York
    Political Art Documentation and Distribution: The PADD Archives

1990 Municipal Art Society, New York
    Up Front/Land Art

1987 Museum of Contemporary Hispanic Art (MOCHA), New York, and tour
    Project Conexus

Women's Building, Los Angeles
    Reflections on Survival

1984 Tompkins Square Gallery, New York
    L'Esprit Encyclopédique

1982 A.I.R. Gallery, New York
    Earth Collage

1979 Otis College of Art and Design Gallery, Los Angeles

*New York: A Selection from the Last
Ten Years*

1977 Aldrich Museum of Contemporary Art,
Ridgefield, Conn.
Contemporary Collectors (catalogue)

1975 Oakland Museum, Art Division
Six Painters: Six Attitudes (catalogue)

1972 Storm King Art Center, Mountainville,
N.Y.
SoHo Scene

1970 Aldrich Museum of Contemporary Art,
Ridgefield, Conn., and tour
Lyrical Abstraction (catalogue)
Institute of Contemporary Art, Univer-
sity of Pennsylvania, Philadelphia
Two Generations of Color Painting
(catalogue)

SELECTED BIBLIOGRAPHY

1995 Selz, Peter. Review. *Art in America* 83
(December).
Knowlton, Leslie. Article. *Los Angeles
Times*, February 26.

1994 Lacy, Suzanne, ed. *Mapping the Terrain:
New Genre Public Art.* Seattle: Bay
Press.
Torres, Anthony. Review. *Artweek*,
September 26.

1993 "Political Art Documentation and Distri-
bution: PADD Archive Exhibition,
June 1993–May 1994." *Museum of
Modern Art Library Bulletin* (Winter).

1992 Smith, Roberta. "The Earth Ambulance
1982–1992." *The New York Times*,
August 28.

1989 Collin, Françoise. "Lianinnaire du nu-
cléalre—Las Chaiers du Grit 'Survive
& Continue.'" *Le Grif* (Paris) (Winter).
Maksymowicz, Virginia. Review. *Art and
Artists* (March).
McCann, Cecile. "The Loss of Sands
by a Storage Company." *Artweek*,
February 23.
Baker, Kenneth. Article. *San Francisco
Chronicle*, February 17.
Robinson, Walter. "Ecology Art Con-
founds Jury." *Art in America* 74
(February).

"On Common Ground." *Heresies*, no. 23.

1985 Orenstein, Gloria. *Women's Studies
International Forum* 8.

1981 Goldstein, Richard. Review. *The Village
Voice*, July 12.
Review. *Schachaf* (Israel) (July).
Boettger, Suzaan. "From Oil to Stone:
The Making of a Political Artist."
Artbeat (February).

1979 Kingsley, April. "Nature Takes Its
Course." *The Village Voice*, April 1.
Glueck, Grace. "Formations Breaking."
The New York Times, March 16.
Stile, Knute. Review. *Art in America* 67
(March).

1978 Fischer, Hal. Review. *Artforum* 17
(December).

1976 Alloway, Lawrence. "Paintings That
Change in Time." *Womenart Maga-
zine* (Summer).
Phillips, Ann. "Aylon's Paintings Flow
before Your Very Eyes." *Cambridge
Chronicle*, March 25.
Dickson, Joanne. "Paintings in Process."
Artweek, January 17.

1975 Schjeldahl, Peter. Review. *Art in America*
63 (November).
Ellenzweig, Allen. Review. *Arts* 50
(November).

1973 Kingsley, April. "Women Choose
Women." *Artforum* 11 (March).

1972 Ratcliff, Carter. Review. *Art International*
16 (June).
Siegel, Jeanne. Review. *Arts* 71 (May).

1971 Muller, Gregoire. "Materiality and Painter-
liness." *Arts* (September–October).

1970 Ratcliff, Carter. Review. *Art International*
14 (December).
Aldrich, Larry. "Young Lyrical Painters."
Art in America 58 (April).
Glueck, Grace. "Highlights of the Down-
town Scene." *The New York Times*,
April 11.

1966 Campbell, Lawrence. "Ruach." *ARTnews*
65 (December).

NEIL GOLDBERG

Born in Hicksville, New York, 1963

EDUCATION

B.A. Brown University, 1986

SELECTED ONE-PERSON EXHIBITIONS

1995 P.S. 122 Gallery, New York
Hallelujah

SELECTED GROUP EXHIBITIONS

1995 The Jewish Museum, San Francisco
Light Interpretations

1994 S.A.C. Gallery, Cobbleskill, N.Y.
Group Show

1993 The Kitchen, New York
Mix

1992 ABC No Rio, New York
Psychological Assault
Bill Bace Gallery, New York
Artists' Christmas Show
Nomadic Site Project, Los Angeles
Not Working in L.A.

SELECTED PERFORMANCES

1995 The Jewish Museum, New York
*The Third Seder**
The Joyce Theater, New York
Approaching No Calm (stage installa-
tion*)

1993 La MaMa-La Galleria, New York
The Third Seder

SELECTED BIBLIOGRAPHY

1995 Hamlin, Jesse. Review. *San Francisco Ex-
aminer and Chronicle*, November 19.
Jowitt, Deborah. "Men/Women." *The
Village Voice*, January 17.

1993 Solomon, Alisa. "Feast of Freedom." *The
Village Voice*, April 13.
Morris, Bob. "Still Life with Matzoh."
The New York Times, April 11.

Kenneth Goldsmith
Born in Freeport, New York, 1961

EDUCATION

B.F.A. Rhode Island School of Design, 1984

SELECTED ONE-PERSON EXHIBITIONS

1995 Bravin Post Lee, New York
1994 Bravin Post Lee, New York
    Sawhill Gallery, James Madison University, Harrisonburg, Va.
    A Portrait of the Writer as a Young Artist
1993 The Drawing Center, New York, and tour
    73 Poems
    Sue Spaid Fine Art, Los Angeles
1992 John Post Lee Gallery, New York
1990 Mincher/Wilcox Gallery, San Francisco
    Paula Allen Gallery, New York
1988 Schreiber/Cutler, Inc., New York

SELECTED GROUP EXHIBITIONS

1995 Art Gallery, Beaver College, Glenside, Pa.
    Word for Word
    Deutches Haus, Columbia University, New York
    Collaborations between Artists and Writers
1994 Independent Curators, Inc. (ICI) 20th Anniversary, Sonnabend Gallery, New York
    Up the Establishment: Reconstructing the Counterculture
1993 The Artist's Museum, Lodz, Poland
    Construction in Process IV: My Home is Your Home
    The Drawing Center, New York
    Selections/Winter 1993
    Gallery 400, School of Art and Design, University of Illinois at Chicago
    In The Spirit of Fluxus
    Interart Center, New York
    The Rag Trade
    Elizabeth Koury Gallery, New York
    Confessional
    John Post Lee Gallery, New York
    Between

Turman Art Gallery, Indiana State University, Terre Haute
    Is Poetry a Visual Art? (catalogue)
1992 BlumHelman Warehouse, New York
    Group Show
    Edwin A. Ulrich Museum of Art, Wichita State University, Kansas
    Volumination
    Galerie van Orsouw, Zurich
    Multiple Choices
    The Sculpture Center, New York
    The Wall Project
1991 Ezra and Cecile Zilkha Gallery, Center for the Arts, Wesleyan University, Middletown, Conn.
    The Good, the Bad, and the Ugly: Knowledge and Violence in Recent American Art
    Penine Hart Gallery, New York
    Comments on Nomos (catalogue)
    HOME for Contemporary Art and Theatre, New York
    HOME for June
1990 l'Espace-Dieu, Paris
    All Quiet on the Western Front? (catalogue)
    Andrea Rosen Gallery, New York
    Stendahl Syndrome: The Cure (catalogue)
    White Columns, New York
    Brute '90
1989 The Gallery at Bristol-Myers Squibb, Princeton, N.J.
    Fictive Strategies
    Barbara Toll Fine Arts, New York
    A Good Read: The Book as Metaphor
1988 F Train East Broadway Station, New York
    The Advertising Show
    Schreiber/Cutler, Inc., New York
    Kenneth Goldsmith: The Plain Truth
1987 P.S. 122 Gallery, New York
    Avant-Garde-O-Rama
1986 Franklin Furnace Archive, Inc., New York
    Snap Series

SELECTED WRITINGS BY THE ARTIST

1993 *73 Poems* (Brooklyn, N.Y.: Permanent Press)

No. 105 (New York: Beans Dear? Press)
Tizzy Boost, a collaboration with Bruce Andrews (Great Barrington, Mass.: The Figures)
No. 109 2.7.93–12.15.93 (New York: Bravin Post Lee)

SELECTED BIBLIOGRAPHY

1994 Smith, Roberta. "ICI at Sonnabend." *The New York Times*, June 3.
    Anderson, Michael. *Grammarians.* Catalogue accompanying exhibition, Guggenheim Gallery, Chapman University, Orange, Calif., February.
    Myers, Terry. "Construction in Process." *Flash Art* (January–February).
1993 Miles, Eileen. "Prints of Words." *Print Collectors Newsletter* (September–October).
    Saltz, Jerry. "10 Artists for the '90s." *Art and Auction* (May).
    Borum, Jenifer, P. "Kenneth Goldsmith at John Post Lee Gallery." *Artforum* 31 (February).
    Schwartzman, Alan. "Selections/Winter 1993." *The New Yorker*, February 1.
1990 Geer, Suvan. "Kenneth Goldsmith: Measures of Life." *Los Angeles Times*, November 24.
1988 Rose, Matthew. "Successful Opposites." *Art Gallery International* (Summer).

Dennis Kardon
Born in Des Moines, Iowa, 1950

EDUCATION

Whitney Museum Independent Study Program, 1973
B.A. Yale University, 1973

SELECTED ONE-PERSON EXHIBITIONS

1996 Richard Anderson Fine Arts, New York
1991 A/D, New York
    A Conversation with Rococo Mirrors

DEBORAH KASS

Born in San Antonio, Texas, 1952

1991 Richard F. Brush Gallery, Saint Lawrence
　　　University, Canton, N.Y.
　　　From Desire: A Queer Diary
　　　Galeria Fernando Alcolea, Barcelona
　　　Rope
　　　Hyde Collection, Glens Falls, N.Y.
　　　*Just What Is It That Makes Today's
　　　Home So Different, So Appealing?*
　　　(catalogue)
1990 Massimo Audiello Gallery, New York
　　　*The Last Laugh: Irony, Humor, Self-
　　　Mockery, and Derision*
　　　White Columns, New York
　　　*Fragments, Parts, and Wholes: The
　　　Body and Culture*
1989 Bellarte, Helsinki
　　　Young New York
　　　Galerie Rahmel, Cologne, Germany
　　　*Painting Between the Paradigms—Part
　　　One: Between Awareness and Desire*
　　　Jersey City Museum
　　　*The Mirror in Which Two Are Seen as
　　　One*
　　　Simon Watson Gallery, New York
　　　*Erotophobia: A Forum of Contempo-
　　　rary Sexuality*
1988 Jacob Javits Center, New York
　　　Five Corners of Abstraction
　　　Postmasters, New York
　　　Meaningful Geometry
1987 One Penn Plaza, New York
　　　Romantic Science
　　　Solo Gallery, New York
　　　Major Acquisitions, Small Appliances
　　　Carl Solway Gallery, Cincinnati
　　　Dreams of the Alchemist
1986 Ben Shahn Galleries, William Paterson
　　　College, Wayne, N.J.
　　　A Radical Plurality
1984 Exit Art, New York
　　　Fantastic Landscape
1982 Green Space, New York
　　　Landscape/Cityscape
　　　Institute for Contemporary Art, P.S. 1
　　　Museum, Long Island City, N.Y.
　　　Critical Perspectives
1981 Institute for Contemporary Art, P.S. 1
　　　Museum, Long Island City, N.Y.
　　　Heads

1980 Pratt Manhattan Center, Pratt Institute,
　　　New York and Brooklyn, N.Y
　　　*First Person Singular: Recent Self-
　　　Portraiture*

SELECTED WRITINGS BY THE ARTIST

1993 "Color Me Barbra." *10 Percent* (Winter).

SELECTED BIBLIOGRAPHY

1995 Smith, Roberta. "Void, Self, Drag,
　　　Utopia (And 5 Other Gay Themes)."
　　　The New York Times, March 26.
　　　Cembalest, Robin. "Warhol Meets
　　　Streisand, Deborah Kass Makes Pop
　　　Art Ethnic." *The Forward*, March 17.
1994 Cottingham, Laura. *The Power of Femi-
　　　nist Art.* New York: Harry N. Abrams,
　　　Inc.
　　　Goldberg, Vicki. "A Pair of Saints Who
　　　Refuse to Stay Dead." *The New York
　　　Times*, December 18.
　　　Wise, Michael. "Double Yentls, Chanel
　　　Kippahs, and P.C. Torahs." *The For-
　　　ward*, July 1.
　　　Cotter, Holland. "Art after Stonewall, 12
　　　Artists Interviewed." *Art in America*
　　　82 (June).
　　　Avgikos, Jan. "Review of Ciphers of
　　　Identity." *Artforum* 32 (March).
1993 Cronin, Patricia. "A Conversation on Les-
　　　bian Subjectivity and Painting (with
　　　Deborah Kass)." *M/E/A/N/I/N/G*, no.
　　　14 (November).
　　　Waddington, Chris. "A Woman's Work
　　　Is . . ." *Lagniappe*, October 1.
1992 Mifflin, Margot. "Feminism's New Face."
　　　ARTnews 91 (November).
　　　Liu, Catherine. "Diary of the Pop Body:
　　　Dandy Darlings and New Pop Strate-
　　　gies." *Flash Art* 25 (October).
　　　Smith, Roberta. "Women Artists Engage
　　　the 'Enemy.'" *The New York Times*,
　　　August 16.
　　　Cameron, Dan. "The Outlaw Academy."
　　　Art and Auction 14 (May).
　　　Cameron, Dan. "Don't Look Now."
　　　frieze (January).

Cameron, Dan. "The Changing Tide."
　　　Art and Auction 14 (January).
1990 Westfall, Stephen. "Subject Matters."
　　　Contemporanea (November).
1987 Saltz, Jerry. *Beyond Boundaries: New York,
　　　New Art.* New York: Alfred Van der
　　　Mark Editions.
1986 Cameron, Dan. "Second Nature: New
　　　Paintings by Deborah Kass." *Arts
　　　Magazine* 61 (April).
1985 Masheck, Joseph. "Observations on
　　　Harking Back (and Forth)." *New
　　　Observations*, no. 28.
1982 Cohen, Ronny. "A Survey of What, How,
　　　and Why Artists Are Drawing So
　　　Much Today." *Drawing* 3, no. 2.

CARY S. LEIBOWITZ/CANDYASS
Born in New York, New York, 1963

EDUCATION

Pratt Institute, 1981–1983
Fashion Institute of Technology, 1983–1984
B.F.A. University of Kansas, 1987

**SELECTED ONE-PERSON EXHIBITIONS
AND COLLABORATIONS**

1995 I.D. Gallery, Dusseldorf
　　　*My Third One-Person Show in Dussel-
　　　dorf*
　　　Shoshana Wayne Gallery, Santa Monica
　　　*HOT DOG!! (Please don't forget
　　　Eleanor Roosevelt)*
1994 Bravin Post Lee, New York
　　　Schlock of the New
　　　Ynglingagtan I, Stockholm
　　　CandyAss Math Team
1993 Galerie Vier, Berlin
　　　I Slept with Martin Kippenberger
　　　Gallery Cellar, Nagoya, Japan
　　　*Don't Hate Me Because I Don't Speak
　　　Japanese* (catalogue)
1992 Barneys (17th Street windows), New York
　　　April Fools
　　　Galerie Antoine Candau, Paris
　　　Paris Retrospective (Candyass Cemetery)

Galerie Snoei, Rotterdam
Winners and Losers (collaboration
with Lily van der Stokker)
Gallery Samuel Lallouz, Montreal
Being a Grown-Up Is Hard
1991 Stux Gallery, New York
*Candyass Carnival (and Warehouse
Retrospective)* (collaboration)
Shoshana Wayne Gallery, Santa Monica
*I Think I'm the Only Artist Discovered
on The Gong Show*
1990 Galerie Antoine Candau, l'Espace-Dieu,
Paris
U Can't Be Dead All the Time
(catalogue)
I.D. Gallery, Dusseldorf
Some Rules
Stux Gallery, New York
Bric-A-Brac
1989 Stux Gallery, New York
World's Best Fried Chicken
1987 Art and Design Building, University of
Kansas, Lawrence
I Love You More Than Michael Jackson

SELECTED PERFORMANCES

1994 Four Walls, New York
"Fear of a Jewish Planet" (with
Rhonda Lieberman)*

SELECTED GROUP EXHIBITIONS

1995 Cabinet Gallery, London
Please Don't Hurt Me (catalogue)
Cyber-exhibition, organized in Helsinki
Rzguia Muu-ltiples Production
Künstlewerkstatt, Munich
Outburst of Signs (catalogue)
Memory/Cage Editions, Zurich
The Pleasures of Merely Circulating
(catalogue)
Paço Imperial, Rio de Janeiro
Correspondèncias (catalogue)
Phœnix Art Museum, and tour
It's Only Rock and Roll (catalogue)
Regin Gallery, Moscow
On Beauty
Southeastern Center for Contemporary

Art (SECCA), Winston-Salem,
and tour
Civil Rights Now (catalogue)
University Art Museum, University of
California at Berkeley
In a Different Light (catalogue)
Vienna Secession, Vienna
How Is Everything?
1994 The New Museum of Contemporary Art,
New York (in conjunction with
UCLA Wight Art Gallery, Los
Angeles)
Bad Girls (catalogue)
1993 Exit Art, New York
The Design Show
Frankfurter Kunstverein, Frankfurt
Prospect 93
The Jewish Museum, New York
*Bridges and Boundaries: African Amer-
icans and American Jews*
(catalogue)
Le Cappellaine Gallery, New York
The Wasteland
The Space, Boston
4 Artists: An Exhibition and Edition
Washington Project for the Arts (WPA),
Washington, D.C.
Beyond Loss: Art in the Era of AIDS
1992 Aldrich Museum of Contemporary Art,
Ridgefield, Conn.
X 6: New Multiple Makers (catalogue)
Casa della citta, Rome
Molteplici Culture Arte Critica 1992
(catalogue)
Hôtel des Arts, Paris
Génériques: Le visuel & l'écrit
Institute for Contemporary Art, P.S. 1
Museum, Long Island City, N.Y.
Small Talk
Holly Solomon Gallery, New York
People Pleasers
Stux Gallery, New York
The Fake Chanel Show
1991 Claudio Botello Gallery, Turin
A New Low
Galerie im Margarethenhof,
Friedrich-Naumann-Stiftung,
Koenigswinter
Vier Kunstler aus New York

Gallery 400, School of Art and Design,
University of Illinois at Chicago
Fay Gold Gallery, Atlanta
Outside America: Going into the '90's
(catalogue)
1990 Massimo Audiello Gallery, New York
The Last Laugh (brochure)
Galerie Antoine Candau, l'Espace-Dieu,
Paris
U.S.A. Années, 90 (catalogue)
Bennet Siegel Gallery, New York
*The Exotic Image: Modern Masters and
Mistresses*
Shoshana Wayne Gallery, Santa Monica
Whitney Museum of American Art,
Downtown at Federal Plaza,
New York
*The Charade of Mastery: Deciphering
Modernism in Contemporary Art*
(catalogue)
1989 Deichtorhallen Museum, Hamburg
Einleuchten (catalogue)
List Visual Arts Center, Massachusetts
Institute of Technology, Cam-
bridge
Trouble in Paradise (catalogue)
Stux Gallery, New York
Althea Viafora Gallery, New York
The Second Second
1988 Institute of Contemporary Art, Boston
Boston Now (catalogue)

SELECTED BIBLIOGRAPHY

1994 Cotter, Holland. "Art after Stonewall, 12
Artists Interviewed." *Art in America*
82 (June).
1993 Lieberman, Rhonda. "Springtime for
Grunge." *Artforum* 31 (April).
1992 Lieberman, Rhonda. "The Loser Thing."
Artforum 31 (September).
Hess, Elizabeth. "Chutes and Ladders."
The Village Voice, April 7.
1991 Kilian, Michael. "Rude Enlightenment."
Chicago Tribune, September 5.
Burchard, Hank. "What You Get: What
You See." *The Washington Post*, June 14.
Sommer, Von Christa. "Ein Teddybar für
Wien." *Wochenpresse*, May 16.

Knight, Christopher. "Leibowitz Seeks Success Through Failure." *Los Angeles Times*, April 16.

Roulette, Todd. "Dear CSL/Candyass." *THING* (Spring).

Collins, Tricia, and Richard Milazzo. "From Kant to Kitsch and Back Again." *Tema Celeste* (January–February).

Humphrey, David. "New York/Gilbert & George, Larry Clark, Pruitt & Early, Cary S. Leibowitz/Candyass, 'American Artists of the 80's.'" *Art Issues* (January).

1990 Cottingham, Laura. "Negotiating Masculinity and Representation." *Contemporanea* (December).

Schwendenwien, Jude. "Trouble in Paradise, The Art Gallery, University of Maryland." *Contemporanea*, no. 21 (December).

Johnson, Ken. "Cary S. Leibowitz/Candyass at Stux." *Art in America* 78 (November).

Aletti, Vince. "The Schlemiel of SoHo." *The Village Voice*, October 9.

1989 Als, Hilton. "Cary Leibowitz/CANDYASS." *Artforum* 28 (December).

Temin, Christine. "Uncensored." *The New York Observer*, October 2.

1988 Cameron, Dan. "The Sexual Is Cultural." *Art and Auction* 7 (December).

Bonetti, David. "Paper Prophets." *Boston Phoenix*, July 1.

Rhonda Lieberman

Born in New York, New York, 1960

EDUCATION

Ph.D. candidate Yale University
M.A. Yale University, 1985
B.A. Brandeis University, 1982

SELECTED GROUP EXHIBITIONS

1994 Barneys, New York
Red Windows

The New Museum for Contemporary Art, New York, in conjunction with UCLA Wight Art Gallery, Los Angeles
Bad Girls (catalogue)

1993 The Drawing Center, New York
Exquisite Corpse

The Museum of Art, Palm Beach Community College
Art, Money, Myth

1992 Stux Gallery, New York
The Fake Chanel Show

SELECTED PERFORMANCES

1993 Four Walls, New York
"Fear of a Jewish Planet" (with Cary Leibowitz)*

SELECTED WRITINGS BY THE ARTIST

(See also general Bibliography to this volume)
1994 "Shiksa Goddess (Forever Barbie)." *Mirabella* (November).

1993 "Another Oedipus Wreck." Catalogue essay for the Venice Biennale, ed. Christian Leigh and Pedro Almódovar.

1992 "Shopping Disorders." In *The Politics of Everyday Fear*, ed. Brian Massumi. Minneapolis: University of Minnesota Press.

1991 "Other People's Pictures." *Flash Art* (Fall).

1990 "Capital, the Void, Your Mother." *Lusitania* 1 (Fall).

"MacDonna." Catalogue essay for "The Stendhal Syndrome: The Cure." New York: Andrea Rosen Gallery, reprinted in *Lusitania* 4 (1992).

SELECTED BIBLIOGRAPHY

1993 Jacobs, Karrie. "Coco: The Column." *Metropolis* (March).

1992 Vogel, Carol. "The Art Market." *The New York Times*, December 18.

Beverly Naidus

Born in Salem, Massachusetts, 1953

EDUCATION

M.F.A. Nova Scotia College of Art and Design, Halifax, N.S., Canada, 1978
B.A. Carleton College, 1975

SELECTED ONE-PERSON EXHIBITIONS

1993 Highways, Santa Monica
One Size Fits All?

1992 Angels Gate Cultural Center, The Gate Gallery, San Pedro, Calif.
A Klug Tzu Columbus (A Curse on Columbus)

1991 Envy Salon, Long Beach, Calif.
The Fat Book Series (catalogue)

South Bay Contemporary Museum, Torrance, Calif.
Remote Control

1990 Central Coast Plaza, sponsored by Alternatives, San Luis Obispo, Calif.
Please Take a Number

Unitarian Church, Long Beach, Calif.
Taking the Empire's New Clothes to the Laundry

1989 The Art Gallery, California State University, Northridge
Will You Stop Depressing Me?!

1988 Todd Madigan Gallery, California State University, Bakersfield
You're So Negative

Saddleback College, Mission Viejo, Calif.
You're Such a Complainer

1985 M.A.D. Gallery, Carleton College, Northfield, Minn.

Y.W.C.A., Minneapolis, sponsored by Peace Links/Peace Child
This Is Not a Test

1981 Printed Matter, New York
No More Mr. Nice Guy

1980 Franklin Furnace Archive, Inc., New York
Apply Within

1979 22 Beaver Street Space, New York
Daily Reminder

1978 Nova Scotia College of Art and Design
Gallery, Halifax
This Is Not a Test

SELECTED GROUP EXHIBITIONS

1995 Highways, Santa Monica
Show Your Self
Municipal Gallery, Barnsdell Art Park,
Hollywood, Calif.
Social Engagements (catalogue)
University Art Museum, California State
University at Long Beach
Verde Que Te Quiero Verde (catalogue)
1994 Side Street Projects, Santa Monica
*Just Take This—Women/Pain/Medical
Histories* (catalogue)
1993 Santa Barbara Contemporary Arts
Forum, Calif.
Backtalk: Women's Voices in the 90's
(catalogue)
1992 Muckenthaler Museum, Fullerton, Calif.,
and tour
World News (catalogue)
New Gallery, Santa Monica, and Artists
Space, New York
Remapping Tales of Desire
1991 A.I.R. Gallery, New York
Choice
Orange County Center for Contempo-
rary Art, Santa Ana, Calif.
Teetering Relationships: Earth/People
(catalogue)
St. Luke's Gallery, Long Beach, Calif.
Children of War
1990 Couturier Gallery, Los Angeles
The Environment in Crisis
University Art Museum, University of
California at Berkeley
Free Speech Movement Exhibition
1989 Long Beach Museum of Art, Calif.
LA Free Waves
1988 Long Beach Museum of Art, Calif.
This Is Not a Test
1987 Installation Gallery, San Diego, and tour
Projections in Public
1986 M.A.D. Gallery, Carleton College,
Northfield, Minn.
Landscapes

1985 Group Material, New York
MASS
1984 The New Museum of Contemporary Art,
New York
*The End of the World: Contemporary
Visions of the Apocalypse* (catalogue)
1983 ABC No Rio, New York
Suburbia Show
Women's Interart Center, New York
Consumer Beware
1982 Brooklyn Museum, New York
Joint Forces (catalogue)
Loeb Student Center Gallery, New York
University
Radical Humor
University Art Museum, State University
of New York at Binghamton
Nine Women Artists (catalogue)
1981 Gallery 1199, New York
Who's Laffin Now
P.S. 122 Gallery, New York
Scale-ing (catalogue)
1980 Institute of Contemporary Art, London
*Issue—Social Strategies by Women
Artists* (catalogue)

SELECTED WRITINGS BY THE ARTIST

1993 *One Size DOES NOT Fit All*. Littleton,
Colo.: Aigis Publications, Ltd.
1987 "The Artist Teacher as Decoder and
Catalyst." *Radical Teacher* (Fall).

SELECTED BIBLIOGRAPHY

1995 Von Blum, Paul. *Other Visions, Other
Voices: Women Political Artists in
Greater L.A.* Oakland, Calif.: Univer-
sity Press.
"Review." *Lilith* 20 (Summer).
1993 Burnham, Linda. "One Size DOES
NOT Fit All." *High Performance*
(Fall).
Leddy, Pat. "Flesh and Blood." *Artweek*,
September 21.
1991 Gablik, Suzi. *The Reenchantment of Art*.
New York: Thames & Hudson.
Curtis, Cathy. "The Nature of Man." *Los
Angeles Times*, May 9.

Von Blum, Paul. "Women Political
Artists in LA: Eva Cockcroft, Shelia
Pinkel, and Beverly Naidus." *Z Magazine* (February).
1990 Lazzari, Margaret. "Signs of the Times."
Artweek, April 6.
Geer, Suvan. "Endangered Earth." *Los
Angeles Times*, March 16.
1989 Ziaya, Christine. "Audience Participa-
tion . . ." *Los Angeles Times*, January
27.
1988 Spiegel, Judith. "An Antidote for Cyni-
cism." *Artweek*, September 8.
1987 McMannus, Michael. "An Anxious
Space." *Artweek*, April 25.
1984 Lippard, Lucy R. *Get the Message: A
Decade of Art for Social Change*. New
York: Dutton.
Brenson, Michael. "Can Political Passion
Inspire Great Art?" *The New York
Times*, April 29.
Gablik, Suzi. "Art Alarms: Visions of the
End." *Art in America* (April).
Glueck, Grace. "When Artists Portray
Utopia and Armageddon." *The New
York Times*, Arts and Leisure section,
January 15.
1983 Lippard, Lucy R. "Too Close to Home."
The Village Voice, June 14.
1980 Schoenfeld, Ann. "Art and Politics, Do
We Need to Choose?" *Women Artists
Newsletter* 6 (Summer).

NURIT NEWMAN
Born in New York, New York, 1962

EDUCATION

M.F.A. Rutgers, The State University of New
Jersey, 1993
B.F.A. New York University, 1984

SELECTED ONE-PERSON EXHIBITIONS

1995 ABC No Rio, New York
boilingpoints
Franklin Furnace Archive, Inc., New York
Complex Princess

1993 South Gallery, New Brunswick, N.J.
Between Planes and Passages
1989 Synchronicity Space, New York

SELECTED GROUP EXHIBITIONS

1995 Foramen Magnum Gallery, New York
Post Beuys
Gallery Korea, New York
Makers of Identity
1994 Art in General, New York
Animated (catalogue)
Bronx Museum of the Arts, N.Y.
Artists in the Marketplace (catalogue)
East West Cultural Studies, New York
18 Inches and Up
148 Gallery, New York
10 x 10
1993 494 Gallery, New York
Beyond Body
Jane Voorhees Zimmerli Art Museum,
Rutgers University, New
Brunswick, N.J.
24 artists (catalogue)
1992 Chattanooga School of the Arts, Chat-
tanooga, Tenn.
1991 Raritan Gallery, Raritan, N.J.
[S]PACE[S]
The Weatherholt Gallery, Washington,
D.C.

SELECTED BIBLIOGRAPHY

1994 Tagami, Ty. "Helping Emerging Artists
Learn Their Marketplace." *New York
Newsday*, August 16.
Zimmer, William. "A Religious Spirit
Vies in the Bronx." *The New York
Times*, July 31.

RONA PONDICK
Born in Brooklyn, New York, 1952

EDUCATION

M.F.A. Yale University School of Art, 1977
B.F.A. Queens College, 1974

SELECTED ONE-PERSON EXHIBITIONS

1995 Cincinnati Art Museum, Cincinnati
(brochure)
Jose Freire Fine Art, New York
1993 Jose Freire Fine Art, New York
Howard Yezerski Gallery, Boston
1992 Galerie Thaddaeus Ropac, Paris, and tour
The Israel Museum, Jerusalem
Pink and Brown (catalogue)
1991 Art Gallery, Beaver College, Glenside, Pa.
Scrap (catalogue)
Asher-Faure Gallery, Los Angeles
fiction/nonfiction, New York
Foot and Mouth (catalogue)
1990 Asher-Faure Gallery, Los Angeles
mamamamama
1989 fiction/nonfiction, New York
Bed Milk Shoe (catalogue)
Institute of Contemporary Art, Boston
Currents (catalogue)
1988 Sculpture Center, New York
Beds (catalogue)

SELECTED GROUP EXHIBITIONS

1995 Armory, Philadelphia
*The Figure/The Body—American Art,
1945–1999*
Erfurt, Germany
Configura 2: Dialog der Kulturen
(catalogue)
Galerie Enrico Navarra, Paris
Autour de Roger Vivier (catalogue)
Galerie Thaddaeus Ropac, Salzburg
*The Muse? Transforming the Image of
Women in Contemporary Art*
(catalogue)
Herter Art Gallery, University of Massa-
chusetts at Amherst, and tour
Imperfect (catalogue)

The Main Gallery and the Huntington
Gallery, Massachusetts College of
Art, Boston
*Object Lessons: Feminine Dialogue
with the Surreal* (catalogue)
The Museum of Contemporary Art
(MOCA), Los Angeles
*Intersections: The Personal and the
Social in the Permanent Collection*
New Jersey Center for Visual Arts,
Summit
The Outer Layer (catalogue)
Rosemont College Art Gallery, Rose-
mont, Pa.
Foundations: Underwear/Under Where?
(catalogue)
The South Bank Centre, London, and
tour
Fetishism (catalogue)
Whitney Museum of American Art,
New York
Altered and Irrational
Elga Wimmer, New York
Women on the Verge (Fluxus and Not)
1994 Aldrich Museum of Contemporary Art,
Ridgefield, Conn.
In the Lineage of Eva Hesse (catalogue)
Stedelijk Museum Bureau, Amsterdam
Puber Alles (Why Am I Who I Am?)
Turman Gallery, Indiana State University,
Terre Haute
Object Bodies
UCLA Wight Art Gallery, Los Angeles,
in conjunction with The New
Museum for Contemporary Art,
New York
Bad Girls West (catalogue)
1993 Aldrich Museum of Contemporary Art,
Ridgefield, Conn., and tour
Fall from Fashion (catalogue)
Bonner Kunstverein, Bonn
UBER-LEBEN (catalogue)
The Drawing Center, New York
Return of the Cadavre Exquis
(catalogue)
Exit Art, New York
1920
Rhona Hoffman Gallery, Chicago
Legend in My Living Room

Palazzo delle Stelline, Milan
Normality as Art (catalogue)
Arthur Roger Gallery, New Orleans
Regarding Masculinity
Thread Waxing Space, New York
I Am the Enunciator
The Venice Biennial
Slittamenti: I Love You More Than My Own Death, A Melodrama in Parts by Pedro Almódovar

1992 AB Galerie, Paris
Erotiques
alternative space, Frankfurt am Main
Spielholle: Aesthetics and Violence (catalogue)
Carnegie Museum of Art, Pittsburgh
Effected Desire (catalogue)
Fullerton Art Gallery, California State University, Fullerton
Bedroom Eyes: Room with a View (catalogue)
The Gallery of the Art Institute of Chicago
Power Play
Heckscher Museum, Huntington, N.Y.
The Edge of Childhood (catalogue)
Kunsthalle, New York
Psycho (catalogue)
List Visual Arts Center, Massachusetts Institute of Technology, Cambridge
Corporal Politics (catalogue)
Thread Waxing Space, New York
Mssr. B's Curio Shop (catalogue)

1991 BlumHelman Warehouse, New York
Plastic Fantastic Lover (Object A) (catalogue)
Galeria Fernando Alcolea, Barcelona
Rope (catalogue)
The Hudson River Museum of Westchester, Yonkers, N.Y.
Experiencing Sculpture: The Figurative Presence in America, 1870–1990
Hyde Collection, Glens Falls, N.Y.
Just What Is It That Makes Today's Homes So Different, So Appealing? (catalogue)
Solo Press, New York
Sense and Sensibility

Jack Tilton Gallery, New York
Forbidden Games
Whitney Museum of American Art, New York
The Whitney Biennial (catalogue)

1990 Galerie Thaddaeus Ropac, Paris
Vertigo (catalogue)
Galerie Thaddaeus Ropac, Salzburg
Vertigo II
The Morris Museum, Morristown, N.J.
Diverse Representations (catalogue)
Marc Richards Gallery, Los Angeles
Spellbound
Emily Sorkin Gallery, New York
Body, Once Removed
Jack Tilton Gallery, New York,
Detritus: Transformation and Reconstruction
White Columns, New York
Fragments, Parts, and Wholes: The Body and Culture

1989 Emily Sorkin Gallery, New York
Form and Fetish
Simon Watson Gallery, New York
Erotophobia: A Forum in Contemporary Sexuality

1988 The New Museum of Contemporary Art, New York
Girls Night Out (Femininity as Masquerade) (catalogue)
Sculpture Center, New York
Beds (catalogue)

1987 Sculpture Center, New York
Small Works
Carl Solway Gallery, Cincinnati
The Level of Volume

1986 Richard Green Gallery, New York
Transformations

1985 alternative space, New York
The Non-Objective World

SELECTED BIBLIOGRAPHY

1995 Fineberg, Jonathan. *Art Since 1940: Strategies of Being.* Englewood Cliffs, N.J.: Prentice-Hall.
Lippard, Lucy R. *The Pink Glass Swan: Selected Feminist Essays on Art.* New York: The New Press.

Nixon, Mingon. "Bad Enough Mother." *October* 75 (Winter).
Riddell, Jennifer L. "The Abject Object." *The New Art Examiner* (October).
Murdoch, Sadie. "New York in Brief." *Woman's Art* (July–August).
Hagen, Charles. "Review of 'Inside Out.'" *The New York Times*, June 14.
Wilson, Elizabeth. "Strange Objects of Desire." *The Independent* (London), May 30.
Cork, Richard. Objects of Obscure Desire." *The Times* (London), May 16.

1994 Kuspit, Donald. "The Decline, Fall and Magical Resurrection of the Body." *Sculpture* 13 (May–June).
Smith, Roberta. "Sculptures in the Shadow of a Minimalist Master." *The New York Times*, March 18.
Zaya, Octavia. "'I can express it any way I want': An Interview with Rona Pondick." *AtlAnticA* (February).

1993 Seward, Keith. Review. *Artforum* 32 (November).
Smith, Roberta. "Examining Culture Through Its Castoffs." *The New York Times*, November 28.
Saltz, Jerry. "Critic's Diary, Mayday, Mayday, Mayday." *Art in America* 81 (September).

1992 Smith, Roberta. "Women Artists Engage the 'Enemy.'" *The New York Times*, August 16.
Myers, Terry R. "Abstraction Gets a Life." *Tema Celeste* (Summer).
Schwabsky, Barry. "Shamelessness." *Sculpture* 11 (July–August).
Cameron, Dan. "Don't Look Now." *frieze*, no. 3 (January).

1991 Schor, Mira. "You Can't Leave Home Without It." *Artforum* 30 (October).

1989 Spector, Buzz. "A Profusion of Substance." *Artforum* 28 (October).

1988 Brenson, Michael. "Rona Pondick—Beds." *The New York Times*, September 9.
Raap, Jurgen. "The Other New York." *Kunstforum* (July).
Hess, Elizabeth. "Ladies' Room." *The Village Voice*, May 24.

1984 Raynor, Vivien. "Exceptional and New." *The New York Times*, June 2.

ARCHIE RAND

Born in New York, New York, 1949

EDUCATION

City College of New York, 1965–1966
Art Students League, 1966–1967
B.F.A. Pratt Institute, 1968–1970

SELECTED ONE-PERSON EXHIBITIONS

1996 Girona Museum, Girona, Spain (catalogue)

1995 Tricia Collins, Grand Salon, New York (catalogue)

1993 The Montclair Art Museum, N.J. (catalogue)

1992 John Post Lee Gallery, New York
Philadelphia Museum of Judaica at Congregation Rodeph Shalom (catalogue)

1991 Exit Art, New York, and tour
Spertus Museum of Judaica, Chicago (catalogue)

1989 Memorial Art Gallery, University of Rochester, Rochester, N.Y. (catalogue)

1988 Phyllis Kind Gallery, New York

1987 Phyllis Kind Gallery, New York

1986 Phyllis Kind Gallery, New York

1984 The Contemporary Arts Center, Cincinnati (catalogue)
Tibor de Nagy Gallery, New York

1983 The Carnegie Museum of Art, Pittsburgh (catalogue)

1982 Tibor de Nagy Gallery, New York

1979 Tibor de Nagy Gallery, New York

1978 Tibor de Nagy Gallery, New York

1974 Tibor de Nagy Gallery, New York

1972 Tibor de Nagy Gallery, New York

SELECTED GROUP EXHIBITIONS

1996 Phoenix Art Museum, Phoenix
It's Only Rock and Roll (catalogue)

Smithsonian Institution, Washington, D.C., and tour
Jazz (catalogue)

1995 Deutsches Haus, Columbia University, New York
Collaborations: Artists and Writers
Exit Art, New York
. . . It's How You Play the Game

1994 Brooklyn Union Gallery at One Metrotech Center, Brooklyn, N.Y. (catalogue)
Fawbush Gallery, New York

1993 Centre l'Echange de Perrache, Lyon, France, and tour
Autoportraits Contemporain (catalogue)

1992 Decker and Meyerhoff Galleries, Maryland Institute, College of Art, Baltimore
Three of a Perfect Pair: James Grashow, Archie Rand, Frank Smith (catalogue)
James Howe Gallery, Kean College, Union, N.J.
The Word-Image in Contemporary Art
Jamaica Arts Center, Queens, N.Y., and tour
Malcolm X: The Man, the Meaning
Max Protetch Gallery, New York
A New American Flag
Arthur Roger Gallery, New York
Fear of Painting (catalogue)
Wexner Center for the Arts, Ohio State University, Columbus
Re: Framing Cartoons

1991 Brooke Alexander Editions, New York
Poets/Painters Collaborations
Baumgartner Gallery, Washington, D.C.
The Figure in the Landscape
Hyde Collection, Glens Falls, N.Y.
Just What Is It That Makes Today's Homes So Different, So Appealing? (catalogue)
Tony Shafrazi Gallery, New York, Invitational

1990 Grand Palais, Paris, and tour
SAGA-FNAC, Collectif Génération (catalogue)
Laing Art Gallery, Newcastle, and tour
Painters and Poets in Print

1989 Scott Hanson Gallery, New York (catalogue)
Hillwood Art Museum, C. W. Post Campus, Long Island University, Brookville, N.Y., and tour
Unknown Secrets, 1988–1991
Washington Projects for the Arts (WPA), Washington, D.C., and tour
The Blues Aesthetic: Black Culture and Modernism (catalogue)

1986 The Jewish Museum, New York, and tour
Jewish Themes/Contemporary American Artists II (catalogue)
Museum of the Baseball Hall of Fame, Gallery 53, Smithy Artworks, Cooperstown, N.Y.
Line Drives

1983 The Artists' Choice Museum, New York
Bodies and Souls (catalogue)
Thorpe Intermedia Gallery, New York
Humor in Art

1982 The Hudson River Museum of Westchester, Yonkers, N.Y.
Contemporary Realism

1979 Société des Artistes Indépendents, Grand Palais, Paris
L'Amérique aux Indépendents
Thorpe Intermedia Gallery, New York
Religious Art, Contemporary Directions

SELECTED WRITINGS BY THE ARTIST

1995 "A Good Dream." From *In the Night*, 1919, by Moyshe Leyb-Halpern, illustrations by Archie Rand. In *Hanging Loose* (November).

1993 *Appointment in Wipe-Ola*. New York: Hot Press.

1991 With John Yau. *Mug City Moves*. New York and Detroit: Monkey Choir Maestros.

1989 "Word and Image." *Arts* 63 (May).

SELECTED BIBLIOGRAPHY

1994 Prescott, Theodore, ed. "In Public View." *Christians in the Visual Arts Bulletin*
Cembalest, Robin. "Taking an Air Gun to the Eyes of Jesus." *The Forward*, May 6.

1993 Silver, Larry. *Art in History*. Englewood Cliffs, N.J.: Prentice-Hall.

Harris, Ellen. "Archie Rand: The Old Testament." *The Montclair Museum Bulletin* (November–December).

Rubinstein, Raphael. "A Muse in the Room, or Poets Are Poor." *Art Journal* 52 (Winter).

Yau, John. "Interactions Between Artists and Writers." (Debra Bricken Balken, ed.) *Art Journal* 52 (Winter).

1992 Knubel, Fred. "Collectif Génération: Painters, Writers, and Books, 1988–1992." *Pin* (December).

Heartney, Eleanor. "Fear of Painting." *ARTnews* 91 (November).

Sall, Joan. "Archie Rand: The Chapter Paintings." *Philadelphia Museum of Judaica Newsletter* (Fall).

Russell, John. "The Secret Life of Art Is Led in Drawings." *The New York Times*, June 28.

1991 Yau, John. *Archie Rand: The Letter Paintings*. New York.

Lattes, Abby. "Profile: Archie Rand." *Contact* (Fall–Winter).

Westfall, Stephen. "Archie Rand at Exit Art." *Art in America* 79 (October).

Pruvost-Massardier, Marylene. "Pourquoi des paillons ont-ils des ailes?" *Nouvelles de L'Estampes* (June).

Collins, Tricia, and Richard Milazzo. "From Kant to Kitsch and Back Again." *Tema Celeste* (January–February).

1990 Stella, Rachel. "Collectif Génération: Artists' Books as Objects d'Art." *Journal of Art* (December).

Schwabsky, Barry. "Forwarding Address." *Arts* 65 (November).

Kuspit, Donald. "Archie Rand." *Artforum* 29 (October).

Reid, Calvin. "Kind of Blue." *Arts* 64 (February).

1989 Yau, John. "Archie Rand: The Figure of the Artist." *Sulfur*, no. 25 (Fall).

Yau, John. "The Phoenix of the Self." *Artforum* 27 (April).

Smith, Roberta. "Tales of Ordinary People Told in Bits and Pieces." *The New York Times*, March 31.

1988 McCormick, Carlo. "Exits and Entrances." *Artforum* 26 (January).

1987 Schwabsky, Barry. "What Is Painting About? A Conversation with Archie Rand." *Arts* 61 (April).

1986 Howell, John. "Holy Art, Hot Images." *Elle* (December).

1985 Schwabsky, Barry. "Exotica: A Different World." *Arts* 59 (March).

1980 Shanks, John Arthur. "In the Shadow of God." *Midstream* 26 (January).

1979 Lane, John. "Archie Rand: The Consistency of Choice." *Arts* 54 (November).

1977 Feld, Ross. "On the Hook: The Work of Archie Rand." *Arts* 52 (December).

1974 Kramer, Hilton. "Archie Rand." *The New York Times*, November 2.

1973 Lippard, Lucy R. "Archie Rand." *ARTnews* 72 (January).

1972 Kramer, Hilton. "Archie Rand." *The New York Times*, December 2.

ELAINE REICHEK

Born in New York, New York

EDUCATION

B.F.A. Yale University
B.A. Brooklyn College

SELECTED ONE-PERSON EXHIBITIONS AND COLLABORATIONS

1995 Michael Klein Gallery, New York
Form Security Administration

1994 Center for Research in Contemporary Art, University of Texas, Arlington
At Home in America

The Jewish Museum, New York, and tour
Elaine Reichek: A Postcolonial Kinderhood (brochure)

Stichting de Appel, Amsterdam, and tour
Model Homes

1993 The Irish Museum of Art, Dublin, and tour
Home Rule (catalogue)

Norton Gallery of Art, West Palm Beach, Fla.
Sign Languages (brochure)

1992 Grey Art Gallery, New York
Native Intelligence (catalogue)

1986 Institute of Contemporary Art, University of Pennsylvania, Philadelphia
Investigations (catalogue)

1985 Center for Contemporary Art, Seattle
Collaboration with Nancy Spero (catalogue)

Snug Harbor Cultural Center, Newhouse Center for Contemporary Art, Staten Island, N.Y.
Houses

1979 Institute for Contemporary Art, P.S. 1 Museum, Long Island City, N.Y. .
Special Projects: Artist's Bedroom

SELECTED GROUP EXHIBITIONS

1995 Bronx Museum of the Arts, N.Y.
Division of Labor: Women's Work in Contemporary Art (catalogue)

Center for Contemporary Art, Seattle
KunstKabinett

1994 Art Gallery, Beaver College, Glenside, Pa.
The Social Fabric

Michael Klein Gallery, New York
An American Landscape

Museum of Contemporary Art, Sydney
Localities of Desire (catalogue)

Ruskin School of Art, Oxford University, Oxford
The Reading Room: Consider the Lilies

1993 Richard Anderson Gallery, New York
Songs of Retribution

Art Museum, Florida International University, Miami
American Art Today: Clothing as Metaphor (catalogue)

The Contemporary Arts Center, Cincinnati
The Figure as Fiction: The Figure in Visual Art and Literature (catalogue)

The Drawing Center, New York, and tour
The Return of the Cadavre Exquis (catalogue)

Fine Arts Gallery, University of Mary-
land–Baltimore County,
Catonsville, and tour
Ciphers of Identity (catalogue)
Independent Curators, Inc. (ICI),
New York, and tour
The Empty Dress (catalogue)
Barbara Krakow Gallery, Boston
*Myths and Legends as Told and
Retold*
1992 Independent Curators, Inc. (ICI),
New York, and tour
Dark Decor (catalogue)
Longwood Arts Gallery, Bronx, N.Y.
Imaging Indians
1991 Franklin Furnace Archive, Inc., New York
Burning in Hell
Lieberman & Saul Gallery, New York,
and tour
*Constructing Images: Synapse between
Photography and Sculpture*
(brochure)
The New Museum of Contemporary Art,
New York
The Interrupted Life (catalogue)
University Galleries, Illinois State Uni-
versity, Normal
Constructions of Hug
Simon Watson, New York
The Subversive Stitch
Whitney Museum of American Art
Downtown at Federal Plaza,
New York
*Site Seeing. Travel and Tourism in Con-
temporary Art* (catalogue)
1990 Ezra and Cecile Zilkha Gallery, Center
for the Arts, Wesleyan University,
Middletown, Conn.
Exoticism (brochure)
Carlo Lamagna Gallery, New York
Landscape/Mindscape
1989 Rena Bransten Gallery, San Francisco
The Big Picture
Jan Turner Gallery, Los Angeles
*Photocollage/Photomontage: The
Changing Picture 1920–89*
1988 Greenville County Museum of Art,
Greenville, S.C.
Just Like a Woman (catalogue)

Helander Gallery, Palm Beach, Fla.
Figure It Out
North Dakota Museum of Art, Grand
Forks, and tour
Frontiers in Fiber—The Americans
(catalogue)
1986 Carlo Lamagna Gallery, New York
Traps: Elements of Psychic Seduction
Bernice Steinbaum Gallery, New York
Let's Play House
Three Rivers Arts Festival, Pittsburgh
Connections: Works in Fiber
(catalogue)
1985 Laforet Art Museum, Tokyo, and tour
New York Art Now: Correspondences
(catalogue)
1984 Frauen Museum, Bonn
Neue Stofflichkeit (catalogue)
1981 Grey Art Gallery, New York
Heresies Benefit Exhibition
Lund Konsthalle, Lund, Sweden
National Women's Hall, Seneca Falls, N.Y.
*Home Work: Domestic Environment
Reflected in the Seneca Work of
Contemporary Artists* (catalogue)
1980 McIntosh Drysdale Gallery, Washington,
D.C.
Structure, Narrative, Decoration
Touchstone Gallery, New York
System, Inquiry, Translation
1978 Artists in Space (in conjunction with
New York City Department of
Transportation), New York
Ten Cases on Eighth Avenue
Whitney Museum of American Art
Downtown at Federal Plaza,
New York
Out of the House

SELECTED WRITINGS BY THE ARTIST

1995 Artist's page. *Art Journal* 54 (Spring).
1992 "Elaine Reichek." *Tema Celeste* (Fall).
"Red Delicious." *Aperture* (Fall).

SELECTED BIBLIOGRAPHY

1995 "People and Ideas: All the Nude That's
Fit to Print: Elaine Reichek and *The*

New York Times." *Aperture*, no. 129
(Winter).
Cotter, Holland. "Feminist Art, 1962
until Tomorrow Morning and Inter-
national." *The New York Times*,
March 17.
1994 Broude, Norma, and Mary D. Garrard.
The Power of Feminist Art. New York:
Harry N. Abrams.
Mahoney, Robert. "Elaine Reichek:
Assimilation in America." *Fiberarts* 21
(September–October).
Liebman, Lisa. "A Fashion Gallery: Eight
New York Artists Interpret the New
York Fall Collections." *The New York
Times Magazine*, September 18.
Corrin, Lisa G. "Installing History." *Art
Papers* 18 (July–August).
Glueck, Grace. "Consumerama's Seduc-
tive Styling; Postcolonial Kinder-
hood." *The New York Observer*,
March 21.
1993 Mensing, Margo. "Close to Home."
Fiberarts 20 (November–December).
Mensing, Margo. "Elaine Reichek, Na-
tive Intelligence." *Art Papers* (March).
1992 Olalquiaga, Celeste. *Megalopolis. Contem-
porary Cultural Sensibilities*. Min-
neapolis: University of Minnesota
Press.
Isaak, Jo-Anna. "Who's 'We,' White
Man?" *Parkett*, no. 34 (Fall).
Princenthal, Nancy. "Elaine Reichek's
'Native Intelligence.'" *The Print Col-
lector's Newsletter* (July–August).
Avgikos, Jan. "Elaine Reichek, Native
Intelligence." *Art Papers* (March).
1991 Goldberg, Vicki. "Context Is All—or
Nothing." *The New York Times*, July 7.
Handy, Ellen. "Photography's
History/History's Photography." *Pho-
tography Center Quarterly* 12 (Fall).
1990 Solnit, Rebecca. "Postmodern Primitive."
Artweek, July 9.
Morgan, Susan. "Colonialism." *Aperture*
(Spring).
1989 Smith, Roberta. "Galleries Paint a
Brighter Picture for Women." *The
New York Times*, April 14.

Miller, Charles V. "Domestic Science." *Artforum* 27 (March).

Handy, Ellen. "Installations and History." *Arts Magazine* 63 (February).

1987 McEvilley, Thomas. "Marginalia." *Artforum* 26 (December).

1985 Downey, Roger. "On Visual Arts: The Arts of Politics and Propaganda." *Seattle Times*, June 26.

1984 Robins, Corrine. *The Pluralist Era: American Art 1968–1981*. New York: Harper & Row.

1983 Moufarrege, Nicolas A. "X Equals Zero, as in Tic-Tac-Toe." *Arts Magazine* 57 (February).

1981 Perreault, John. "Homespun." *SoHo Weekly News*, December 15.

Robins, Corinne. "Verbal Image/Written Object: Connection as Meaning in the Work of Elaine Reichek." *Arts Magazine* 55 (February).

1980 Rice, Shelley. "System/Inquiry/Translation." *Artforum* 9 (September).

Perreault, John. "Old Wine, New Bottles, Bad Year." *SoHo Weekly News*, June 18.

1979 Dallier, Aline. "La Couture et la Broderie dans l'Art Contemporain." *Bulletin des Arts Plastiques* (October).

1978 Marter, Joan. "Elaine Reichek." *Arts Magazine* 52 (January).

ADAM ROLSTON

Born in Los Angeles, California, 1962

EDUCATION

B.A. Syracuse University, 1985

SELECTED ONE-PERSON EXHIBITIONS

1995 Monte Clark Gallery, Vancouver
1994 Fawbush Gallery, New York
1992 Fawbush Gallery, New York
Serial Killings
Shoshana Wayne Gallery, Santa Monica
Trojans
1991 New Era Space, New York
I Love Jody Foster

Wessel O'Connor Gallery, New York
Trojans
1990 Wessel O'Connor Gallery, New York
Sell Homosexuality

SELECTED GROUP EXHIBITIONS

1995 Fawbush Gallery, New York
Greg Kucera Gallery, Seattle
Sex
1994 The New York Public Library
Becoming Visible
Pittsburgh Center for the Arts
Working around Warhol
1993 Arena Gallery, New York
Contemporary Drawing Part III
Barbara Braathan Gallery, New York
Fawbush Gallery, New York
Gallery Artists
Fawbush Gallery, New York
John Lindell, Donald Moffett, Adam Rolston
Henie-Onstad Kunstsenter, Oslo, and tour
Tema: AIDS (catalogue)
White Columns, New York
Markets of Resistance
1992 Fawbush Gallery, New York
Summer Group Exhibition
Kunstverein, Hamburg, and Kunstmuseum, Lucerne
Ethik und Asthetik im Zeitalter von AIDS
Tramway, Glasgow
Read My Lips
1991 Jane Voorhees Zimmerli Art Museum, Rutgers University, New Brunswick, N.J.
Outrageous Desire
Regione Autonoma Della Valle D'Aosta, Italy
Theoretically Yours
1990 Aldrich Museum of Contemporary Art, Ridgefield, Conn.
The Art of Advocacy (catalogue)
Stedelijk Museum, Amsterdam
Commitment: Posters, Documents, and Video against AIDS
Simon Watson Gallery, New York
Looking at a Revolution

SELECTED WRITINGS BY THE ARTIST

1990 *AIDS Demo Graphics*, by Douglas Crimp with Adam Rolston. Seattle: Bay Press.

SELECTED BIBLIOGRAPHY

1992 Morgan, Stuart. "Queer." *frieze* (January).
1991 Wollen, Joe. Review. *Artscribe* (December).

Faust, Gretchen. Review. *Arts Magazine* 12 (December).

Rimanelli, David. Review. *Artforum* 10 (December).

Petrow, Steven. "Art Without Shame." *The Advocate* (December).

Hilditch. Review. *Downtown Express,* September 26.

Aletti, Vince. Review. *The Village Voice*, September 24.

Hirsh, David. "Desire and Emotion." *New York Native*, September 23.

Smith, Roberta. "A Plea for Safe Sex." *The New York Times*, September 20.

Goldstein, Richard. "Young Blood." *The Village Voice*, July 2.

Bordowitz, Greg. "Against Homosexuality." *Parkett* (March).

1990 Nalley, Jon. "In Your Face." *Philadelphia Au Courant*, December 10.

Raven, Arlene. "It's Been a Queer Fall." *The Village Voice*, November 13.

Hirsh, David. "Symbols, Ancient to Pop." *New York Native*, November 5.

Meyer, Richard. "Representing Ourselves." *Outweek*, August 15.

Heller, Steven. "AIDS Guerrillas." *The New York Times*, August 5.

ILENE SEGALOVE
Born in Los Angeles, California, 1950

EDUCATION

M.A. Loyola University, 1975
B.F.A. University of California, Santa Barbara, 1972

SELECTED ONE-PERSON EXHIBITIONS

1990 Laguna Museum of Art, Laguna Beach, Calif., and tour
Ilene Segalove: Why I Got into TV and Other Stories (catalogue)
1987 Saxon-Lee Gallery, Los Angeles
1983 CEPA Gallery, Center for Exploratory and Perceptual Art, Buffalo, N.Y.
Ilene Segalove
1981 China Club, Los Angeles
Ilene Segalove
1977 Arco Plaza, presented by Carp, Los Angeles
California Casual

SELECTED AUDIO PERFORMANCES

1989 *Mother's Day*
Baseball Cards
1988 *Domestic Intelligence*
1987 *TV Times*
1986 *Body Parts*
1985 *Hanukkah*
Boys

SELECTED GROUP EXHIBITIONS

1994 Long Beach Museum of Art, Calif.
Women in Video, Pioneers
1993 Santa Barbara Contemporary Arts Forum, Calif.
Love and Other Fatal Attractions
1992 Houston Center for Photography
Icons and Idols: TV Images
Independent Curators, Inc. (ICI), New York, and tour
Good Stories, Well Told: Video Art for Young Audiences (brochure)
1989 California Museum of Photography, University of California at Riverside
Biennial I

Laforet Art Museum, Tokyo
Images of American Pop Culture Today III
Los Angeles Municipal Art Gallery
About TV: Appropriation and Parody in Contemporary Video Art
Whitney Museum of American Art, New York
Identity: Representations of the Self (catalogue)
Whitney Museum of American Art, New York
Suburban Home Life: Tracking the American Dream (catalogue)
1988 Institute of Contemporary Art, Boston
Meditated Narrative: Constructed and Invented Myth (catalogue)
Irvine Fine Arts Center, Calif.
Bare Facts, Sly Humor
Kijkhuis, The Hague, Netherlands
More TV Stories
Long Beach Museum of Art, Calif.
Personal Histories: Ilene Segalove and Skip Sweeney
Santa Barbara Contemporary Arts Forum
Home Show
1987 The Los Angeles County Museum of Art
Avante-Garde in the Eighties (catalogue)
The Museum of Contemporary Art (MOCA), Los Angeles, and tour
The Arts for Television (catalogue)
Taipei Fine Arts Museum, Taiwan
Contemporary Southern California Art (catalogue)
1985 Institute of Contemporary Art, Boston, and tour
Revising Romance: New Feminist Video
International Center of Photography, New York
Video Feature
Museum of Modern Art, New York
Video from Vancouver to San Diego
1983 Galleries of the Claremont Colleges, Montgomery Gallery, Calif.
Contemporary Collage: Extensions (catalogue)
Institute of Contemporary Art, Boston
New Soap Video
Institute of Contemporary Art, Boston
Portraits (brochure)

Long Beach Museum of Art, Calif.
At Home
Museum of Modern Art, New York, and tour
New Narrative
1982 Contemporary Arts Museum, Houston
Some Contemporary Portraits
Museum of Art, Rhode Island School of Design, Providence
California Photography
Windows on White, New York
Post-Romance: Artists' Valentines (catalogue)
1981 Newport Harbor Art Museum, Newport Beach, Calif.
InsideOut: Self Beyond Likeness (catalogue)
1979 Los Angeles Institute of Contemporary Art
Real Angelinos
1978 California State University, Los Angeles
The Oriental Mystique
Contemporary Arts Museum, Houston, and tour
American Narrative/Story Art: 1967-77
Independent Curators, Inc. (ICI), New York, and tour
The Sense of the Self: From Self-Portrait to Autobiography (catalogue)
Whitney Museum of American Art Downtown at Federal Plaza, New York
Out of the House (brochure)
1977 California State University, Los Angeles
Miniature (catalogue)
Los Angeles Institute of Contemporary Art
Hildegard Duane and Ilene Segalove
Whitney Museum of American Art, New York
Biennial Exhibition (catalogue)
1976 San Francisco Museum of Modern Art
Video Art: An Overview (brochure)
1975 Long Beach Museum of Art, Calif., and tour
Southland Video Anthology
Whitney Museum of American Art, New York
Biennial Exhibition (catalogue)
1974 Womanspace, Los Angeles

In an Attempt to Recognize Myself
(performance)

1973 California Institute of the Arts, Valencia
     How to Look Prettier in a Picture
     California Institute of the Arts, Valencia
     Mother's Gifts (performance)

SELECTED WRITINGS BY THE ARTIST

1989 "Last Words: Sweet Radio Reminders."
     Radio Guide 1 (March).
1987 "Learning about Great Art." *Journal:*
     A Contemporary Art Magazine.

SELECTED BIBLIOGRAPHY

1993 Leddy, Pat. "Television Universe."
     Artweek, July 8.
     Frank, Peter. "Art Pick of the Week."
     L.A. Weekly, July 2–8.
     Kapitanoff, Nancy. "Ilene Segalove's Pho-
     tographic Stories." *Los Angeles Times*
     Calendar, June 20.
     Pincus, Robert L. "Proof Artists Attacked
     Photography's Image." *The San Diego*
     Union Tribune, January 3.
1990 Grundberg, Andy. "Talent for Making
     the Ordinary Seem Offbeat." *The*
     New York Times, August 31.
1989 Goldring, Nancy. "Identity: Representa-
     tions of the Self." *Arts Magazine* 64
     (March).
1986 Reidy, Robin. "TV Stories: The Adven-
     tures of Ilene Segalove." *Afterimage* 14
     (October).
1985 Lewis, Louise. "Where Are the Dau-
     miers of Video Art?" *Media Arts* 1
     (Fall).
     King, Susie. "A Successful Model Ignored?"
     Media Arts 1 (Spring–Summer).
1984 Ohland, Gloria. "Segalove's Latest Is a
     Riot." *L.A. Weekly* 6 (April).
1981 Brown, Gillian, and Sidney Jason.
     "What's Wrong with This Picture?"
     Obscura 1 (January–February).
1979 Larsen, Susan C. "The Nation—Los An-
     geles: A Fantasy Life." *ARTnews* 78
     (May).
1977 "Ilene Segalove's Portraits." *Artweek* 8
     (October 15).

Frueh, Joanna. "Art in the Me Decade."
     [Chicago] *Reader* (October 7).
Battcock, Gregory, ed. *New Artists' Video:*
     A Critical Anthology. New York: Dut-
     ton.
1976 Ollman, Leah. "A Wry Look at Life."
     Artweek, October 8.
     Marmer, Nancy. "Los Angeles." *Artforum*
     14 (April).

ART SPIEGELMAN
Born in Stockholm, Sweden, 1948

EDUCATION

State University of New York at Binghamton,
     1965–1968
Honorary degree, State University of New York
     at Binghamton, 1995

SELECTED ONE-PERSON EXHIBITIONS

1994 Galerie St. Etienne, New York
     Drawn to Text (brochure)
1992–93 Galerie St. Etienne, New York, and
     tour
     The Road to Maus (brochure)
1991 Mercat del Born, Barcelona
     Museum of Modern Art, New York
     Making Maus (brochure)
1988 Martyrs Memorial and Museum of the
     Holocaust, Los Angeles
     Maus
1987 Smith Gallery, London
1986 Museum of Cartoon Art, Port Chester,
     N.Y.

SELECTED GROUP EXHIBITIONS

1995 Karl Hammer Gallery, Chicago
     Cold/Mix Art
1991 Aldrich Museum of Contemporary Art,
     Ridgefield, Conn.
     Art of Advocacy (catalogue)
     Institute of Contemporary Art, Univer-
     sity of Pennsylvania. Philadelphia
     Devil on the Stairs (brochure)
1990 Exit Art Gallery, New York
     Personal Commix!

Loughelton Gallery, New York
     Re: Framing Cartoons
1989 The Ohio State University Cartoon,
     Graphic, and Photographic Arts
     Research Library, and Smithson-
     ian Institution Traveling Exhibi-
     tion Service, and tour
     Great American Comics: 100 Years of
     Cartoon Art (catalogue)
1987 The Jewish Museum, New York, and tour
     Jewish Themes/Contemporary American
     Artists II (catalogue)
     New York Institute of Technology,
     New York, and tour
     Raw: Images from the Graphix Maga-
     zine That Overestimates the Taste of
     the American Public (catalogue)
1986 Kulturhuser, Stockholm
     Avante-Garde Comics
1983 Hallwalls Gallery, Buffalo, N.Y.
     Comic Relief
     Seibu Gallery, Tokyo
     Raw N.Y.
     Whitney Museum of American Art,
     New York
     The Comic Art Show (catalogue)
1971 New York Cultural Center
     Seventy-five Years of the Comics
1969 Corcoran Gallery of Art, Washington,
     D.C.
     Phonus Balonus

SELECTED WRITINGS BY THE ARTIST

1994 *Maus: CD ROM.* New York: The Voyager
     Company.
     The Wild Party, by Joseph M. March, il-
     lustrations by Art Spiegelman. New
     York: Raw Books.
1991 *Maus II: And Here My Troubles Began.*
     New York: Pantheon.
1987 *Read Yourself Raw: Comix Anthology for*
     Damned Intellectuals. New York: Pan-
     theon.
1986 *Maus I: A Survivor's Tale.* New York: Pan-
     theon.
1980 *Two-Fisted Action Painters.* New York:
     Raw Books.
1979 *Every Day Has Its Dog.* New York: Raw
     Books.

1979 *Work and Turn*. New York: Raw Books.

1977 *Breakdowns*. New York: Belier Press.

1974 *Ace Hole, Midget Detective*. San Francisco: Apex Novelties.

1973 *Whole Grains: A Book of Quotations*. Ed. with Bob Schneider. New York: Douglas/Links.

1970 *The Complete Mr. Infinity*. San Francisco: San Francisco Book Company.

SELECTED BIBLIOGRAPHY

1988 Gitlin, Todd. "Hip Deep in Post Modernism." *The New York Times*, November 6.

1987 Cantor, J. "Kat and Maus." *The Yale Review* 77 (Autumn).

Gerber, D. A. "Of Mice and Jews." *American Jewish History* 77.

Summerfield, G. "Comics and Tragedy." *Tikkun* 2 (July).

Gapnic, A. "The Holocaust Comic Book." *The New Republic*, June 22.

B.R. "Richard Gehr on Art Spiegelman." *Artforum* 25 (February).

Grossman, R. "Mauschwitz." *The Nation*, January 10.

1986 Dale, I. "Trapped by Life: Pathos and Humor among Mice and Men." *The Comics Journal*.

ALLAN WEXLER
Born in Bridgeport, Connecticut, 1949

EDUCATION

M.A. Pratt Institute, 1976

B.A. Rhode Island School of Design, 1972

B.F.A. Rhode Island School of Design, 1971

SELECTED ONE-PERSON EXHIBITIONS

1994 Ronald Feldman Fine Art, New York
Allan Wexler: Buckets, Sinks, Gutters
Hochschule der Kunste, Berlin, Germany
The Small Buildings, Furniture, and Utensils of Allan Wexler

1993 Karl Ernst Museum, Hagen, Germany, and tour
Allan Wexler—Structures for Reflection (catalogue)

1992 DeCordova Museum and Sculpture Park, Lincoln, Mass.
Table/Building/Landscape and Proposals for a Picnic Area

1991 San Diego Museum of Contemporary Art, La Jolla, Calif.

1990 Ronald Feldman Fine Arts, New York
Table/Building/Landscape
Horace Richter Gallery, Old Jaffa, Israel
Allan Wexler: Furniture Prototypes for Production

1989 Institute of Contemporary Art, University of Pennsylvania, Philadelphia
Allan Wexler (catalogue)
University Gallery, University of Massachusetts, Amherst
Allan Wexler: Dining Rooms and Furniture for the Typical House

1988 Ronald Feldman Fine Arts, New York
Small Buildings, Furniture and Proposals for the Typical House (catalogue)
The Jewish Museum, New York
Sukkah: Allan Wexler

1985 Ronald Feldman Fine Arts, New York
Two Architectures: Susana Torre and Allan Wexler
List Art Center, Brown University, Providence, R.I. (catalogue)

SELECTED GROUP EXHIBITIONS AND COLLABORATIONS

1995 Brattleboro Museum & Art Center, Brattleboro, Vt.
Universe of Meaning (brochure)
Eastern State Penitentiary, Philadelphia
Prison Sentences: The Prison as Subject (brochure)
Three Rivers Art Festival, Pittsburgh

1994 Gwenda Jay Gallery, Chicago
Function-Dysfunction
Katonah Museum of Art, Katonah, N.Y. (in collaboration with Ellen Wexler)
Shelter and Dreams (catalogue)
Museum fur Gestaltung, Zurich
Tedes Haus ein Kunsthaus

Wexner Center for the Arts, Ohio State University, Columbus
House Rules (catalogue)

1993 Aldrich Museum of Contemporary Art, Ridgefield, Conn.
The Fall Fashion
John Michael Kohler Arts Center, Sheboygan, Wis.
Discursive Dress

1992 Four Walls @ Artists Space
The Radio Show/Unrealized Projects
Karl Ernst Osthaus Museum, Hagen, Germany
Trivial Machines

1991 University Galleries, Illinois State University, Normal
Constructions of Meanings (catalogue)
University Gallery, University of Massachusetts, Amherst
Home Rooms (catalogue)
Weatherspoon Art Gallery, University of North Carolina at Greensboro
The Chair: From Object to Artifact (catalogue)

1990 Barbicon Art Gallery, Barbicon Center, London
The Jewish Experience in the Art of the 20th Century

1988 Mattress Factory Gallery, Pittsburgh
Bed/Sitting Room for Artist in Residence (permanent installation) (catalogue)

1987 The Art Museum, Princeton University, Princeton, N.J.
Little Office Building #2
Neuberger Museum of Art, State University of New York at Purchase
Pure Room for the Memory Theater
Parish Art Museum, Southampton, N.Y.
Architects Design Bird Houses
Workbench Gallery, New York
Chair/Building

1986 Art et Industrie, New York
Picket Fence Furniture
Creative Time at Brooklyn Bridge Anchorage, Brooklyn, N.Y.
Pure Room for the Memory Theater of Giulio Camillo

1985 Storefront for Art and Architecture, New York

After Titled Arc

1984 Art on the Beach (Creative Time),
New York
Beach Building
Whitney Museum of American Art
Downtown at the Federal Build-
ing, New York
Metamanhattan
1983 Institute for Contemporary Art, P.S. 1
Museum, Long Island City, N.Y.
Four Proposals for Little Buildings
1979 The Hudson River Museum of West-
chester, Yonkers, N.Y.
1,000 Boxes
Newark Museum, Newark, N.J.
Mind, Child, Architecture
P.S. 1, Institute for Art and Urban Re-
sources, Long Island City, N.Y.,
and tour
New Americans (catalogue)
1978 The Drawing Center, New York
Elements of the House
1976 Institute for Architecture and Urban
Studies, New York
Alternate Positions in Architecture

SELECTED WRITINGS BY THE ARTIST

1990 "September 18, 1990–September 28, 1990."
Harvard Architecture Review.

SELECTED BIBLIOGRAPHY

1995 "Art World: Jailhouse Commissions." *Art
in America* 83 (May).
Seward, Keith. "Allan Wexler." *Artforum*
33 (February).
1994 Nasatir, Judith. *Interior Design* 65 (July).
Louie, Elaine. "Where the House is All
Play." *The New York Times*, May 5.
Becker, Jochen. "Allan Wexler." *Kunstfo-
rum* (January–February).
Morgan, Robert C. "Doing Art in
Poland: Trying Not to Make Sense."
Cover (January).
1993 Christ, Ronald, and Dennis Dollens.
New York: Nomadic Design. New
York: Rizzoli International Publica-
tions, Inc.
Berendsmeier, Jorg. "Absurdes Leben im

Haus aus Kisten." *Recklinghauser
Zeitung*, October 5.
Phillips, Patricia. "Sitting Up: Critical
Chairs." *Sculpture* 12 (Summer).
1992 Cembalest, Robin. "Reviews." *ARTnews*
90 (April).
Levin, Kim. "Voice Choices." *The Village
Voice*, February 4.
Cotter, Holland. "Allan Wexler—On the
Dubious Comforts of Home." *The
New York Times*, January 31.
1991 Podos, Lisa. *Essay in Explorations II: The
New Furniture.* New York: American
Craft Museum.
Smith, Roberta. "Explorations II: The
New Furniture." *The New York Times*,
July 19.
1990 Phillips, Patricia. "Allan Wexler." *Artfo-
rum* 28 (Summer).
Raven, Arlene. "Choices." *The Village
Voice*, July 17.
1988 Muschamp, Herbert. "A Reconsideration
of Beach Houses." *Smart* (Fall).
Aaron, Jane. "Transformation and Con-
nections." *Metropolis* 7 (June).
Vogel, Carol. "Architect's Vision: Pyra-
mid to Suburbia." *The New York
Times*, February 25.
1987 Princenthal, Nancy. "After *Tilted Arc* at
Storefront for Art and Architecture."
Art in America 86 (February).
1986 Phillips, Patricia. *Artforum* 25 (Novem-
ber).
1985 "Portfolio, Allen Wexler: Small Build-
ings." *Gallery Arts* (November).
Phillips, Patricia. *Artforum* 23 (April).
Giovannini, Joseph. Review. *The New
York Times*, February 7.
1981 Perreault, John. Review. *SoHo News*, July 1.
1978 "Recent Work, The Domestication of
Nature." *The Journal of the London
Architecture Club.*
1976 Sky, Alison, and Michelle Stone. *Unbuilt
America. Manhattan Skyline World
Trade Center Transformation.* New
York: McGraw-Hill.

HANNAH WILKE

Born in New York, New York, 1940
Died 1993

EDUCATION

B.A. Tyler School of Art, 1960
B.S. Temple University, 1961

SELECTED ONE-PERSON EXHIBITIONS

1994 Ronald Feldman Fine Arts, New York,
and tour
Intra-Venus (catalogue)
1990 Genovese Graphics Gallery, Boston
Hannah Wilke, Past and Present
1989 Ronald Feldman Fine Arts, New York
About Face
Gallery 210, University of Missouri at
St. Louis
Hannah Wilke: A Retrospective (cata-
logue)
1984 Ronald Feldman Fine Arts, New York
Support Foundation Comfort
Joseph Gross Gallery, University of Ari-
zona at Tucson
1979 Washington Project for the Arts (WPA),
Washington, D.C.
Performalist Self-Portraits, 1942–79
1978 Ronald Feldman Fine Arts, New York
Through the Large Glass
Ronald Feldman Fine Arts, New York
(I Object) Performalist Self-Portraits
P.S. 1, Institute for Art and Urban Re-
sources, Long Island City, N.Y.
So Help Me Hannah
1976 Fine Arts Gallery, University of Califor-
nia at Irvine
*Hannah Wilke, Scarification Pho-
tographs and Videotapes* (and
performance*)
1975 Ronald Feldman Fine Arts, New York
Galerie Gerald Pitzer, Paris
Five American Women in Paris
1974 Ronald Feldman Fine Arts, New York
Margo Leavin Gallery, Los Angeles
Drawings from the Flower Series
1972 Ronald Feldman Fine Arts, New York

1987 *The Starving Artists' Cookbook**
1982 A.I.R. Gallery, New York
*So Help Me Hannah**
1981 Fifth International Congress of Psycho-
analysis, Movimento Freudiano
Internazionale, at the Plaza Hotel,
New York
Sex and Language
1978 Susan Caldwell Gallery, New York
*Give: Hannah Wilke Can—A Living
Sculpture Needs to Make a Living*
(benefit performance for City
Walls)
1977 *The Last Tapes of Marcel Duchamps**
1976 Philadelphia Museum of Art
*Philly** and *C'est la Vie, Rrose**
Philadelphia Museum of Art
*Through the Large Glass**
Whitney Museum of American Art, New
York, and Albright-Knox Art
Gallery, Buffalo, N.Y.
*I'd Be Rich as Rockefeller—My Country
'Tis of Thee*
1975 Paula Cooper Gallery, New York
Invasion Performance (opening of
Linda Benglis show)
1974 The Kitchen, New York
Hannah Wilke, Super T-Art (for the
series "Soup and Tart")
1970 Arts Council of Great Britain
The Great Ice Cream Robbery

SELECTED GROUP EXHIBITIONS

1995 Allen Memorial Art Museum, Oberlin
College, Ohio, and tour
*Action/Performance and the
Photograph*
Exit Art, New York
Endurance
The Helsinki City Art Museum & The
Nordic Arts Centre, Helsinki,
Finland, and tour
Borealis 7—Desire.
The Parrish Art Museum, Southampton,
N.Y.
Face Value: American Portraits

The Swiss Institute, New York
Chocolate! (catalogue)
1994 Cleveland Center for Contemporary Art
*Outside the Fam: Performance and the
Object* (catalogue)
Institute of Contemporary Art, Univer-
sity of Pennsylvania, Philadelphia
Face Off: The Portrait in Recent Art
(catalogue)
Isabella Stewart Gardner Museum, Boston
*Arts Lament: Creativity in the Face of
Death* (catalogue)
Women's Caucus for Art, Denise Bibro
Gallery, New York
Diagnosis: Breast Cancer
1993 Art Contemporain, Lyon, France
Here's Looking at Me
Haines Gallery, San Francisco
Body Parts
Phyllis Kind Gallery, New York
M'Aidez/Mayday
Weatherspoon Art Gallery, University of
North Carolina at Greensboro,
and tour
*Fictions of the Self: The Portrait in
Contemporary Photography*
(catalogue)
Whitney Museum of American Art,
New York
*Abject Art: Repulsion and Desire in
American Art* (catalogue)
David Zwirner Gallery, New York
Coming to Power
1992 494 Gallery, New York
Taboo: Bodies Talk
Ledis Flam, New York
Rubber Soul
Ghia Gallery, San Francisco
*Love and Death: Growing Old in
America Is a Sin*
Tel Aviv Museum of Art
Not for Sale (catalogue)
1991 Alternative Museum, New York
Artists of Conscience (catalogue)
Wright State University, Dayton, Ohio
Parents
1990 The Forum Gallery, Jamestown Commu-
nity College, Jamestown, N.Y.,
and tour

Aging: The Process, The Perception
(catalogue)
Katonah Museum of Art, Katonah, N.Y.
The Technological Muse (catalogue)
1989 Cincinnati Art Museum, and tour
*Making Their Mark: Women Artists
Move into the Mainstream
1970–1985* (catalogue)
Whitney Museum of American Art,
New York
Image World: Art and Media Culture
(catalogue)
1988 Museum Ludwig, Cologne
*Marcel Duchamp and the Avant-garde
Since 1950*
National Portrait Gallery, Washington,
D.C.
*The Artist's Mother: Portraits and
Homage* (brochure)
Whitney Museum of American Art
Downtown at Federal Plaza,
New York
*Modes of Address: Language in Art
Since 1960* (catalogue)
1987 David Winton Bell Gallery, Brown Uni-
versity, Providence, R.I.
*Alternative Supports: Contemporary
Sculpture on the Wall* (catalogue)
Longwood Arts Gallery, Bronx, N.Y., and
tour
*The Blue Angel: The Decline of Sexual
Stereotypes in Post-Feminist Sculp-
ture* (catalogue)
White Columns, New York
Spring Film
1986 Alternative Museum, New York
Liberty and Justice (catalogue)
Snug Harbor Cultural Center, Newhouse
Center for Contemporary Art,
Staten Island, N.Y.
New Liberty Monuments
Bernice Steinbaum Gallery, New York
Let's Play House
Women's Caucus for Art 1986 National
Conference at The Clocktower,
Institute for Art and Urban Re-
sources, Long Island City, N.Y.
Letters
1985 Avenue B Gallery, New York, and tour

Feminists and Misogynists Together at Last

Ronald Feldman Fine Arts, New York
  Benefit Exhibition Sale for Fashion Moda

Münchner Stadtmuseum, Munich, and tour
  Das Akfoto

Schoharie County Arts Council Gallery, Cobbleskill, N.Y.
  Vessels of Meaning

Storefront for Art and Architecture, New York
  After "Tilted Arc"

1984 Franklin Furnace Archive, Inc., New York
  Artist's Call

Ted Greenwald Gallery, New York
  Artists' Weapons

Sidney Janis Gallery, New York
  American Women Artists (catalogue)

Margo Leavin Gallery, Los Angeles
  American Sculpture

The New Museum of Contemporary Art, New York
  Art and Ideology (catalogue)

Sculpture Center, New York
  Sound/Art

World's Fair—Women's Pavilion, New Orleans
  American Women Artists

1983 Linda Farris Gallery, Seattle
  Self Portraits (catalogue)

Whitney Counterweight, No. 4, New York

Windows on White, New York
  Protective Device

1982 Ronald Feldman Fine Arts, New York
  Revolutions Per Minute—The Art Record (and performance)

Institute for Contemporary Art, P.S. 1 Museum, Long Island City, N.Y.
  Sound Corridor

Emily Lowe Gallery, Hofstra University, Hempstead, N.Y.
  Androgyny and Art

Women's Caucus for the Arts, Westbeth Gallery, New York
  Sexuality in Art: Two Decades from a Feminist Perspective

1981 Franklin Furnace Archive, Inc., New York
  The Page as Alternative Space

Franklin Furnace Archive, Inc., New York
  Soundworks

The Kitchen, New York
  Pictures and Promises

P.S. 1, Institute for Art and Urban Resources, Long Island City, N.Y.
  Figuratively Sculpting

1980 Studio Amazone, Amsterdam
  Androgyny

Tangeman Fine Arts Gallery, University of Connecticut, Storrs
  The Sense of Self

1979 Hampshire College of Art Gallery, Amherst, Mass.
  Images of the Self

Museum of Art, Smith College, Northampton, Mass.
  Contemporary Women in the Visual Arts

Washington Project for the Arts (WPA), Washington, D.C.
  Performalist Self-Portraits

1978 Bronx Museum of the Arts, N.Y.
  Personal Visions

Marian Goodman Gallery, New York
  Objects

The High Museum of Art, Atlanta
  19 Galleries

Independent Curators, Inc. (ICI), New York, and tour
  The Sense of the Self: From Self-Portrait to Autobiography (catalogue)

Margo Leavin Gallery, Los Angeles
  Three Generations: Structures in College

P.S. 1, Institute for Art and Urban Resources, Long Island City, N.Y.
  So Help Me Hannah—Snatch Shots with Ray Guns

1977 Rutgers University Art Gallery, Camden, N.J.
  Six Women Artists

Whitney Museum of American Art Downtown at Federal Plaza, New York
  Nothing but Nudes

Women's Building, Los Angeles
  Contemporary Issues—Work by Women on Paper

1976 Fine Arts Gallery, University of California at Irvine
  Art in Landscape

Indianapolis Museum of Art
  Painting and Sculpture Today

Louisiana Museum of Modern Art, Humleback, Denmark
  SoHo—Downtown Manhattan

1975 Bronx Museum of the Arts, N.Y.
  The Year of the Woman

California Institute of the Arts, Valencia
  Anonymous Was a Woman (catalogue)

The Contemporary Arts Center, Cincinnati
  Painting and Sculpture Today 1974

Fine Arts Building, New York
  Photography Not Photography (and performance)

Harcus Kradow Sonnebend Rosen, Boston
  Drawings

Indianapolis Museum of Art
  Painting and Sculpture Today

Landhaus, Graz, Austria
  Art as Living Ritual

Margo Leavin Gallery, Los Angeles
  Drawings

Museum of Art, Smith College, Northampton, Mass.
  Non-traditional Sculpture

Women's Interart Center, New York
  Wall Sculpture

1973 New York Cultural Center, New York
  Women Choose Women (catalogue)

Whitney Museum of American Art, New York
  Whitney Biennial (catalogue)

1972 Kunsthaus, Hamburg, Germany
  American Women Artists

Newark Museum, Newark, N.J.
  Painting or Sculpture?

1971 Richard Feigen Gallery, New York
  10 Painters, 1 Sculptor

1966 Castagno Gallery, New York
  3-D Group Show

SELECTED WRITINGS BY THE ARTIST

1988 "Seura Chaya." *New Observations* (June).

1981 "Thank You from Hannah Wilke." In

"Artists' Valentines: A Portfolio." *The Atlantic Monthly* 247 (February).

SELECTED BIBLIOGRAPHY

1995 Lippard, Lucy R. *The Pink Glass Swan: Selected Feminist Essays on Art.* New York: The New Press.

"Performance Art Survey." *Flash Art* 28 (Summer).

Levin, Kim. "Chocolate." *The Village Voice,* May 23.

"Art World: Awards." *Art in America* 83 (May).

Cooper, Dennis. "Vincent Fecteau." *Artforum* 33 (April).

Glueck, Grace. "The Darker Side of Chocolate." *The New York Observer,* April 19.

Slonim, Jeffrey. "In with the Out Crowd." *Artforum* 33 (March).

1994 Broude, Norma, and Mary D. Garrard, eds. *Power of Feminist Art.* New York: Harry N. Abrams.

Smith, Roberta. "The Year in the Arts." *The New York Times,* December 25.

Schaffner, Ingrid. "Reviews." *Artforum* 33 (September).

Apple, Jacki. "Performance Is Dead. Long Live Performance Art!" *High Performance* (Summer).

"Obituaries." *Art in America* 82 (August).

Cheney, Elyse. "Hannah Wilke: Intra-Venus." *Art Papers* 18 (July–August).

Roberts, Katrina. "Power, Pleasure, Pain." *Harvard Magazine* (July–August).

Hirsch, Faye. "Hannah Wilke." *Flash Art* 27 (May–June).

Kubitza, Annette. "Hannah Wilke: Bildervollstandiger und unvollstadiger Schonheit." *Frauen Kunst Wissenschaft* (May).

Cottingham, Laura. "The Damned Beautiful." *The New Art Examiner* 21 (April).

Perchuk, Andrew. "Reviews: Hannah Wilke, Ronald Feldman Fine Arts." *Artforum* 32 (April).

"Ronald Feldman Fine Arts, Inc." *Likovnebesede* (March).

Smith, Roberta. "An Artist's Chronicle of a Death Foretold." *The New York Times,* January 30.

Hess, Elizabeth. "Fem Fatale." *The Village Voice,* January 25.

1993 Gardner, James. *Culture or Trash?* New York: Carol Publishing Group.

Kelly, James. *Living Materials: A Sculptor's Handbook.* New York: Holt, Rinehart and Winston.

Lippard, Lucy R. "In the Flesh: Looking Back and Talking Back." *Women's Art Magazine* (September–October).

Hess, Elizabeth. "Abject Lessons." *The Village Voice,* July 13.

Glueck, Grace. "Witness to the Making of a Most Glamourous Borough." *The New York Observer,* May 31.

Raven, Arlene. "Marching On." *The Village Voice,* April 6.

Raven, Arlene. "Hannah Wilke, 1940–1993." *The Village Voice,* February 23.

Smith, Roberta. "Hannah Wilke, 52: Artist Dies; Used Female Body as Her Subject." *The New York Times,* January 29.

1992 Brown, Elizabeth. *The Living Object.* Akron, Ohio: Oberlin College.

Meidav, Edie. "Expressing the Inexpressible." *Artweek* 23 (January 30).

Hess, Elizabeth. "Secret Garden." *The Village Voice,* January 28.

1991 Plagens, Peter. "Frida on Our Minds." *Newsweek,* May 27.

1990 *Heresies* 7, no. 1.

Heresies 7, no. 24.

Wooster, Ann-Sargent. "Hannah Wilke: Whose Image Is It?" *High Performance* (Fall).

Kuspit, Donald. "The Only Mortal." *Artforum* 28 (February).

Johnson, Ken. "Hannah Wilke at Ronald Feldman." *Art in America* 78 (January).

1989 Liu, Catherine. "Hannah Wilke." *Artforum* 28 (December).

Danto, Arthur. "Women Artists, 1970–85." *The Nation,* December 25.

Akers, Jama J. "Wilke Uses Nudes and Bubble Gum in Her Female-oriented Work." *The KC View* (September).

Cone, Tim. "Art and the Law: Oldenburg's Privacy, Wilke's Publicity." *Arts* 64 (September).

Kimmelman, Michael. "Hannah Wilke." *The New York Times,* September 29.

Hess, Elizabeth. "Self- and Selfless Portraits." *The Village Voice,* September 26.

Edelson, Mary Beth. "Objections of a 'Goddess Artist.'" *The New Art Examiner* 16 (April).

1988 Heartney, Eleanor. "A Necessary Transgression." *The New Art Examiner* 16 (November).

Wooster, Ann-Sargent. "Attention, Art Shoppers: A Collector's Primer." *Seven Days* 1 (June 8).

1987 Sischy, Ingrid. "Nine Beautitudes on Eight Pages." *Artforum* 25 (March).

1986 Stein, Harvey. *Artists Observed.* New York: Harry N. Abrams.

Nemeczek, Alfred. "Frauenbilder von Kunstlerinnen—Made in New York." *Art, Das Kunstmagazin* (Hamburg) (September).

1984 Levin, Kim. "Hannah Wilke: Support Foundation Comfort." *The Village Voice,* December 18.

Brenson, Michael. "Art: Political Subjects." *The New York Times,* February 24.

1983 Roth, Moira. *The Amazing Decade: Women and Performance Art in America 1970–1980.* Los Angeles: Astro Artz.

1982 Russell, John. "The Critic's Notebook." *The New York Times,* June 3.

1981 Perreault, John. "Good for the Figure." *SoHo Weekly News,* December 1.

Hammond, Harmony. "A Sense of Touch." *Heresies,* no. 12.

"New York: Sexe et Langage." *Spirales* (Milan) (June).

1980 Goldberg, Roselee. *Performance: Live Art 1980 to the Present.* New York: Harry N. Abrams.

Alba, Richard D. *Ethnic Identity: The Transformation of White America.* New Haven: Yale University Press, 1990.

———, ed. *Ethnicity and Race in the U.S.A.: Toward the Twenty-first Century.* London and Boston: Routledge & Kegan Paul, 1985.

Allen, J. *500 Great Jewish Jokes.* New York: Signet, 1990.

Allen, Theodore W. *The Invention of the White Race: Racial Oppression and Social Control.* Vol. 1. New York: Verso, 1994.

Anderson, Benedict. *Imagined Communities: Reflections on the Origin and Spread of Nationalism.* London and New York: Verso, 1983.

Balibar, Etienne, and Immanuel Wallerstein. *Race, Nation, Class: Ambiguous Identities.* Trans. Chris Turner. London and New York: Verso, 1991.

Balka, Christie, and Andy Rose. *Twice Blessed: On Being Lesbian, Gay, and Jewish.* Boston: Beacon Press, 1989.

Baskin, Judith R., ed. *Women of the World: Jewish Women and Jewish Writing.* Detroit: Wayne State University Press, 1994.

Baum, Charlotte, Paula Hyman, and Sonya Michel. *The Jewish Woman in America.* New York: Dial Press, 1976.

Bauman, Zygmunt. *Modernity and Ambivalence.* Ithaca, N.Y.: Cornell University Press, 1991.

Bearden, Romare, and Harry Henderson. *A History of African-American Artists from 1792 to the Present.* New York: Pantheon, 1993.

Berger, Maurice. *How Art Becomes History: Essays on Art, Society, and Culture in Post–New Deal America.* New York: HarperCollins, 1992.

———, ed. *Modern Art and Society: An Anthology of Social and Multicultural Readings.* New York: HarperCollins, 1994.

———, Brian Wallis, and Simon Watson, eds. *Constructing Masculinity.* New York and London: Routledge, 1995.

Berman, Paul, ed. *Blacks and Jews: Alliances and Arguments.* New York: Delacorte Press, 1994.

Bernal, Martin. *Black Athena: The Afroasiatic Roots of Classical Civilization.* Vol. 1: *The Fabrication of Ancient Greece, 1785–1985.* New Brunswick, N.J.: Rutgers University Press, 1987.

———. *Black Athena: The Afroasiatic Roots of Classical Civilization.* Vol. 2: *The Archaeological and Documentary Evidence.* New Brunswick, N.J.: Rutgers University Press, 1991.

Bernstein, Richard. *The Dictatorship of Virtue: Multiculturalism, Diversity, and the American Future.* New York: Knopf, 1994.

Bersani, Leo. *Homos.* Cambridge, Mass.: Harvard University Press, 1995.

Bhabha, Homi K. *The Location of Culture.* London and New York: Routledge, 1994.

Biale, Rachel. *Women and Jewish Law: An Exploration of Women's Issues in Halakhic Sources.* New York: Schocken Books, 1984.

Boyarin, Daniel. *Carnal Israel: Reading Sex in Talmudic Culture.* Berkeley and Los Angeles: University of California Press, 1993.

Broude, Norma, and Mary D. Garrard. *The Power of Feminist Art: The American Movement of the 1970's, History and Impact.* New York: Harry N. Abrams, 1994.

Brown, Wesley, and Amy Ling, eds. *Imagining America: Stories from the Promised Land.* New York: Persea Books, 1991.

———, eds. *Visions of America: Personal Narratives from the Promised Land.* New York: Persea Books, 1992.

Bryson, Scott, Barbara Kruger, Lynne Tillman, and Jane Weinstock, eds. *Beyond Recognition: Representation, Power, and Culture.* Berkeley and Los Angeles: University of California Press, 1992.

Bulkin, Elly, Minnie Bruce Pratt, and Barbara Smith. *Yours in Struggle: Three Feminist Perspectives on Anti-Semitism and Racism.* Brooklyn, N.Y.: Long Haul Press, 1984.

Butler, Judith. *Gender Trouble: Feminism and the Subversion of Identity.* New York and London: Routledge, 1990.

Carter, Stephen L. *The Culture of Disbelief: How American Law and Politics Trivialize Religious Devotion.* New York: Basic Books, 1993.

Castillo-Speed, Lillian, ed. *Latina Women's Voices from the Borderlands.* New York: Simon and Schuster, 1995.

Chapman, Abraham, ed. *Jewish American Literature: An Anthology of Fiction, Poetry, Autobiography, and Criticism.* New York: New American Library, 1974.

Clifford, James. *The Predicament of Culture: Twentieth-Century Ethnography, Literature, and Art.* Cambridge, Mass.: Harvard University Press, 1988.

Cohen, Naomi W. *Jews in Christian America: The Pursuit of Religious Equality.* New York: Oxford University Press, 1992.

Cohen, Steven M. *American Assimilation or Jewish Revival?* Bloomington and Indianapolis: Indiana University Press, 1988.

———. *American Modernity and Jewish Identity.* New York: Tavistock, 1983.

———, and Paula E. Hyman, eds. *The Jewish Family: Myths and Realities.* New York and London: Holmes and Meier, 1986.

Cottingham, Laura. *The Power of Feminist Art.* New York: Harry N. Abrams, 1994.

Cripps, Thomas. *Slow Fade to Black: The Negro on American Film, 1900–1942.* New York: Oxford University Press, 1977.

Cuddihy, Jon Murray. *The Ordeal of Civility: Freud, Marx, Lévi-Strauss, and the Jewish Struggle with Modernity.* 2d ed. Boston: Beacon Press, 1987.

Czitrom, Daniel J. *Media and the American Mind from Morse to McLuhan.* Chapel Hill: University of North Carolina Press, 1982.

Degler, Carl N. *Culture versus Biology in the Thought of Franz Boas and Alfred L. Kroeber.* New York: Berg, 1989.

De Lauretis, Teresa. *Technologies of Gender.* Bloomington and Indianapolis: Indiana University Press, 1987.

Deleuze, Gilles, and Félix Guattari. *A Thousand Plateaus: Capitalism and Schizophrenia.* Trans. Brian Massumi. Minneapolis: University of Minnesota Press, 1987.

Dembo, L. S. *The Monological Jew: A Literary Study.* Madison: University of Wisconsin Press, 1988.

Dent, Gina, ed. *Black Popular Culture.* Seattle: Bay Press, 1992.

De Vos, George, and Lola Romanucci-Ross. *Ethnic Identity: Cultural Communities and Change.* Chicago: University of Chicago Press, 1975.

Early, Gerald, ed. *Lure and Loathing: Essays on Race, Identity, and the Ambivalence of Assimilation.* New York: Viking Penguin, 1992.

Eckardt, A Roy. *Black-Woman-Jew: Three Wars for Human Liberation.* Bloomington and Indianapolis: Indiana University Press, 1989.

Efron, John. *Defenders of the Race: Jewish Doctors and Race Science in Fin-de-Siècle Europe.* New Haven: Yale University Press, 1994.

Ehrenreich, Barbara. *Fear of Falling: The Inner Life of the Middle Class.* New York: Pantheon Books, 1989.

———. *The Hearts of Men: American Dreams and the Flight from Commitment.* New York: Anchor Books, 1983.

Eilberg-Schwartz, Howard. *People of the Body: Jews and Judaism from the Embodied Perspective.* Albany: State University of New York Press, 1992.

———. *The Savage in Judaism: An Anthropology of Israelite Religion and Ancient Judaism.* Bloomington and Indianapolis: Indiana University Press, 1990.

Eisen, Arnold. *The Chosen People in America.* Bloomington and Indianapolis: Indiana University Press, 1995.

Ferguson, Russel, Martha Gever, Trinh T. Minh-ha, and Cornel West, eds. *Out There: Marginalization and Contemporary Cultures.* New York: The New Museum of Contemporary Art; Cambridge, Mass.: MIT Press, 1992.

Ferguson, Russel, William Olander et al. *Discourse: Conversations in Postmodern Art and Culture.* New York: The New Museum of Contemporary Art, 1989.

Fiske, John. *Understanding Popular Culture.* Boston: Unwin Hyman, 1989.

Foster, Hal. *Recordings: Art, Spectacle, Cultural Politics.* Port Townsend, Wash.: Bay Press, 1985.

Frankel, Jonathan, and Steven J. Zipperstein. *Assimilation and Community: The Jews in Nineteenth-Century Europe.* Cambridge: Cambridge University Press, 1991.

Freud, Sigmund. *Briefe, 1873–1939.* Ed. Ernst and Lucie Freud. Frankfurt: Fischer, 1960.

———. *The Complete Psychological Works of Sigmund Freud, Standard Edition.* Ed. and trans. J. Strachey, A. Freud, A. Strachey, and A. Tyson. 24 vols. London: Hogarth Press, 1955–1974.

Fuss, Diana, ed. *Inside/Out: Lesbian Theories, Gay Theories.* New York and London: Routledge, 1991.

Gabler, Neal. *An Empire of Their Own: How the Jews Invented Hollywood.* New York: Crown, 1988.

Garber, Marjorie. *Vested Interests: Cross Dressing and Cultural Anxiety.* New York: Harper Perennial, 1993.

Gates, Henry Louis, Jr. *Loose Canons: Notes on the Culture Wars.* New York: Oxford University Press, 1992.

———. *The Signifying Monkey: A Theory of African American Literary Criticism.* New York: Oxford University Press, 1988.

Gerber, David A. *Anti-Semitism in American History.* Champaign: University of Illinois Press, 1986.

Gilman, Sander L. *The Case of Sigmund Freud: Medicine and Identity at the Fin De Siècle.* Baltimore: The Johns Hopkins University Press, 1993.

———. *Difference and Pathology: Stereotypes of Sexuality, Race, and Madness.* Ithaca, N.Y.: Cornell University Press, 1985.

———. *Freud, Race, and Gender.* Princeton: Princeton University Press, 1993.

———. *The Jew's Body.* New York and London: Routledge, 1991.

Ginsburg, Faye, and Anna Lowenhaupt Tsing, eds. *Uncertain Terms: Negotiating Gender in American Culture.* Boston: Beacon Press, 1990.

Goldberg, David Theo, and Michael Krausz, eds. *Jewish Identity.* Philadelphia: Temple University Press, 1993.

Gordis, David H. and Yoav Ben-Horin. *Jewish Identity in America.* Los Angeles: Wilstein Institute, University of Judaism; Hoboken, N.J.: Ktav, 1991.

Green, Rayna, ed. *That's What She Said: Contemporary Poetry and Fiction by Native American Women.* Bloomington and Indianapolis: Indiana University Press, 1984.

Greenberg, Clement. *Art and Culture: Critical Essays.* Boston: Beacon Press, 1961.

———. *The Collected Essays and Criticism.* Vol. 2: *Arrogant Purpose, 1945–1949.* Chicago: Chicago University Press, 1986.

Grubb, Nancy, ed. *Making Their Mark.* New York: Abbeville Press, 1989.

Guilbaut, Serge. *How New York Stole the Idea of Modern Art.* Chicago: University of Chicago Press, 1983.

———, ed. *Reconstructing Modernism: Art in New York, Paris, and Montreal 1945–1964.* Cambridge, Mass.: MIT Press, 1992.

Guttmann, Allen. *The Jewish Writer in America: Assimilation and the Crisis of Identity.* Oxford and New York: Oxford University Press, 1971.

Hartman, Geoffrey H., and Sanford Budick, eds. *Midrash and Literature.* New Haven and London: Yale University Press, 1986.

Heine, Heinrich. *Werke.* Ed. Klaus Briegleb. 12 vols. Berlin: Ullstein, 1981.

Heinze, A. *Adapting to Abundance: Jewish Immigrants, Mass Consumption, and the Search for American Identity.* New York: Columbia University Press, 1990.

Henry, Sondra, and Emily Taitz. *Written Out of History: Our Jewish Foremothers.* New York: Biblio Press, 1983.

Heschel, Susannah, ed. *On Being a Jewish Feminist.* New York: Schocken Books, 1983.

Hill, Herbert, and James E. Jones Jr., eds. *Race in America: The Struggle for Equality.* Madison: University of Wisconsin Press, 1993.

Hobsbawm, E. J. *Age of Extremes: The Short Twentieth Century, 1914–1991.* New York: Pantheon, 1995.

Hollinger, David A. *Post-Ethnic America: Beyond Multiculturalism.* New York: HarperCollins, 1995.

hooks, bell. *Black Looks: Race and Representation.* Boston: South End Press, 1992.

———. *Killing Rage: Ending Racism.* New York: Henry Holt, 1995.

———. *Yearning: Race, Gender, and Cultural Politics.* Boston: South End Press, 1990.

———, and Cornel West. *Breaking Bread: Insurgent Black Intellectual Life.* Boston: South End Press, 1991.

Hosken, Fran P. *The Hosken Report: Genital/Sexual Mutilation of Females.* Lexington, Mass.: Women's International Network News, 1994.

Howe, Irving. *World of Our Fathers.* New York: Schocken, 1989; Harcourt Brace, illustrated edition, 1989.

Huyssen, Andreas. *After the Great Divide: Modernism, Mass Culture, Postmodernism.* Bloomington and Indianapolis: Indiana University Press, 1986.

Hyman, Paula E. *Gender and Assimilation in Modern Jewish History: The Roles and Representations of Women.* Seattle: University of Washington Press, 1995.

Ignatiev, Noel. *How the Irish Became White.* New York: Routledge, 1995.

Jacobs, Joseph. *Studies in Jewish Statistics, Vital and Anthropometric.* London: D. Nutt, 1891.

Jacobson, Dan. *The God-Fearer.* London: Bloomsbury, 1992.

Joselit, Jenna Weissman. *New York's Jewish Jews: The Orthodox Community in the Interwar Years.* Bloomington and Indianapolis: Indiana University Press, 1990.

Karp, Abraham. *Haven and Home: A History of the Jews in America.* New York: Schocken, 1985.

Katchor, Ben. *Cheap Novelties: The Pleasures of Urban Decay.* New York: Penguin, 1991.

Kaya/Kantrowitz, Melanie, and Irena Kelpfisz, eds. *The Tribe of Dina: A Jewish Women's Anthology.* Montpelier, Vt.: Sinister Wisdom Books, 1986; expanded edition, Boston: Beacon Press, 1989.

Kelley, Robin D. G. *Race Rebels: Culture, Politics, and the Black Working Class.* New York: Free Press, 1994.

Klein, Marcus. *Foreigners: The Making of American Literature, 1900–1940.* Chicago: University of Chicago Press, 1981.

Klingenstein, Susanna. *Jews in the American Academy, 1900–1940: The Dynamics of Intellectual Assimilation.* New Haven and London: Yale University Press, 1991.

Knox, Robert. *The Races of Men: A Fragment.* Philadelphia: Lea and Blanchard, 1850.

Kousser, Morgan, and James M. McPherson. *Region, Race, and Reconstruction: Essays in Honor of C. Vann Woodward.* Oxford and New York: Oxford University Press, 1982.

Kruger, Barbara, and Phil Mariani, eds. *Remaking History.* Seattle: Bay Press, 1989.

Krupnick, Mark, ed. *Displacements: Derrida and After.* Bloomington and Indianapolis: Indiana University Press, 1983.

Kuspit, Donald B. *Clement Greenberg: Art Critic.* Madison: University of Wisconsin Press, 1979.

Lerner, Michael, and Cornel West. *Jews and Blacks: The Hard Hunt for Common Ground.* New York: G. P. Putnam's Sons, 1995.

Levin, Kim, ed. *Beyond Walls and Wars: Art, Politics, and Multiculturalism.* New York: Midmarch Arts Press, 1992.

Levine, Lawrence W. *The Unpredictable Past: Explorations in American Cultural History.* Oxford and New York: Oxford University Press, 1993.

Levine, Peter. *Ellis Island to Ebbets Field: Sport and the American Jewish Experience.* New York: Oxford University Press, 1992.

Lippard, Lucy R. *Mixed Blessings: New Art in Multicultural America.* New York: Pantheon Books, 1990.

———. *The Pink Glass Swan: Selected Feminist Essays on Art.* New York: The New Press, 1995.

———. *Six Years: The Dematerialization of the Art Object, 1966–1972.* New York and Washington, D.C.: Praeger Publishers, 1973.

Lipsitz, George. *Time Passages: Collective Memory and American Popular Culture.* Minneapolis: University of Minnesota Press, 1990.

Lott, Eric. *Love and Theft: Blackface Minstrelsy and the American Working Class.* New York: Oxford University Press, 1993.

Lucie-Smith, Edward. *Movements in Art Since 1945: Issues and Concepts.* 3rd ed. London and New York: Thames and Hudson, 1995.

Lyotard, Jean-François. *The Postmodern Condition: A Report on Knowledge.* Trans. Geoff Bennington and Brian Massumi. Foreword by Fredric Jameson. Minneapolis: University of Minnesota Press, 1984.

McElroy, Guy, ed. *Facing History: The Black Image in American Art.* San Francisco: Bedford Arts Publishers, 1990.

McEvilley, Thomas. *Art & Otherness: Crisis in Cultural Identity.* Kingston, N.Y.: Documentext/McPherson & Company, 1992.

Mamet, David. *Some Freaks.* New York: Viking Press, 1989.

Medding, Peter Y., ed. *Studies in Contemporary*

Jewry, An Annual. Vol. 8: *A New Jewry? America Since the Second World War.* New York: Oxford University Press, 1992.

Miller, Alice. *Banished Knowledge: Facing Childhood Injuries.* Trans. Leila Vennewitz. New York: Doubleday, 1990.

Miller, Daniel, ed. *Unwrapping Christmas.* Oxford: Oxford University Press, 1993.

Moore, Deborah, ed. *To the Golden Cities: Pursuing the American Jewish Dream in Miami and L.A.* New York: The Free Press, 1994.

Mosse, George L. *Toward the Final Solution: A History of European Racism.* New York: Howard Fertig, 1975.

Mulvey, Laura. *Visual and Other Pleasures.* Bloomington and Indianapolis: Indiana University Press, 1989.

Nochlin, Linda, and Tamar Garb, eds. *The Jew in the Text: Modernity and the Construction of Identity.* London: Thames and Hudson, 1995.

O'Brien, Mark, and Craig Little, eds. *Reimaging America: The Arts of Social Change.* Philadelphia: New Society Publishers, 1990.

Okihiro, Gary. *Margins and Mainstreams: Asians in American History and Culture.* Seattle: University of Washington Press, 1994.

Olsen, Tillie. *Silences.* New York: Delacorte/Seymour Lawrence, 1978.

Ortner, S. B., and H. Whitehead. *Sexual Meanings: The Cultural Construction of Gender and Sexuality.* Cambridge: Cambridge University Press, 1981.

Paese, Donald E., ed. *National Identities and Post-Americanist Narratives.* Durham: Duke University Press, 1994.

Parles, Alejandro, and Ruben G. Rumbant. *Immigrant America: A Portrait.* Berkeley and Los Angeles: University of California Press, 1990.

Plaskow, Judith. *Standing Again at Sinai: Judaism from a Feminist Perspective.* San Francisco: Harper & Row, 1989.

Pogrebin, Letty Cottin. *Deborah, Golda, and Me: Being Female and Jewish in America.* Garden City, N.Y.: Doubleday, 1991.

Reed, Ishmael. *Airing Dirty Laundry.* Reading, Mass.: Addison-Wesley, 1993.

Roediger, David R. *Towards the Abolition of Whiteness.* New York: Verso, 1994.

———. *The Wages of Whiteness.* New York: Revolutionary Books, 1991.

Rosenberg, Harold. *Barnett Newman.* New York: Harry N. Abrams, 1978.

———. *Discovering the Present: Three Decades in Art, Culture, and Politics.* Chicago: University of Chicago Press, 1973.

Ross, Andrew. *No Respect: Intellectuals and Popular Culture.* New York: Routledge, 1989.

Roth, Philip. *Reading Myself and Others.* New York: Farrar, Straus and Giroux, 1975.

Rubin, Barry. *Assimilation and Its Discontents.* New York: Random House, 1995.

Russo, Vito. *The Celluloid Closet: Homosexuality in the Movies.* New York: Harper & Row, 1981.

Rutherford, Jonathan, ed. *Identity: Community, Culture, Difference.* London: Lawrence & Wishart, 1990.

Samuel, Raphael, and Gareth Stedman Jones, eds. *Culture, Ideology, and Politics: Essays for Eric Hobsbawm.* London and Boston: Routledge & Kegan Paul, 1983.

Saxton, Alexander. *The Rise and Fall of the White Republic: Class Politics and Mass Culture in Nineteenth Century America.* London and New York: Verso, 1991.

Schlesinger, Arthur M., Jr. *The Disuniting of America: Reflections on a Multicultural Society.* Knoxville, Tenn.: Whittle Communications, 1991; New York: Norton, 1993.

Schneider, S. W. *Jewish and Female: Choices and Changes in Our Lives Today.* New York: Simon and Schuster, 1984.

Schwarzer, Mitchell. *German Architectural Theory and the Search for Modern Identity.* Cambridge: Cambridge University Press, 1995.

Sedgwick, Eve Kosofsky. *Epistemology of the Closet.* Berkeley and Los Angeles: University of California Press, 1990.

Shorris, Earl. *Latinos: A Biography of the People.* New York: W. W. Norton, 1992.

Skerry, Peter. *The Mexican-Americans: The Ambivalent Minority.* Cambridge, Mass.: Harvard University Press, 1993.

Sklare, M., and J. Greenblum. *Jewish Identity and the Suburban Frontier: A Study of Group Survival in the Open Society.* 2d ed. Chicago: University of Chicago Press, 1979.

Sollors, Werner. *The Invention of Ethnicity.* New York: Oxford University Press, 1989.

Sombart, Werner. *The Jews and Modern Capitalism.* Trans. M. Epstein. Glencoe, Ill.: The Free Press, 1951.

Spivak, Gayatri Chakravorty. *In Other Worlds: Essays in Cultural Politics.* New York and London: Routledge, 1987.

Steele, Shelby. *The Content of Our Character: A New Vision of Race in America.* New York: Harper Perennial, 1991.

Suleiman, Susan Rubin. *Subversive Intent: Gender, Politics, and the Avant-Garde.* Cambridge, Mass.: Harvard University Press, 1990.

Takaki, Ronald T. *A Different Mirror: A History of Multicultural America.* Boston: Little, Brown, 1993.

Terkel, Studs. *Race: How Blacks and Whites Think and Feel about the American Obsession.* New York: The New Press, 1992.

Theweleit, Klaus. *Male Fantasies,* 2 vols. Minneapolis: University of Minnesota Press, 1987.

Torgovnick, Marianna DeMarco. *Crossing Ocean Parkway: Readings by an Italian American Daughter.* Chicago: University of Chicago Press, 1994.

Turner, B. *The Body and Society: Explorations in Social Theory.* Oxford: Basil Blackwell, 1984.

Visotzky, Rabbi Burton L. *Reading the Book: Making the Bible a Timeless Text.* Garden City, N.Y.: Doubleday/Anchor Books, 1991.

Wald, Priscilla. *Constituting Americans: Cultural Anxiety and Narrative Form.* Durham: Duke University Press, 1995.

Walker, Alice, and Pratibha Parmar. *Warrior Masks: Female Genital Mutilation and the Sexual Blinding of Women.* New York: Harcourt Brace, 1993.

Wallace, Michelle. *Black Macho and the Myth of the Superwoman.* New York: Dial Press, 1979; new edition, New York: Verso, 1990.

Waters, Mary C. *Ethnic Options: Choosing Identities in America.* Berkeley and Los Angeles: University of California Press, 1990.

Wegner, Judith Romney. *Chattel or Person? The Status of Women in the Mishnah.* New York and Oxford: Oxford University Press, 1990.

Weinberg, Sydney Stahl. *The World of Our Mothers: The Lives of Jewish Immigrant Women*. Chapel Hill: University of North Carolina Press, 1988.

Weindling, Paul. *Health, Race, and German Politics between National Unification and Nazism, 1870–1945*. Cambridge: Cambridge University Press, 1989.

Welch, Susan, and Fred Ullrich. *The Political Life of American Jewish Women*. New York: Biblio Press, 1984.

West, Cornel. *Race Matters*. Boston: Beacon Press, 1993.

Weyr, Thomas. *Hispanic U.S.A.: Breaking the Melting Pot*. New York: Harper & Row, 1988.

Williams, Patricia. *The Alchemy of Race and Rights: Diary of a Law Professor*. Cambridge, Mass.: Harvard University Press, 1991.

Wistrich, Robert. *Anti-Semitism: The Longest Hatred*. London: Thames Metheun, 1991.

Wittig, Monique. *The Lesbian Body*. New York: William Morrow, 1975.

Wolfe, Alan, ed. *America at Century's End*. Berkeley and Los Angeles: University of California Press, 1991.

Young, Crawford, ed. *The Rising Tide of Cultural Pluralism: The Nation-State at Bay?* Madison: University of Wisconsin Press, 1993.

Creators and Disturbers: Reminiscences by Jewish Intellectuals of New York. Drawn from Conversations with Bernard Rosenberg and Earnest Goldstein. New York: Columbia University Press, 1982.

EXHIBITION CATALOGUES

The Art of Memory: The Loss of History. The New Museum of Contemporary Art, New York, 1985–1986.

Bad Girls. The New Museum of Contemporary Art, New York, 1994. Cambridge, Mass.: MIT Press, 1994.

Barnett Newman. Thomas B. Hess, Curator. Museum of Modern Art, New York, 1971.

Biennial Exhibition. Whitney Museum of American Art, New York, 1993.

Biennial Exhibition. Whitney Museum of American Art, New York, 1995.

Black Male: Representations of Masculinity in Contemporary American Art. Thelma Golden, Assistant Curator. Whitney Museum of American Art, New York, 1994.

Bridges and Boundaries: African Americans and American Jews. Ed. Jack Salzman with Adina Back and Gretchen Sullivan Sorin. New York: George Braziller in association with The Jewish Museum, 1992.

Ciphers of Identity. Organized with an essay by Maurice Berger. Fine Arts Gallery, University of Maryland Baltimore County, 1993.

Damaged Goods: Desire and the Economy of the Object. Brian Wallis, Adjunct Curator. The New Museum of Contemporary Art, New York, 1986.

The Decade Show: Frameworks of Identity in the 1980's. Museum of Contemporary Hispanic Art, The New Museum of Contemporary Art, The Studio Museum in Harlem, New York, 1990.

Difference: On Representation and Sexuality. Kate Linker, Guest Curator, Jane Weinstock, Guest Curator/Film and Video. The New Museum of Contemporary Art, New York, 1984–1985.

Dislocations. Ed. Robert Storr. Museum of Modern Art, New York, 1991.

From Inside Out: Eight Contemporary Artists. Ed. Susan Tumarkin Goodman. The Jewish Museum, New York, 1993.

Getting Comfortable in New York: The American Jewish Home, 1880–1950. Ed. Susan L. Braunstein and Jenna Weissman Joselit. The Jewish Museum, New York, 1990.

Jewish Themes/Contemporary American Art. Ed. Susan Tumarkin Goodman. The Jewish Museum, New York, 1982.

Jewish Themes/Contemporary American Art II. Ed. Susan Tumarkin Goodman. The Jewish Museum, New York, 1986.

Mistaken Identities. Abigail Solomon-Godeau and Constance Lewallen, Curators. University Art Museum, University of California at Santa Barbara, 1992–1993.

Points of Entry: A Nation of Strangers. Museum of Photographic Arts, San Diego, 1995.

Points of Entry: Reframing America. Center for Creative Photography, Tucson, 1995.

Points of Entry: Tracing Cultures. The Friends of Photography, San Francisco, 1995.

A Postcolonial Kinderhood: An Installation by Elaine Reichek. Exhibition brochure text by Emily Whittemore. The Jewish Museum, New York, 1994.

Race and Representation: Art/Film/Video. Hunter College Art Gallery, New York, 1987.

States of Loss: Migration, Displacement, Capitalism, and Power. Gary Sangster, Curator. Jersey City Museum, 1993–1994.

ARTICLES

Adler, Jerry. "Sweet Land of Liberties." *Newsweek*, July 10, 1995, 18–23.

Adler, R. "The Jew Who Wasn't There: Halacha and the Jewish Woman." *Response: A Contemporary Jewish Review* 3, no. 18 (1973): 77–83.

Akam, Everett. Review of *Multiculturalism and the Canon of American Culture*, edited by Hans Bak. *Journal of American History* 81 (December 1994): 1278–1279.

Alloway, Lawrence. "Women's Art in the 70's." *Art in America* 64 (May–June 1976): 64–72.

———. "More on Women's Art: An Exchange" (responses and reply to Alloway's "Women's Art in the 70's"). *Art in America* 64 (November-December 1976): 11–23.

Appiah, Kwame Anthony, and Henry Louis Gates, Jr. "Multiplying Identities." *Critical Inquiry* 18 (Summer 1992): 625.

Appleby, Joyce. "Recovering America's Historic Diversity: Beyond Exceptionalism." *Journal of American History* 79 (September 1992): 419–431.

Aronowitz, Stanley. "Reflections on Identity." *October* 61 (Summer 1992): 91–101.

"The Artist as Jew." *The Economist*, April 16, 1988, 113.

Atlas, James. "Memo to Clinton: Intellectuals." *Tikkun* 8 (January 1993): 11.

Avgikos, Jan. Review of *Ciphers of Identity*. *Artforum* 32 (March 1994): 91.

Bartky, S. "Women, Bodies, and Power: A Research Agenda for Philosophy." *Newsletter on Feminism and Philosophy* (American Philosophical Association) 89, no. 1 (1989): 79–80.

Bhabha, Homi. "Freedom's Basis in the Intermediate." *October* 61 (Summer 1992): 46–57.

———. "Of Mimicry and Man: The Ambivalence of Colonial Discourse." *October* 28 (Spring 1984): 125-133.

Biale, David. "Jewish Identity in the 1990s" (response to Ilene Philipson's "What's the Big I.D.? The Politics of the Authentic Self"). *Tikkun* 6 (November 1991): 60–62.

Bourne, Jennie. "Homelands of the Mind: Jewish Feminism and Identity Politics." *Race and Class* 29, no. 1 (1987).

Bowman, James. "Small Wars, No Jokes: *The Dictatorship of Virtue: Multiculturalism and the Battle for America's Future,* by Richard Bernstein." *Times Literary Supplement*, June 23, 1995, 14.

Brubach, Holly, moderator. "Whose Vision Is It, Anyway?" (a conversation between Linda Nochlin and Thierry Mugler). *The New York Times Magazine*, July 17, 1994: 46–49.

Cembalest, Robin. "Goodbye, Columbus?" *ARTnews* 90 (October 1991): 104–109.

Chicago Cultural Studies Group. "Critical Multiculturalism." *Critical Inquiry* 18 (Spring 1992): 530–555.

Cohen, L. "Encountering Mass Culture at the Grassroots: The Experience of Chicago Writers in the 1920s." *American Quarterly* 41 (March 1989): 6–33.

Cohen, S. B. "Philip Roth's Would-be Patriarchs and Their Shikses and Shrews." *Studies in American Jewish Literature* 1 (Spring 1975): 16–29.

Davis, Douglas. "Issues & Commentary: Multicultural Wars." *Art in America* 83 (February 1995): 35–45.

Drucker, Johanna. Review of *Mixed Blessings: New Art in a Multicultural America*, by Lucy Lippard. *Art Journal* 50 (Winter 1991): 109–111.

Ducille, Ann. "Dyes and Dolls: Multicultural Barbie and the Merchandising of Difference." *Differences: A Journal of Feminist Cultural Studies* 6 (Spring 1994): 46–68.

Dundes, Alan. "The J.A.P. and the J.A.M. in American Jokelore." *Journal of American Folklore* 98, no. 390 (1985): 456–475.

Einzig, Barbara. "Tom Tom Club: *Art & Otherness: Crisis in Cultural Identity,* by Thomas McEvilley." *The Village Voice*, January 26, 1993, 79–80.

Epstein, Steven. "Gay Politics, Ethnic Identity: The Limits of Social Construction." *Socialist Review* 17 (May–August 1987): 9–54.

Fishkin, Shelley Fisher. Review of *Jews in the American Academy, 1900–1940: The Dynamics of Intellectual Assimilation,* by Susanne Klingenstein. *Journal of American History* 79 (September 1992): 693.

Foucault, Michel. "Friendship as a Lifestyle." *Gay Information* 7 (1981). Rpt. in *Foucault Live*. New York: Semiotexte, 1989.

Fuchs, Lawrence H. "The Secrets of Citizenship: *Out of the Barrio: Toward a New Politics of Hispanic Assimilation*, by Linda Chavez." *The New Republic*, March 23, 1992, 37–41.

Galchinsky, Michael. "Glimpsing Golus in the Golden Land: Jews and Multiculturalism in America." *Judaism* 43 (Fall 1994): 360–368.

Gates, Henry Louis, Jr. "Blacklash?" *The New Yorker*, May 17, 1993, 42–44.

———. "The Culture of Politics and the Politics of Culture: *Discourse and the Other*, by W. Lawrence Hogue/*Duties, Pleasures, and Conflicts*, by Michael Thelwell." *Callaloo* 14 (Summer 1991): 752–754.

———. "The Meaning of America: *Culture of Complaint,* by Robert Hughes," *The New Yorker,* April 19, 1993, 113–117.

———. "Multicultural Madness" (response to Ilene Philipson's "What's the Big I.D.? The Politics of the Authentic Self"). *Tikkun* 6 (November 1991): 55–58.

———. "What's in a Name?" *Dissent* 36 (Fall 1989): 487–495.

———. "Whose Canon Is It, Anyway?" *New York Times Book Review*, February 26, 1989, 1, 44ff.

Glazer, Nathan. "In Defense of Multiculturalism." *The New Republic*, September 2, 1991, 18–22.

Hacker, Andrew. "'Diversity' and Its Dangers: *A Different Mirror: A History of Multicultural America*, by Ronald Takaki/*Race Matters*, by Cornel West/*The Scar of Race*, by Paul M. Sniderman and Thomas Piazza/and others." *The New York Review of Books*, October 7, 1993, 21–25.

Hall, Ronald E. "The 'Bleaching Syndrome': Implications of Light Skin for Hispanic American Assimilation." *Hispanic Journal of Behavioral Sciences* 16 (August 1994): 307–314.

Heartney, Eleanor. "Identity Politics at the Whitney." *Art in America* 81 (May 1993): 42–47.

———. "Multicultural Survey: *Mixed Blessings: New Art in a Multicultural America,* by Lucy R. Lippard." *Art in America* 80 (September 1992): 35–39.

Heschel, Susannah. "A Few Universals, A Few Particulars" (review of *Where Are We?: The Inner Life of America's Jews*, by Leonard Fein and *American Assimilation or Jewish Revival?* by Steven M. Cohen). *New York Times Book Review*, June 19, 1988, 19.

Hutcheon, Linda. "Productive Comparative Angst: Comparative Literature in the Age of Multiculturalism." *World Literature Today* 69 (Spring 1995): 299–303.

Jacobs, Jack. Review of *Assimilation and Community: The Jews in Nineteenth-Century Europe*, edited by Jonathan Frankel and Steven J. Zipperstein. *Journal of Interdisciplinary History* 24 (Autumn 1993): 315–316.

Jaher, R. C. "The Quest for the Ultimate Shiksa." *American Quarterly* 35 (Winter 1983): 518–541.

Johnson, Charles. "The Color Black." *New York Times Book Review*, May 23, 1993, 7.

Jonas, George. "The End of Jewry?" *Saturday Night* 110 (March 1995): 18–26.

Kantrowitz, Barbara (with Jeanne Gordon, Lori Rotenberk, Kate Robins, and Karen Springen). "The Ultimate Assimilation." *Newsweek*, November 24, 1986, 80.

Kelly, Mary. "On Femininity." *Control* 11 (November 1979): 14–15.

Kleeblatt, Norman L. "Multivalent Voices." *Art in America* 83 (December 1995): 29–31, 35.

Lerner, Michael. "Jews Are Not White." *The Village Voice*, May 18, 1993, 33–34.

Lieberman, Rhonda. "Glamorous Jewesses." *Artforum* 31 (January 1993): 5–6.

———. "Goys and Dolls: On the Further Adventures of Jewish Barbie." *Artforum* 33 (April 1995): 21–22.

———. "Je M'Appelle Barbie: On the Other American Princess." *Artforum* 34 (March 1995): 20–21.

———. "The Loser Thing." *Artforum* 31 (September 1992): 78–92.

———. "Miami Fantasia, Part I: The Fountainbleau." *Artforum* 31 (February 1993): 8–9.

———. "Miami Fantasia, Part II: Rhonda Lieberman on the Jew Beat Again." *Artforum* 31 (March 1993). 5–6.

———. "Revenge of the Mouse Diva: Karen Kilimnik's Favorite Things." *Artforum* 32 (February 1994): 76–82, 111.

———. "Springtime for Grunge." *Artforum* 31 (April 1993): 8–9.

McDonald, Terrence J. "History under the Sign of Assimilation: *Speaking of Diversity: Language and Ethnicity in Twentieth-Century America*, by Philip Gleason/*The Disuniting of America: Reflections of a Multicultural Society*, by Arthur M. Schlesinger, Jr." *Reviews in American History* 22 (June 1994): 358–364.

McEvilley, Thomas. "Same Difference." *Artforum* 31 (May 1993): 14.

Maddox, Richard. "Religious Transformations: *Unwrapping Christmas*, edited by Daniel Miller." *Sociology of Religion* 55 (Winter 1994): 496.

Min, Yong Soon. "Territorial Waters: Mapping Asian American Identity." *Cultural Studies* 4 (October 1990).

Miron, Susan. "Jewish Anatomy: Is It Destiny?" (review-essay of three books by Sander L. Gilman). *Congress Monthly* 59 (November–December 1992).

Mooney, Carolyn J. "America's Many Religions." *Chronicle of Higher Education*, June 9, 1995, A10–A11.

Morrison, Toni. "Unspeakable Things Unspoken: The Afro-American Presence in American Literature." *Michigan Quarterly Review* 28 (Winter 1989): 1–34.

Murray, Wendy. "The Holiday Dilemma." *Instructor* 102 (November 1992): 50–53.

New, Elisa. "Killing the Princess: The Offense of a Bad Defense." *Tikkun* 4 (March 1988): 17–18.

Newfield, Christopher. "What Is Political Correctness? Race, the Right, and Managerial Democracy in the Humanities." *Critical Inquiry* 19 (Winter 1993): 308–336.

Nochlin, Linda. "Learning from 'Black Male'." *Art in America* 83 (March 1995): 86–91.

Norwood, Stephen H. "My Son the Slugger: Sport and the American Jew: *Ellis Island to Ebbets Field: Sport and the American Jewish Experience*, by Peter Levine." *Reviews in American History* 21 (September 1993): 465–470.

Ockman, Carol. "Two Large Eyebrows à l'Orientale: Ethnic Stereotypes in Ingres' *Baronne de Rothschild*." *Art History* 14 (December 1991): 525.

Owens, Craig. "A la Recherche du Récit Perdu." In *Beyond Recognition: Representation, Power, and Culture*, ed. Scott Bryson, Barbara Kruger, Lynne Tillman, and Jane Weinstock. Berkeley and Los Angeles: University of California Press, 1992.

———. "The Discourse of the Other: Feminists and Postmodernism." In *Beyond Recognition: Representation, Power, and Culture*.

Philipson, Ilene. "What's the Big I.D.?: The Politics of the Authentic Self—Comment/Reply." *Tikkun* 6 (November 1991): 51–55.

Piper, Adrian. "Passing for White, Passing for Black." *Transition* 58 (1992): 4–32.

Podhoretz, Norman. "My Negro Problem and Ours." *Commentary* (February 1963).

Pogrebin, Letty Cottin. "Anti-Semitism in the Women's Movement." *Ms. Magazine* (June 1982). Rpt. in *Deborah, Golda and Me: Being Female and Jewish in America*. Garden City, N.Y.: Doubleday, 1991.

Prell, Riv-Ellen. "Rage and Representation: Jewish Gender Stereotypes in America." In *Uncertain Terms: Negotiating Gender in American Culture*, ed. Faye Ginsburg and Anna Lowenhaupt Tsing. Boston: Beacon Press, 1990.

"Race and Racism: American Dilemmas Revisited." *Salamagundi*, nos. 104–105 (Fall 1994–Winter 1995).

Ravitch, Diane. "Multiculturalism Yes, Particularism No." *Chronicle of Higher Education*, October 24, 1990, A44.

Robinson, Walter. "Venice Preview, 1993." *Art in America* 81 (March 1993): 29.

Rockland, Michael Aaron. "The Jewish Side of Philip Roth." *Studies in American Jewish Literature* 1 (Spring 1975): 29–37.

Rogin, Michael. "The Sword Became a Flashing Vision: D. W. Griffith's *The Birth of a Nation*." *Representations*, no. 9 (Winter 1985).

Said, Edward. "An Ideology of Difference." *Critical Inquiry* 12 (Autumn 1985): 38–58.

Sarna, Jonathan D. "The Secret of Jewish Continuity." *Commentary* 98 (October 1994): 55–58.

Sawislak, Karen. Review of *A Different Mirror: A History of Multicultural America*, by Ronald Takaki. *Journal of American Ethnic History* 13 (Summer 1994): 49–50.

Schlesinger, Arthur, Jr. "The Cult of Ethnicity, Good and Bad." *Time*, July 8, 1991, 21.

Schneider, S. W. "'In a Coma! I Thought She Was Jewish': Some Truths and Some Speculations about Jewish Women and Sex." *Lilith: The Jewish Women's Magazine* 5 (Spring–Summer 1977): 5–8.

Scott, Joan. "Multiculturalism and the Politics of Identity." *October* 61 (Summer 1992): 12–19.

Selz, Peter. "Saint Louis: 'Recovering the Holy'." *ARTnews* 92 (February 1993): 42.

Shapiro, Edward S. "Jewishness and the New York Intellectuals." *Judaism* 38 (Summer 1989): 282–292.

Slayer, Monte. "Educators and Cultural Diversity: A Six-Stage Model of Cultural Versatility." *Education* 112 (Summer 1992): 506–511.

Spiegelman, Barbara. "Video Reviews: I Am a Jew." *Library Journal*, October 1, 1989, 128.

"Three Other-Visioned Mice: *The Disuniting of America*, by Arthur Schlesinger/*Kindly Inquisitors*, by Jonathan Rauch/*Culture of Complaint*, by Robert Hughes." *The Economist*, April 17, 1993, 89–90.

Tonner, Leslie. "The Truth about Being a Jewish Princess." *Cosmopolitan Magazine* (September 1976): 226.

Wa-Khasis, Kothar. "Choosing Your Names." *Raritan* 11 (Winter 1992): 17–30.

Walden, D. "Goodbye, Columbus, Hello, Portnoy—and Beyond: The Ordeal of Philip Roth." *Studies in American Jewish Literature* 3 (Winter 1977–78).

Wallace, Michele. "Beyond Assimilation." *The Village Voice*, September 17, 1991, 41–42.

Waxman, Barbara Frey. "Jewish American Princesses, Their Mothers, and Feminist Psychology: A Re-reading of Roth's *Goodbye, Columbus.*" *Studies in American Jewish Literature* 7, no. 1 (1988): 90–104.

Weinstein, Andrew. "Art after Auschwitz." *Boulevard* 9, no. 1–2 (1994): 187–196

West, Cornel. "Critical Reflections." *Artforum* 28 (November 1989): 120–121.

———. "The Dilemma of a Black Intellectual." *Cultural Critique* 1 (Fall 1985).

———. "The Identity in Question: Discussion." *October* 61 (Summer 1992): 33–41.

———. "A Matter of Life and Death." *October* 61 (Summer 1992): 20–27.

———. "The New Politics of Difference." *October* 53 (Summer 1990): 109.

Wieseltier, Leon. "Against Identity." *The New Republic*, November 28, 1994, 24–32.

Willis, Ellen. "Multiple Identities" (response to Ilene Philipson's "What's the Big I.D.? The Politics of the Authentic Self"). *Tikkun* 6 (November 1991): 58–60.

Wolfe, Alan. "Books & the Arts: The Return of the Melting Pot" (review of *Ethnic Identity: The Transformation of White America*, by Richard D. Alba and *Ethnic Options: Choosing Identities in America*, by Mary C. Waters). *The New Republic*, December 31, 1990, 27–34.

Wright, Charles A., Jr. "The Mythology of Difference: Vulgar Identity Politics at the Whitney Biennial." *Afterimage* 21 (September 1993): 4–8.

Young, James E. "The Counter-Monument: Memory Against Itself in Germany Today." *Critical Inquiry* 18 (Winter 1992): 267–296.

PLATES

3, 10, 12, 34: John Parnell; 4: Oren Slor; 5: John Bessler; 6, 7: Erma Estwick; 11: Courtesy Stux Gallery; 14, 15: John Lamka; 16: Jennifer Kotter/Courtesy Sidney Janis Gallery; 31: Richard Loesch/Courtesy Wexner Center for the Arts, July 1995; 32: Tom Warren; 35, 36: D. James Dee.

FIGURES

Page xviii: Courtesy of Jean Paul Gaultier.

Pages 10, 21: Liz Deschenes; page 11: John Behrens; page 12 top: Denis Courley/Courtesy Max Protetch Gallery; page 12 bottom: Erma Estwick; pages 13, 17, 26 left, 30: John Parnell; page 14: © 1996 by The Andy Warhol Foundation, Inc./ARS; page 18: Jennifer Kotter/Courtesy Sidney Janis Gallery; page 23: Dana Byerly; page 26 right: Richard Loesch/Courtesy Wexner Center for the Arts, July 1995; page 27: D. James Dee/Courtesy Holly Solomon Gallery; pages 31, 32: Oren Slor; page 33: Beth Phillips Studio.

Page 45: Courtesy Department of Special Collections. University of Chicago Library, Chicago; page 46: © 1996 by ARS, New York/ADAGP, Paris; page 48: Courtesy Mouton de Gruyter, a division of Walter de Gruyter & Co.

Pages 62, 63, 64, 65, 68, 71: Courtesy Private Collection, Chicago; page 70: Courtesy National Library of Medicine, Bethesda, Md.

Page 87: © 1969 by Paramount Pictures Corporation. All rights reserved. Courtesy Museum of Modern Art/Film Stills Archive.

Page 95 left: © 1984 by NBC, Inc. All rights reserved; page 95 right: Courtesy Paramount Pictures Corporation. All rights reserved; pages 97: ©B/Romy Achituv; page 98: © 1995 Capital Cities/ABC, Inc.; page 99: © 1960 by Universal City Studios, Inc. Courtesy MCA Publishing Rights, a division of MCA, Inc. All rights reserved/Romy Achituv; page 102: Courtesy Columbia Pictures Television/Romy Achituv; page 103: Courtesy MGM Worldwide Television, Inc./Romy Achituv.

Pages 109, 110, 111: Dana Byerly/Courtesy Rhonda Lieberman. Hair and makeup (photos pages 109 and 111) by Dan Sharp.

Page 114: Oren Slor.